D1617010

French Philosophy of the Sixties

Luc Ferry and Alain Renaut

French Philosophy of the Sixties

An Essay on Antihumanism

Translated by Mary H. S. Cattani

The University of Massachusetts Press / Amherst

Original title:

La pensée 68:

Essai sur l'anti-humanisme contemporain

© 1985 by Gallimard

"Preface to the English Translation" and

translation, copyright © 1990 by

The University of Massachusetts Press

All rights reserved

Printed in the United States of America

LC 89-38173

ISBN 0-87023-694-6 (cloth); 695-4 (paper)

Designed by Edith Kearney

Set in Linotron Bodoni Book

by Keystone Typesetting, Inc.

Printed and bound by Thomson-Shore, Inc.

Library of Congress Cataloging-in-Publication Data

Ferry, Luc.

    [Pensée 68. English]

    French philosophy of the sixties : an essay on antihumanism / Luc
Ferry and Alain Renaut : translated by Mary H.S. Cattani.

    p. cm.

    Translation of: La pensée 68.

    Includes bibliographical references.

    ISBN 0–87023–694–6 (alk. paper). — ISBN 0–87023–695–4
(pbk. : alk. paper)

    1. Philosophy, French—History—20th century—Controversial
literature. 2. France—Politics and government—1958–   I. Renaut,
Alain. II. Title. III. Title: French philosophy of the '60s.

    B2421.F4713   1990

    194—dc20   89–38173

                                      CIP

British Library Cataloguing in Publication data are available.

For Tzvetan Todorov

A Frenchman, an Englishman, and a German each undertook a study of the camel.

The Frenchman went to the Jardin des Plantes, spent half an hour there, questioned the guard, threw bread to the camel, poked it with the point of his umbrella, and, returning home, wrote an article for his paper full of sharp and witty observations.

The Englishman, taking his tea basket and a good deal of camping equipment, went to set up camp in the Orient, returning after a sojourn of two or three years with a fat volume, full of raw, disorganized, and inconclusive facts which, nevertheless, had real documentary value.

As for the German, filled with disdain for the Frenchman's frivolity and the Englishman's lack of general ideas, he locked himself in his room, and there he drafted a several-volume work entitled: *The Idea of the Camel Derived from the Concept of the Ego.*

Le Pèlerin, September 1, 1929, p. 13

Contents

Preface to the
English Translation

When this book was published in France it was misunderstood in so many different ways that it would be impossible to take care of them all in a preface. Because we were attempting to write, perhaps for the first time in the French context, a philosophical critique of certain aspects of the student rebellions of the 1960s (which in France, through a kind of metonymy, we refer to under the general heading "May '68"), our book aroused "political" reactions. In 1985 one still could not speak of May '68 without immediately being assigned a position on the political chess board. To distance oneself from the events was to be seen by some as a sign of one's allegiance to the political Right.

It is unfortunate that political and intellectual life, particularly in the French context, are often so closely linked that there is virtually no way to avoid the suspicion of biased readings. But to dispel the crudest misunderstandings, it nevertheless seems useful for the American edition to mention how we see our book situated with respect to French intellectual history since World War II.

The logic of this history cannot be grasped if one does not see that it has been dominated since 1945, more or less surreptitiously, by a critique of the modern world and of the values of formal democracy, a critique inspired mainly by Marx and Heidegger, successively, and sometimes simultaneously. For this reason, it is important to understand clearly how a Marxian critique of bourgeois idealism and the Heideggerian deconstruction of the "technical world" could have gone together in spite of everything that separates them.

In contemporary neo-Marxism, from Althusser to Bourdieu, modern humanism was simply assimilated to bourgeois ideology. We are all familiar with the doctrine that states that valorizing man as such masks differences of class—a doctrine that one can find even in Marx himself, and one that he uses with great skill in *The Jewish Question* for a radical critique of the Declaration of the Rights of Man of 1789. We also know how the theme of a critique of instrumental reason, which is associated with the first motif, is found all through the Marxist tradition, even in the Frankfurt school, of course.

It is on the basis of this twofold critique, of abstract man and of instrumental (or technical) reason, that the Heideggerian deconstruction of the metaphysics of subjectivity could join Marxism in a common rejection of humanism. The Nietzschean-Heideggerian components of contemporary thought do date humanism to Descartes rather than to the rise of capitalism. They intentionally include Marxism itself in the metaphysical project of a subject that posits itself as "master and possessor of nature" and that proclaims its pretension to be self-transparent and to make reality transparent, as well. It is nevertheless the case that on these two points (the critique of abstract man and that of modern rationality), the two main currents of contemporary thought were able to find a common ground. Two books, which were symbols in their times, demonstrate this in the most emblematic way: *One Dimensional Man*, by Marcuse, and *Discipline and Punish*, by Foucault. They share a particular feature, which is that they can be read through a twofold interpretative grid: they are of interest to a Marxist because they pursue an unequivocal critique of the bourgeois universe of modern industrial societies; a Nietzschean-Heideggerian can read them as deconstructions of this modern humanism (which in fact they are, at their most profound) whose final form is the "technical world"—a deconstruction applied for once outside the usual field of the history of philosophy.

Here it is important to understand that this critique of modern rationality was absolutely inseparable from a critique of the subject (of man) defined as conscience and as will, that is, as man as the author of his acts and ideas. In order to understand this, one must refer back to the considerable trauma represented by the Second World War for European intellectuals. Immediately after the war, in fact, it is no exaggeration to say that "civilized societies," that is the entire Western world, could legitimately be accused of having engendered, or at least of having been unable to stop, two of the greatest political catastrophes of this century: colonialist imperialism and Nazism. The idea of a "dialectic of Enlightenment" managed to acquire a legitimacy in philosophy that it had never had before, even at the time of the counterrevolution: Far from having effected the emancipation of man, the Enlightenment was turned inside out, universalism became Eurocentrism and rationalism became irrational, an irrationality unavoidable in a world thoroughly dominated by a purely instrumental or technical reason.

It is in this context that the importance of Marxist theory in France should be conceived, it being the only world vision that, though it is of European origin, even up to the 1960s could not be accused of compromising with colonialism and Nazism. Otherwise it is impossible to understand how the Communist party was able, if not to become the "party of the intellectuals," at least to attract philosophers who, by all the evidence, should have been led to criticizing the premises of a system of thought that reduces man to a history, and history itself to a logical succession of stages geared to the realization of a classless society.

Marxism's domination of French intellectuals in the postwar period is well illustrated, for example, by an article by Simone de Beauvoir published in 1956 in the journal *Les Temps Modernes* concerning rightist thought. Without further commentary, here are the first two lines of the article: "The truth is one, only error is multiple. It is no accident that the right professes pluralism."

It is also in this period of our intellectual history that the structural anthropology of Lévi-Strauss, though also philosophically entirely alien, and even hostile, to Marxism, was able to join it in a critique of Eurocentrism. Lévi-Strauss did indeed vigorously criticize the idea of a teleology of history, to which Marxism was still captive, demonstrating the inevitably Eurocentrist consequences of such a teleology which made the most industrially developed nations the only possible model for primitive societies, societies that were, from this perspective, then inevitably regarded as underdeveloped rather than as *other* or *different*. Still, the common enemy was identified as colonialism and, at the cost of a structuralist revision of its presuppositions (a revision that was undertaken by Althusser, as we know), Marxism freed of economism and of the Hegelian ruse of reason could combine all forms of legitimacy.

There is no need to point out that today in France, Marxism has collapsed. The reasons for this collapse, which has reached such proportions as to permit one to imagine that a revised Marxism may reappear, should be mentioned: they depend in part on the internal mutations of a French society which in the last thirty years has been substantially democratized, whatever may be said, and which has lived through the emergence, in 1968, of a new political force— youth—inspired by simultaneously individualist and democratic ideals that are incompatible in every respect with the authoritarian images and symbols traditionally associated in the political arena with Marxism. It is in this new intellectual atmosphere that the popularizing of critiques of totalitarianism and the discourse of dissidents about the Gulag have acquired a broad following, through the "new philosophy" of Bernard-Henri Levy and André Glucks- mann, which at least had this "generally positive" effect. It is also in this context that the events in Afghanistan and Poland were able to reveal what neither Budapest nor Prague had entirely succeeded in revealing to French intellectuals: the true nature of "real social- ism," not a worker state whose accidental degeneration should be concealed from the workers at Renault, to use Sartre's formula, but a totalitarian and even imperialistic State.

Here the Heideggerian critique of the subject took over for the critique that had been led by Marxism. In fact, those who for a long time had entertained more than just suspicions about the demo- cratic nature of the Soviet regime and about the communist critique of liberal societies, had not waited for the times to be favorable to the deconstruction of the two faces of the "administered world" (Ador- no), capitalist in the West, bureaucratic in the East. Whether by way of the work of H. Arendt or by the late work of Merleau-Ponty, the influence of Heideggerian phenomenology is thus to be found in writers as different as Claude Lefort, Cornelius Castoriadis, and Michel Foucault.

It is clear, for example in Foucault—and he made no mystery of it—that the designation of Cartesian reason as the metaphysical norm from which only unreason, and thus this difference and this otherness that madness is, could be marginalized, then "isolated," is impossible to understand apart from Heidegger's "history of Being" in which Descartes had already been made the primary instigator of the forgetting of difference.

The history of Heidegger's influence in France remains, for the most part, to be written: It goes far beyond the circle of orthodox Heideggerians (Jean Beaufret and his students) and even dissident ones (Derrida and his students). What is clear, nonetheless, is that the retreat of Marxism has made the presence of Heideggerianism in France more and more visible. It would be difficult to underestimate here the politically purifying effect on Heidegger's thought of his translation into a "leftist" intellectual context, most notably in Derrida and Foucault, but also in Lefort and Castoriadis: The great themes of Heidegger's thought were thus freed from the political connotations that, even in his style, are perceptible to any German reader. But in addition, utilized as a critique of the totalitarianism of the East and of the bureaucratic, repressive disciplinary and consumerist society of the West, Heidegger could, without further ado, inhabit the most powerful critical position after the death of Marxism.

We know that Victor Farias in his new book, with all its irritating platitudes, has recently come to put a stop to thinking in the same old rut and to sound a discordant note in the new consensus of critical intellectuals (see on this point our book *Heidegger et les Modernes*, to be published in English translation by the University of Chicago Press). The scenario is already known: What is happening to Heidegger today, happened to Marxism in the 1970s.

For what is now in fact forty years, two critiques of the democratic world have always been competing: the Marxist one, conducted in the name of an ideal future, and the Heideggerian one, depending more openly on traditions dating from before the advent of the modern world (for example, on the Greeks). Since the (recent) collapse of the Marxist dream of a radiant future, it is the neoconservative critique of the Heideggerian type that is in turn being politically compromised. That the two major critiques of modern humanism have proven to be linked with totalitarian adventures is most significant: *Whether conducted in the name of a radiant future or a traditionalist reaction, the total critique of the modern world, because it is necessarily an antihumanism that leads inevitably to seeing in the democratic project, for example in human rights, the prototype of ideology or of the metaphysical illusion, is structurally incapable of taking up, except insincerely and seemingly in spite of itself, the promises that are also those of modernity.*

For it is here too, and not only in the sphere of theoretical philosophy, that the most urgent stakes in the question of the subject, understood as the question of humanism, can be found: between "collaboration" and external criticism, is there really no place for an internal critique?

Let us be quite clear: There is no question of giving up criticism, but of taking note of the fact that the democratic world endlessly makes promises that it does not keep, to parody Adorno's formulation. It is in the name of these promises, then, that one should perhaps criticize it, in the name of the present, the subversive potential of such an attitude being more powerful than the one formerly believed was to be found in the future, or in the past.

It is true that to legitimize such a change of philosophical paradigm, one would also have to be able to grant a minimum of legitimacy to a reference to the subject which is inherent in any democratic thought, a legitimacy that is still missing today due to the confusion between metaphysics (or idealism) and humanism brought about by the two dominant traditions, Marxian and Heideggerian.

On the philosophical level it is impossible to return, after Marx, Nietzsche, Freud, and Heidegger, to the idea that man is the master and possessor of the totality of his actions and ideas. Today we know the illusions and the danger inherent in such a denial of the unconscious in its various forms. But how can we not acknowledge that this assertion must in no way encourage us to place ourselves in a philosophical position, which, though apparently radical, in fact, consists of quietly conducting a critique of subjectivity when today it is a question of rethinking—*after this critique and not only against it*—the question of the subject.

Foreword

The Philosophy of the '68 Period

First, some specifics: French philosophy of the 1960s cannot easily be reduced to what we call " '68 philosophy." Philosophically, the sixties were as notable for the works of Paul Ricoeur[1] or Emmanuel Lévinas[2] as for the contribution of J. Beaufret in acclimatizing French thought to Heidegger, for the revival of epistemological inquiry (G. Canguilhem, Michel Serres, and J. Bouveresse), and for Raymond Aron's concerted attempt to open philosophy to the rigors of ideological criticism and political theory,[3] to mention a few. By '68 philosophy—or, if we may use the expression, "French philosophy of the '68 period"—we refer exclusively to a constellation of works which are in chronological proximity to May or, even more

Translator's note: Unless otherwise indicated, translations of citations in French, including citations from the French translations of German sources, are the translator's own. The English translation of a source has always been given when it has been used. For references to the German sources, both the French editions used by the authors and the German originals are cited. Occasionally, additional bibliographical information is given for the readers' convenience.

I wish to thank Dennis Porter for his generous help with the preparation of this manuscript.

1. Cf. *La Symbolique du mal*, Aubier, 1960; *De l'Interprétation: Essai sur Freud*, Ed. du Seuil, 1965; *Le Conflit des interprétations*, Ed. du Seuil, 1969.
2. *Totalité et infini*, M. Nijhoff, and *Difficile Liberté: Essais sur le judaïsme*, Albin Michel; both appeared in 1963.
3. A very large number of Aron's works appeared during the sixties; for example: *Paix et guerre entre les nations*, Calmann-Lévy, 1961; *Le Grand Débat: Initiation à la stratégie atomique*, Calmann-Lévy, 1963; *Dix-huit Leçons sur la société industrielle*, Gallimard, 1963; *La Lutte des classes*, Gallimard, 1964; *Démocracie et totalitarisme*, Gallimard, 1966; *Trois Essais sur l'âge industriel*, Gallimard, 1966; *Essais sur les libertés*, Calmann-Lévy, 1965; *Les Désillusions du progrès*, Calmann-Lévy, 1966; *Les Etapes de la pensée sociologique*, Gallimard, 1967, etc.

precisely, to works whose authors acknowledged, usually explicitly, a kinship of inspiration with the movement.

Most of the typical or basic works of what we regard today as a "philosophical generation" are in fact nearly contemporaneous with the May crisis, coming either just before or immediately after it. Foucault, whose *Madness and Civilization* had appeared in 1961, published *The Order of Things* in 1966 and *The Archaeology of Knowledge* in 1969. Althusser, whose *For Marx* and first volumes of *Reading Capital* had been published in 1965, delivered and published his lectures *Lenin and Philosophy* and *Marx before Hegel* the following year. In 1967 Derrida's *Writing and Difference* and *Of Grammatology* appeared; in October of 1968, while he was presenting his text entitled *The Ends of Man* at a conference in New York, Derrida made a point of mentioning, in order to clarify "the historical and political horizon" of the talk, that it was written in April 1968 and typed when "the universities of Paris were invaded by the forces of order—and for the first time at the demand of a rector— then reoccupied by the students in the upheaval you are familiar with."[4] In 1966 Lacan gathered some of his principle texts together in *Ecrits*, at the moment that would later be considered the greatest period of his "Seminar." *The Inheritors: French Students and Their Relation to Culture* by Pierre Bourdieu and Jean-Claude Passeron dates to 1964, and their *Reproduction in Education, Society, and Culture* to 1970. So, too, in the aftermath of May, Deleuze's first works to abandon the area of the history of philosophy would appear: *Différence et répétition* and *Logique du sens* (1969). This chronological concentration is surely striking. In the years and months immediately preceding the May crisis, the philosophy was being created which, although it may be an exaggeration to claim it influenced the course of events,[5] may have had a less immediate but no less

4. Jacques Derrida, *Marges de la philosophie*, Ed. de Minuit, 1972, p. 135 (*Margins of Philosophy*, trans. Alan Bass, University of Chicago Press, Chicago, 1982, p. 114).
5. The denial of intellectual influences was a constant in the discourse of the participants in the events of 1968. See, for example, Daniel Cohn-Bendit and Jean-Paul Duteuil, in *La Révolte étudiante: Les Animateurs parlent*, Ed. du Seuil, June 1968, p. 70: "People wanted to blame Marcuse for being our mentor: that's a joke. Not one of us had read Marcuse. Some of us read Marx, maybe Bakunin,

revealing relationship to them: These publications and the revolt in May may have belonged to the same cultural phenomenon and may indeed have constituted it in different modes, like symptoms.

This hypothesis, which is merely suggested by a simple look at the chronology, is confirmed to a remarkable extent by various declarations of the most visible protagonists of the 1960s philosophical generation. We have already referred to Derrida's emphasis on "the historical and political horizon." Another example is particularly significant: In an interview in 1977, Foucault cogently described the predominant reception of the events of '68 on the part of philosophers: The explanation his work had given of the links between knowledge and power, notably in *Madness and Civilization*, had been greeted "by a great silence on the French intellectual left." He acknowledges, however, that this indifference, feigned or real, may have been a function of the limitations of his earlier work in view of the fact that, "despite the Marxist tradition and the P.C. [French Communist party] it was not until around 1968 that these questions took on their political significance with a sharpness I had not suspected, revealing how timid and diffident my earlier works still were."[6] So it is: the month of May as the self-revealer of French philosophy and, at least for Foucault, the confirmation of and decisive impulse for his choice of problematics. This is true to such an extent that, as he adds, "Without the political opening of those years, I would perhaps not have had the courage to take up the thread of these problems and to pursue my inquiry in the direction of punishment, prisons, and discipline."[7]

This type of celebration of the profound commonality of inspiration between the philosophy of the sixties and the political movement of 1968, is not, after all, unique to the times. There are

and among contemporary writers Althusser, Mao, Guevara, Lefebvre. The political militants of the March 22 movement have almost all read Sartre. But you can't really call any writer the inspiration for the movement."

6. "Vérité et pouvoir, entretien avec M. Fontana," *L'Arc*, no. 70, 1977, p. 17.
7. Cf. on this point, ibid., p. 20: The mechanisms of power were never really analyzed until "after '68, that is, starting from everyday struggles and at the local level, with those who had to defend themselves in the finest webs of the network of powers," and this was because, due to May, "the concrete of power was revealed."

examples right up to the most recent works of, for example, Jean-François Lyotard. Recalling in 1984 what still seemed "vital" about Marxism, in the sense of the "difference" between what society is made up of and what "intellectual pursuits" have to give testimony to (including the philosophers'), he thought it useful to clarify: "Something like that happened in '68,"[8] thus demonstrating once again that the May movement fundamentally turned the mind back to what it is "devoted" to thinking about. Even Althusser, who for obvious political reasons could not display the same enthusiasm for the leftisms of May, allowed himself to demonstrate a certain intellectual sympathy toward the movement now and then. For example, in an article that appeared in May/June 1969 he said, in opposition to the prevailing orthodox communist condemnation of the student revolt (as lacking the necessary "class enlightenment" and therefore destined to be reabsorbed by the bourgeoisie), that the rebellion was nevertheless "profoundly progressivist"; in questioning the "apparatus for inculcating bourgeois ideology that the capitalist education system supremely represents," the movement, which cannot be reduced to mere manipulation by bourgeois ideology, deserves to see "its unprecedented newness, its reality, and its progressivist importance recognized," as an intellectual revolt that is objectively able to help "the revolutionary struggle of the working class, on the national and international scale."[9] On this point Althusser might also have written, with Foucault, "that with May, the concrete of power appeared," in this case the concrete aspect of that ideological power whose workings are analyzed in his celebrated last article, "Ideology and Ideological State Apparatuses,"[10] which claimed in a number of respects to be the theorization of what May had revealed on the subject. Each in his own way, the philosophers of the sixties, in their interpretations of May '68, attempted to suggest that the movement had some type of philosophical bearing, in their view

8. Jean-François Lyotard, *Le Tombeau de l'intellectuel et autres papiers*, Galilée, 1984, p. 29.
9. Louis Althusser, "A propos de l'article de Michel Verret sur 'Mai étudiant,'" *La Pensée*, May–June 1969, pp. 11 ff.
10. Louis Althusser, "Idéologie et appareils idéologiques d'État," *La Pensée*, June 1970; reprinted in *Positions*, Ed. sociales, 1976 ("Ideology and Ideological State Apparatuses," in *Essays on Ideology*, trans., Verso, London, 1984).

closely linked with what they themselves, proceeding from their particular philosophical interests, claimed were the essential objects of their theoretical preoccupations.

May '68: Humanism or Individualism?

Examples of this claim could be multiplied with no effort, but it is nonetheless problematic. First of all, it is obvious that, beyond the consensus we have just elucidated, these thinkers each had a different relationship to May '68 in terms of their theoretical judgments and evaluations. But this is not the main thing: What still seems to us today to be the real problem is the meaning attributed to the events of May with respect to the question running all through " '68 philosophy," the question of humanism.

There are good reasons why one might be inclined to regard May '68 as a resurgence of humanism, if we exclude certain failed attempts at forms of political action whose consequences in Italy and Germany we are well aware of.[11] Today, as everyone knows, the spirit of the 1980s is thriving on rediscovering the virtues of "subjectivity": Whether it is the rediscovered consensus around the morality of human rights, or the growing demand even on the left for individual or social autonomy from the state, everything seems to confirm the current revival of a number of values that seem to be in opposition to '68. And yet, is it not true that a closer look reveals one of the leitmotifs of May to be the defense of the person against the "system"? Merely rereading today those curious documents that appeared as events were unfolding is enough: There we see the repeated insistence that the "gears of the system" be uncovered so as to accuse the system of transforming individuals into "cogs in the wheels that guarantee society's functioning,"[12] and if the revolution

11. Cf. on this point François Furet, A. Liniers, and P. Raynaud, *Terrorisme et démocratie*, Fayard, 1985.
12. D. Cohn-Bendit, "Entretien avec J.-P. Sartre," in *La Révolte étudiante*, p. 95. Cf. also p. 96: May as a "rupture in the cohesion of the system," a rupture that "can be used to open up gaps." The theme of gaps has also been fully explored by E. Morin, C. Lefort, and J.-M. Coudray (C. Castoriadis) in the collection *Mai 1968: La Brèche: Premières réflexions sur les événements*, Fayard, 1968.

often had the appearance of a disintegration (of the university, of society), it was because for the revolutionary the old world had to be exploded, and also because of the refusal to let oneself be "integrated" into anything that might deny one's individuality. [13] In all these aspirations for a "dis-integrated" existence, in these critiques of bureaucracy as a "tendency to limit man to a function," [14] beyond the confused formulations and the contingent absurdities, there is the affirmation of a revalorization of the "person." This line leading directly from the May protests to the neohumanism of the eighties is further confirmed by the fact that, since the sixties, criticisms of the Communist party have always accompanied the formulation of ideals. From denunciations of the party as a bureaucratic apparatus, treasonous to the cause of the revolution (and thus an instrument of integration), [15] to condemnations of the party as an accomplice in the threats to human rights in Poland and Afghanistan, we find the direct line leading to the truth of the May revolt, namely, neohumanism as the development of leftism, the evidence being the paths taken by the most celebrated media figures of the "new philosophy," who were emblematic in this respect.

The interpretation of the real meaning and inheritance of the May crisis is more complex, however. It requires a most careful rethinking since, from other points of view, a comparison of the late sixties and the early eighties seems to contradict the hypothesis of a direct link, suggesting rather that one speak of a break, or a reversal from for to against. Did not the demands made in 1968 always contain a public project (that of the overthrow of society and its institutions, or at least some of them, starting from the university), whereas in the ideology of the eighties the primacy of the cult of private happiness and the very liberal pursuit of individual projects

13. *La Révolte édudiante*, p. 95: Cf. the ritualized opposition between "well-integrated executives" and the "revolutionaries." Cf., on the same point, pp. 107 ff., the criticism of the Fouchet Plan, which was denounced by SNESup [Syndicat National D'Education Supérieure] as intending to make education one "factor in social integration."
14. Lefort, *La Brèche*, p. 41 (on the "myth of the system's rationality").
15. Cf. A. Geismar, in *La Révolte étudiante*, p. 52; and J.-P. Sartre, *Les Communistes ont peur de la révolution*, Ed. J. Didier, 1968, pp. 9 ff.

is widely recognized?[16] The reality of this discontinuity cannot be immediately defended as more certain than the hypothesis of an eventual direct link without further examination, but there is enough material for thought so that any hasty diagnoses should be avoided. We believe, however, that to attribute a "more or less humanist" overall intention to the May movement, which is after all infinitely diverse, is to risk being trapped by a simple formula: It may be that 1968, in its defense of the subject against the system, is linked in a certain way to contemporary individualism as it is to the humanist tradition. In Rousseau's words, "natural freedom" is not "moral freedom"; the right to do whatever one wants beyond any restraint (individualism) is not necessarily the same thing as the auto-nomy that humanist man, rightly or wrongly, believed distinguished him from the animals.

Antihumanism in '68 Philosophy

Whatever remains of this question, which we postpone for the moment, at least one thing is clear: French philosophy of the '68 period resolutely chose the antihumanist position.[17]

From Foucault's declaration of the "death of man" at the end of *The Order of Things* to Lacan's affirmation of the radically antihumanist nature of psychoanalysis since "Freud's discovery" that "the true center of the human being is no longer in the same place assigned to it by whole humanist tradition,"[18] the same conviction is upheld: The autonomy of the subject is an illusion. Thus, as J.-F. Lyotard still emphasizes today, it behooves contemporary philosophy "to be at risk beyond the limits of anthropology and humanism,

---

16. Cf. on this point G. Lipovetsky's excellent analyses in *L'Ère du vide: Essais sur l'individualisme contemporain*, Gallimard, 1983. We discuss them in chapter 2 of this book.
17. M. Dufrenne is right in referring to this major component of French philosophy, from 1968 on, and property refers to its Heideggerian heritage. Later developments in '68 philosophy have merely confirmed his hypothesis. Cf. *Pour l'homme*, Ed. du Seuil, 1968.
18. Jacques Lacan, *Écrits*, Ed. du Seuil, 1966, p. 401.

with no concession to the spirit of the times."[19] Since his 1968 treatise *The Ends of Man*, J. Derrida has always called for "rebuilding humanism," for an effective elimination of the "shadows of humanist metaphysics,"[20] and for tracking down even in Heidegger, however expert an antihumanist he was,[21] the relics of a "philosophy of man": Whereas Heidegger thinks "against humanism" only because in his view "humanism does not place man's *humanitas* high enough,"[22] now it is a matter of unsettling humanism much more profoundly, for the purpose of "the reevaluation or revalorization of the essence and dignity of man,"[23] by refusing to assign any "proper" (attribute) to man, by resolutely considering the end or the "relifting of man" as "the end of its proper."[24] If today we can still hear Althusser praising, in *For Marx*, the "definition of humanism as an ideology"[25] presenting "the rupture with every *philosophical* anthropology or humanism" as one with Marx's scientific discovery,"[26] and "openly speaking" of a "theoretical anti-humanism" or of "Marx's philosophical anti-humanism," which reduces "to ashes the philosophical (theoretical) myth of man,"[27] our diagnosis of a general antihumanism can hardly be in doubt.

Why Antihumanism? Why Humanism Once Again?

In an article that appeared in the early eighties, M. Gaucher expresses, and for good reason, his surprise at the "sudden success of the rediscovered theme and policy of human rights, which had

19. Letter of July 1, 1985, to teachers and researchers qualified to apply for a position at the Collège international de philosophie.
20. "The Ends of Man," in *Margins of Philosophy*, p. 117.
21. M. Heidegger, *Lettre sur l'humanisme*, trans. R. Munier, Ed. Aubier, 1964, p. 119: "It is precisely no longer man, taken solely as such, that matters" (*Brief über den Humanismus*, in *Collected Works*, vol. 9, Frankfurt/M., 1976, p. 345).
22. Ibid., p. 75.
23. Derrida, *Margins*, p. 128.
24. Ibid., p. 134.
25. L. Althusser, *Pour Marx*, Maspero, 1965, p. 233; *For Marx*, trans. Ben Brewster, Verso, London, 1979, p. 227.
26. Ibid.
27. Ibid., p. 229.

been thought just a short while ago to be among the most dis-
credited." He adds: "Just imagine the almost universal smile of
commiseration the idea of raising this issue would have occasioned
only three or four years ago. . . . The alleged 'rights' as much as the
so-called 'human' would have seemed either surprisingly incongruous to the benevolent or suspiciously obscurantist to the vigilant,"
so clear is it that "since the beginning of the sixties, antihumanism
is what any good summary of the culminating phase of structuralism
would axiomatically present as the finest of contemporary thought
from Lacan to Foucault, via Althusser."[28]

This diagnosis is not in question. However, we have to acknowledge some difficulty in deciding which of the two is strangest
from the perspective of today, the return to humanism in the sixties
or its radical critique. The basic question is: Why was it declared by
the sixties generation that the valorization of man had to be disturbed or denounced? It goes without saying that the opposition of
'68 philosophy to humanism never meant that it intended to defend
barbarianism and plead for the inhuman. In fact, it is because of the
supposedly catastrophic effects (for whom if not for man?) of modern
humanism that it must have appeared to be the enemy of philosophy.

Without going into the analysis of the specific modalities of
this antihumanism again, it has to be pointed out, in order to
understand the reason, that it was always based on a line of argumentation according to which the humanism of modern philosophy,
although apparently the liberator and defender of human dignity,
actually succeeded only in becoming its opposite: the accomplice, if
not the cause, of oppression. There are as many illustrations as one
could want of this "dialectics" in '68 philosophy: in Foucault's
Madness and Civilization, with his interpretation of the birth of
modern reason as imposing the negation/expulsion/reduction of
everything viewed as external in terms of a universal norm, in spite
of the apparent emancipating intention of the Enlightenment; in
Derrida, with his designation of the "violence" necessarily hidden
within the modern emergence of reason based on identity, con-

28. "Les Droits de l'homme ne sont pas une politique," *Le Débat*, July–Aug.
1980.

strained to reject anything that threatens it from within, whether it be ontological or sexual difference (logocentrism as well as phallocentrism); even in the Marxist tradition, where it would be so easy to demonstrate how, even where one might have expected a bit more prudence (for example, in the Frankfurt school, which is, nevertheless, the origin of the theme of the "dialectics of the Enlightenment"), they persisted in denouncing as bourgeois ideology the most difficult challenge to forms of "formal" democracy, the emergence of which is linked with modernity.

On the horizon of humanism, proliferating each time according to specific logic, is the barbarism, already denounced by Heidegger, of an epoch when "deserts spread, devastated by technology" (or, in another register, by "instrumental reason"), subjugated to the total domination of the "Führer" in control of every district of the social space. And as a result, since the real barbarians are not who one thinks they are, how can one not be resolutely antihumanist?

We admit that the theme of a "dialectics of the Enlightenment" has its own force: We do not deny that it accounts very well for the failure of naive ideologies of progress in view of the political catastrophes running through the twentieth century. What is more, this theme legitimately emphasizes the dangers inherent in the illusion of total mastery that has been conveyed by modern metaphysics, and perhaps even more by the world it developed (we should add that the theme is not at all new in philosophy).

Things, however, are much more complex here than is suggested by the reappearance during the 1960s of the theme of a dialectics of the Enlightenment, whatever degree of refinement one brings to its elaboration. Indeed, the real theme of this book is the question of humanism, which is no doubt *the* central question in contemporary philosophy and which seems to us to need rethinking for at least two reasons.

First, it seems impossible (both impractical and unthinkable) simply to confuse humanism with metaphysics (as the Heideggerian tradition does) or with the ideology of the petite bourgeoisie. It is indeed a possibility that the philosophy of the subject and the valorization of man might have such consequences, but it is not at all a necessity. We will demonstrate in what follows that this reductive assimilation is theoretically untenable.[29] Practically, it leads to absurd consequences, as simple common sense should be enough to demonstrate: Is it reasonable to believe, as Althusser unfortunately invites us to do,[30] that the millions of victims of Stalinism paid with their lives so that petit-bourgeois humanism could survive within a Marxism that was still ideologized by the leaders of the Soviet Union? Is it really because he was still too "humanistic" that Stalin unleashed the "great purge" of 1936–38? And, in another chapter, who can believe that it was because Heidegger had not yet sufficiently deconstructed humanism by 1933 that he was capable of joining the Nazi party and pronouncing, along with many others, a Profession of Faith in Hitler of University Professors? In view of these aberrations, we have to remember, as C. Lefort does, that, if in totalitarian regimes man finds himself "isolated from man and separated from the collective as never before . . . , it is certainly not because he is consigned to the limits of private life, like a monad, not because he enjoys the right to opinions, freedoms, properties, and security, but because he is forbidden this pleasure."[31] This does not mean (do we need to say it?) a defense and illustration of the virtues of primitive capitalism!

If we cannot today (this is obvious but has to be emphasized in view of the predictable criticism) simply return to the values of the philosophy of the Enlightenment, it is equally impossible not to refer to them, as '68 philosophy tried to do, and to effect a tabula rasa of the tradition. Let us also note that the problem is not entirely absent today from the preoccupations of those who were nevertheless contemptuous of humanism. This is how, it seems to us, one has to interpret Derrida's confusion when, in January 1982, as he was describing his encounters with the Czechoslovakian police in the Center for Research on Politics, he acknowledged, with a great deal of honesty, his own difficulty articulating his philosophical method of the deconstruction of metaphysics, including, according to him,

29. Cf. chapter 7, herein.
30. Cf., on this point, A. Renaut, "Marxisme et 'déviation stalinienne': Remarques sur l'interprétation du stalinisme dans l'école althussérienne," in E. Pisier-Kouchner, *Les Interprétations du stalinisme*, P.U.F., 1983.
31. Cf. "Droits de l'homme et politique," *Libre*, 7, 1980.

his radical questioning of any philosophy of the "proper" of man and his political practice of an antitotalitarian reference to human rights (as such): In order to qualify this uncomfortable situation, he even proposed the category "baroque," perceived as inevitably provisional. Even while we willingly acknowledge this moment of self-analysis as a lucid one, it has to be said that it was merely a first, positive, but oddly timid step toward really taking account of the problem. And one wonders if the issue is not condemned to remain at this level of confusion, given how previous critiques of humanism have ended up "without remains."

The problem, formulated in the sharpest way, consists of searching for the conditions for what a *nonmetaphysical humanism* might be. In other words, it is a matter of conferring a coherent philosophical status on the promise of freedom contained in the requirements of humanism that its metaphysical development—far from being the truth of it, as '68 philosophy naively thought—led it to betray. One can be convinced that this is indeed the real philosophical problem of contemporary thought when one understands that it affects at the same time the status of subjectivity in a democracy, at the political level, and the status of reason in its relations to the Other, at the speculative level.

That said, we should not be misled by the recent return to the humanist mode any more than we might have let ourselves be carried away by the certitudes of yesterday's antihumanism: A critique of '68 philosophy cannot find enough legitimation in the whims of the moment. French philosophy of the '68 period had the value (if it had only one, this would be it) that it brought into focus the questioning of the metaphysical foundations of *traditional naïve humanism*, if only to the extent that Heidegger's deconstruction of modernity is often its determining component. If today, in view of the aporias and the disastrous effects of antihumanism, returning its rights to a philosophy of man as such is an issue, this influence of the sixties, at least, must not be lost. For this reason, and because this seems to us the most important philosophical question, our examination of '68 philosophy does not intend to be exclusively, or even primarily, polemical: Even though we believe disagreements have to be asserted clearly in their full radicalness, the goal of this reading is to integrate a dimension of what it rejects while searching for a definition of humanism that can *today* only attempt to protect itself against the old naivete. *Today* means: not only after the many deconstructions of humanism practiced throughout the sixties but also at the end of a century when, as Adorno said, "after Auschwitz" it became impossible merely to write hymns to the grandeur of man.

1 /
The Ideal Type for Sixties Philosophy

The ideal type, in relation to the entire group of objects to be studied, does not denote, as we know, merely a set of average characteristics of the kind a simple statistical study would reveal; rather than necessarily retaining all, or even the most frequently occurring characteristics, it is an intelligible reconstruction of a unique historical reality which, through a process of selection, brings together the fundamental (and in this sense typical) characteristics that can "constitute an intelligible whole."[1] Thus it is a *model* whose relevance is determined both by its coherence (by the intelligibility of the relations uniting the elements of the whole) and by the way it allows an understanding of those particular realities (to which it can never, by definition, perfectly correspond) to be obtained.

The ideal type of the philosophy of '68 we have constructed here is not the goal of our analysis; it is the instrument of the research on the philosophical productions of the sixties we subsequently undertake, which we view in their uniqueness as so many specifications of the ideal type (whose evolution itself also has to be understood). As a result, it goes without saying that what we present here does not claim to exhaust the subject concerned, nor does it claim to take all of those specifications fully into account. Basically, we are concerned with a concept that these realities always manifest in incomplete form. Let us add that constructing this ideal type also serves a delimiting function, allowing us to explain again what we mean by "the philosophy of '68": We mean what such a type, or at least a certain number of its elements, can be applied to with a

---

1. Raymond Aron, *Les Etapes de la pensée sociologique*, Gallimard, 1967, "Tel," p. 521.

greater or lesser degree of adequacy (but always to at least some degree). Having made these methodological remarks, we now come to what it seems to us must make up the four essential characteristics of the philosophy of '68.

The Intellectual Structure of the Sixties

1. The Theme of the End of Philosophy   This seems virtually a common ground for French philosophy at the time. The content though radical, at least is rather simple and can be summarized by the following statement: The philosophical tradition, as it developed and was exhausted (in the sense of exhausted of possibilities) from Plato through Hegel, must be done away with. This theme of "the death of philosophy" had numerous variants throughout the sixties but received above all two great interpretations corresponding to the two great deconstructive models in force at the time: Marxism and Nietzschean/Heideggerian genealogy.

On the Marxian side, Althusser began his address to the French Philosophical Society, *Lenin and Philosophy,* in February 1968, with a challenge: "My talk will not be philosophical." It will be, he explained, "a talk on philosophy," which is no longer a "philosophical talk" but claims to be "science" and anticipates what will perhaps one day be "a nonphilosophical theory of philosophy." Quoting Lenin (who himself was quoting Dietzgen), he added that this theory of philosophy will have the prime task of showing how philosophy has after all been limited to following a "path leading nowhere," a *"Holzweg."*[2] In passing, we point out that we are aware of the deliberate sounding of a theme and a term here, *Holzwege,* which is typical of this other deconstructive practice inspired not by Marx or Lenin but by Heidegger, an excellent example of an "effect of language" so typical of the philosophy of '68 where, within one of the two dominant types of deconstruction, suddenly the language of the other type is used.

2. L. Althusser, *Lenine et la philosophie,* pp. 11, 15 (*Lenin and Philosophy, and Other Essays,* trans. Ben Brewster, Monthly Review Press, New York, 1972, pp. 26 ff.).

Another example from Althusser of what might be called an allegorical practice, in the sense of speaking another's language, is also pertinent to the theme of the "end of philosophy." The closed circle that is the history of philosophy, he gravely explains in the same lecture, today appears to be the "history of the displacement of the indefinite repetition of a null trace."[3] The meaning of this formulation can be deduced from the speaker's personal idiom, of course, since what is infinitely repeated in the history of philosophy is the ideology of the petite bourgeoisie. It is obvious that even the style of the formulation forges a link between this interpretation of the end of philosophy and the one that Derridean deconstruction developed in very similar terms (though the contents are quite different). The philosophy of '68, although it is certainly not reducible to these linguistic effects, was first of all, however, the result of them.

In the same period, back to back with a Heideggerian representation of the end of philosophy as metaphysics, Derrida's *Of Grammatology* explained that deconstructing metaphysics should finally allow philosophy to be released from its captivity "within the epoch of ontotheology, within the philosophy of presence, that is to say, within philosophy *itself*."[4] As opposed to philosophy that "in the past" had always been a "philosophy of presence," characterized by its obsession with the meaning behind words and appearances, Derrida was making an appeal for a philosophical practice "which means nothing," which is understood as pure trace, pure meaning, without an original signified. In contrast to what Althusser was outlining (science as the successor to philosophy/ideology), for Derrida the succession was to be accomplished within a discourse that is no longer conceived of in terms of a naively rationalist theory of meaning (the tangible as a sign of the intelligible). Thus aphoristic or poetic writing, for example, has a privileged place as the antithesis of the linear and demonstrative discourse of

3. Ibid., p. 63 (English trans.).
4. J. Derrida, *De la grammatologie*, Ed. de Minuit, 1967, p. 24 (*Of Grammatology*, trans. Gayatri Spivak, Johns Hopkins University Press, Baltimore, 1976, p. 12).

traditional metaphysics. From this perspective it is easier to understand why the only task that seemed to remain for philosophy *as such* would be found in deconstructing the *history* of philosophy. Philosophy *itself* was thus becoming a strangely problematic activity (a remark equally valid for the Marxist side), condemned for its very survival to the eternal celebration of its own death.

2. The Paradigm of Genealogy Here too, as within the Nietschean/Heideggerian tradition, Marxists and Freudians were proclaiming their conviction that the philosophical activity par excellence is to be defined today by the genealogical method as Nietzsche understood it. In Nietzsche's words, explicitly appropriated by Foucault among others, the fundamental philosophical question is no longer "what" but "who." In other words, it is no longer a matter of extracting the content of a given discourse but one of questioning the external conditions for its production. So different currents of French philosophy agree that conscious discourse is to be treated as a symptom, whether what is outside it is conceived of as infrastructure, as libido, as physiological instinct, or as Being. And we can even identify what, in 1964, were the two fundamental texts of this practice of suspicion, which have in common that they drew attention to the trinity of philosophers of genealogy, Marx, Nietzsche, and Freud. Althusser's "Freud and Lacan" and, most importantly, Foucault's lecture "Nietzsche, Freud, Marx" at the Royaumont Colloquium on Nietzsche retrospectively seem to have inaugurated the style that was to become most characteristic of the '68 period.[5] For example, the following statement of Foucault's in a 1968 interview is indicative of the surprising legitimacy the paradigm of genealogy gained from the very start. In it, Marxian, Nietzschean, and Freudian references combine (we have indicated their presence with the help of brackets):

> The history of science, the history of knowledge, does not simply obey the general law of the progress of reason; human conscious-

---

5. L. Althusser, "Freud and Lacan," in *Lenin and Philosophy*, pp. 189–219. Foucault's text can be found in the collection *Nietzsche*, Actes du Colloque de Royaumont, Ed. de Minuit, 1967.

ness does not somehow retain the laws of its own history [a transparent allusion to the genealogy of the Marxian style]. Beneath what science knows of itself [we recognize here a famous Nietzschean metaphor], there is something it does not know, and its history, its future, its events, its accidents obey a certain number of laws and determinations. These I have tried to bring to light. I have tried to identify an autonomous domain [this time the horizon is Freudian], that of the unconscious of science, the unconscious of knowledge, which could have its own rules, much as the unconscious of the human individual also has its own rules and determinations.[6]

The theme is well known, though it is perhaps useful to mention once again the distance separating Marxism from the rest in the practice of genealogy, and this distance makes problematical the amalgamation of the different figures of the practice of suspicion, which was so characteristic of the sixties. The history of modern philosophy in fact puts in place two types of genealogy, and the philosophy of '68 continually oscillates between them.

One type is a rationalistic genealogy, inspired by a model supplied by Hegelianism, since *The Phenomenology of Mind* is indeed an explanation of the various figures of consciousness through a consideration of their origins and of what precedes and produces them within a historical process. Within this first position, historical process is still dominated by reason (it is its means of deployment), and the genealogy is carried out in terms of *truth*, each figure of consciousness finding its ultimate justification in absolute Knowledge.

Paradoxically opposed to this rationalistic genealogy is the Nietzschean genealogy, which served as the model for Foucault in the above-quoted interview but also, in part, for Lacanian psychoanalysis: It is conducted with no reference to absolute Knowledge. Taking the form of an *infinite hermeneutics*, it draws its inspiration from the paragraph in Nietzsche's *Gay Knowledge* entitled "Our New Infinite" (para. 374: "The world has become infinite for us once

6. *Magazine littéraire*, March 1, 1968.

again in the sense that we cannot refuse to lend it the possibility of an infinite number of interpretations"). This version of the idea of genealogy develops from a conviction that can be readily explained within the register of psychoanalysis. At first glance, analytic interpretation might be regarded as consisting of the unveiling of an unconscious; but since any psychic activity (including that of interpretation) is considered to be motivated by an unconscious, no single interpreter can claim to occupy the (still "naive") position held by the Hegelian absolute Subject. The interpretation of any interpreter is also the function of an unconscious, which has to be interpreted in its turn, and so on to infinity, so that no single interpretation can attain the status of ultimate truth. This displacement (from Hegel to Nietzsche) in the notion of genealogy very logically leads to the disappearance of even the idea of a "subject of knowledge," and to the return once again to Nietzsche's conclusion that "there are no facts, only interpretations." Thus Foucault could write, "If interpretation can never be achieved, it is simply because there is nothing to interpret . . . , since after all everything is already interpretation,' and the allusion to the "new infinite" in *Gay Knowledge* can then be clear: "Interpretation has finally become transparent."[7] To repeat: there is only signifying, and one can never attain the original position of a signified.

The hesitation between these two types of genealogy is particularly prominent in the Marxian component of "sixties" discourse. We will return to this question later, but the reasons for this wavering are quite clear: The Hegelian model of genealogy has the advantage (not a negligible one in the Marxist register) of holding up the idea of science as the interpretative reference, whereas the Nietzschean model is interesting in that it dissolves traditional oppositions at the heart of what Engels called the "old metaphysical bric-a-brac" (appearance/truth, signifier/signified, etc.). Whatever this wavering may mean, it must be added that emphasizing the reference to Nietzschean genealogy leads toward a third characteristic of the ideal type: What is being questioned, along with the idea

7. M. Foucault, "Nietzsche, Freud, Marx," pp. 189, 187.

of an original signified, is nothing other than the idea of truth itself, at least in its traditional form.

3. *The Disintegration of the Idea of Truth*   Traditionally, or, if one prefers, "metaphysically," the truth is defined as adequation (of subject to thing) and as noncontradiction (or coherence of discourse). Now, from the point of view of a genealogical method, both these claims of this theory of truth can be challenged: If there is no referent, adequation loses any meaning; and, on the other hand, the requirement for coherence is shown to depend on the illusion of the potential mastery of a wholly self-transparent discourse, which the hypothesis of an unconscious, or more generally of an exterior that motivates all discourse without the speaker's knowledge, specifically excludes. The practice of genealogy thus requires reference to another concept of the truth. Already present in Nietzsche, it would not, however, be thematized until Heidegger, in his definition of truth as *aletheia* or an unveiling, which is inseparable from the act of veiling. As an image to illustrate this theory of truth, according to which any revelation "is at the same time and in itself a concealment,"[8] we might recall the notorious example of the cube, well known in the phenomenological tradition, which hides three of its sides from view, screened from presence, no matter which way it is turned: Anything visible is thus based on the invisible, any presence on absence, any appearance on withdrawal—condemning from then on as naive the idea of absolute transparency and mastery. Any conscious discourse possesses, like the cube, its hidden side, its beyond.

Here, again, French Marxism visibly hesitated between these two theories of truth, the traditional and the phenomenological ("Heideggerian"), and for very good reason. Moreover, it is a constant problem in the Marxist tradition, a problem the Frankfurt school had already confronted and which we again confront not only in Althusser's *Eléments d'autocritique* but also in Bourdieu's various efforts to work out a sociology of sociology. This difficulty, which can

8. M. Heidegger, *Questions I*, Gallimard, p. 188 ("Vom Wesen der Wahrheit," in *Collected Works*, vol. 9, Frankfurt/M., 1976, p. 198).

be analyzed using Habermas's work as a point of departure, can be stated in terms of an alternative.

On the one hand, to lay the foundation for hermeneutic work (the critique of ideology in the circumstances of the Marxist context), we concede that interpretation rests on an established scientific truth, that of the "science of history" presumed founded by Marx through the gesture of the (epistemological) "rupture" between science and ideology: "Marx put an end to the reign of conceptual errors he could call errors because he advanced truths, scientific concepts. . . . Only on condition of having discovered THE truth [*sic*], then and only then can the scholar turn to the prehistory of his science to call it, wholly or in part, error, a 'tissue of errors' (Bachelard)."[9] All the same, it is clear that proceeding in this way one runs the very real risk of falling back into what had already been denounced as an idealist (thus ideological) myth: the idea of a subject of science that would radically transcend sociohistorical determinants and, once and for all, be conscious of itself and certain of its truth.

On the other hand, in order to avoid this fall back into ideology ("the theoreticist deviation"), we are led into the claim that science itself, even Marxism, is a product of history and thus a discourse that is also conditioned and determined by history. In this case, however, it is the rupture between ideology and science that becomes impossible to establish, even while it is precisely this latter attitude that is required for genealogical discourse to assume all its coherence and force.

French Marxism has been and remains, among the various currents of '68 thought, the most reluctant to accept the logic of this option. However, within this logic, a fourth and last trait appears whose close tie to the previous ones completes the construction of the ideal type as an "intelligible whole": what might be called the historicism or historism of the '68 period.

4. The Historicizing of Categories and the End to Any Reference to the Universal   This is in fact the very emergence of genealogy as

9. L. Althusser, *Eléments d'autocritique*, Hachette, 1973, pp. 26–46.

an effort to return discourses to their concrete historical conditions of production. Foucault always strongly emphasized that "Genealogy does not oppose history, . . . on the contrary, it opposes the metaphysical deployment of ideal meanings."[10] And also: "Do we believe in the universality of feelings? But they all have a history, and particularly those that appear noblest and most detached," such that "Real historical meaning recognizes that we live with neither signposts nor original addresses in the myriads of lost events."[11] Yet, if all the components of '68 philosophy agree in their historicizing of categories, due to their common genealogical bias, it is still important to differentiate the two types of historicism between which Marxism, here again, will waver. Modernism in fact experienced two quite different forms of historicism:

> Rationalistic historicism of the Hegelian type had stated that categories are historical, but on the basis of a conception of their unfolding as obeying a perfectly systematic logic.

> Nietzschean/Heideggerian historicism also conceives of categories as intrinsically linked to time, as historical, or, if one prefers, as "historic," but refuses to see in this historicity/historicalism any type of continuous and necessary development, in the sense of a causal linking.

Inseparable from the conviction that in history "everything happens rationally," the first model has the advantage of being able to accommodate without too much difficulty the goal of a scientific approach to history, which could include *explaining* the future. But measured by the requirements for a radical critique of idealism or metaphysics, this representation of history has the disadvantage that it is too easily deconstructed as being a moment (if not the culminating moment) in a philosophical current that it should be a break away from, as we have seen. From this the attempt is derived to construct an epistemology around the ideal of discontinuity, as in, for example, Veyne, who relies principally on Foucault—the entire

10. M. Foucault, "Nietzsche, la généalogie, l'histoire," in *Hommage à J. Hyppolite*, P.U.F., 1971, p. 146.
11. Ibid., p. 159.

12

problem being to understand whether the breaking up of history into multiple histories remains compatible with the idea of intelligibility that defines science.[12] From this a hesitation between the two models on the part of the Marxists, the more striking because of the claim that it is a science of history, is also derived. This hesitation is best illustrated by Althusser's desperate efforts to elaborate the concept of a causality, which is really no longer one and which he calls "structural causality."

Such, then, is the basic configuration of what we call '68 philosophy, framed by these four characteristics. Having outlined the characteristics, we must now look for and consider their most obvious potential effects. Moving from the most superficial (yet meaningful) to the deepest (or at least the most serious), we will identify for this purpose *effects of style* and *properly intellectual effects*, the second of which will take us directly to the question of antihumanism.

On the Style of the Philosophy of the Sixties

By "effects of style," we mean here effects of writing as well as of style in the larger sense, as for example with "lifestyle," understood here as a style of philosophical life, of course. Thus two points seem to need attention, which might suggest that they should be placed among the characteristics of the ideal type. However, the first four elements define an intellectual structure, whereas here we are dealing not with additional elements of this structure but with its most immediate effects, in some sense its visible signs.

1. The most obvious effects in the writing are *the cult of paradox and the insistent demand for complexity if not, in fact, for a rejection of clarity*. It is the case that "things are not so simple,"[13] as

---

12. Cf. Paul Veyne, *Comment on écrit l'histoire*, Ed. du Seuil, 1971. On this reduction of historical continuity to a "prejudice," cf. Aron's important objections in "Comment l'historien écrit l'épistémologie: A propos du livre de Paul Veyne," in *Annales*, Nov.–Dec. 1971. Aron's critique of the radical negation of historical unity has been carefully analyzed by S. Mesure, *R. Aron et la raison historique*, Vrin, 1984, pt. 2 (on the Spengler example).
13. J. Derrida, *Eperons*, Flammarion, 1978, p. 89.

Derrida said so well. In answer to our questions during the colloquium at Cerisy in 1980 concerning his demand for "another coherence," one which would not be "logicometaphysical," he said: "I cannot tell you what it is."[14] It would be wrong to think these characteristics are unimportant, given how easy it would be to attach this fascination for the unutterable to the second and third characteristics of the ideal type. If in fact deconstruction refers a manifest discourse to an unsaid that does not have the status of a signified or of a definable/identifiable "fact," any demand for a discourse governed by the simple requirements of the identity principle or of noncontradiction smacks of almost provincial naivete. And on this basis it would be so simple to multiply the examples of deliberately paradoxical statements or of discourses that refuse the test of clarification (the taste for transparency being suspect here, by definition). The search for a philosophy that "means nothing," asserted as such, is best expressed in *Glas*, the no doubt quintessential "sixties" discourse: "Sous l'effet de l'obliquide, l'érection est toujours en train de s'épancher pour tomber. Voire s'inverser. gl protège contre la schize que gl produit. L'anthérection, c'est aussi ce 'pén-dant féminin de la grappe de Stilitano.'"[15] In our chapter on French Heideggerianism we will return to considerations of what might have nourished this kind of writing. For the moment it is enough to show that this taste for provocation through absurdity is a widely shared propensity among the philosophical generation of the sixties: When Bourdieu, who has no sympathy for the verbal acrobatics of the discourses of "*différance*," wrote that what guides his work is "the conviction, which is itself a product of a history, that it is in history that one must seek the reason for the paradoxical progress of a reason that is fundamentally historical but yet not reducible to history,"[16] the reader would need to be quite credulous to find any depth there beyond that of an old contradiction disguised as a complex tension or a striking paradox. We will refrain from giving more examples, which would be of no use, in any case, to anyone

14. *Les Fins de l'homme: A partir du travail de J. Derrida*, Galilée, 1981, p. 52.
15. J. Derrida, *Glas*, Galilée, 1974, p. 264.
16. P. Bourdieu, "Le Champ scientifique," *Actes*, June 1976, p. 88.

who had not already been reminded of the sophists when confronted with this kind of discourse. The "philosophists" of the '68 period gained their greatest success through accustoming their readers and listeners to the belief that incomprehensibility is a sign of greatness and that the thinker's silence before the incongruous demand for meaning was not proof of weakness but the indication of endurance in the presence of the Unsayable.

2. The style of the sixties is also a certain philosophical lifestyle, characterized, let us say, by *the search for marginality* and *the phantasm of conspiracy*. To claim to be saying the unsayable, and for this reason to be breaking from all the traditions that still inform our daily lives, to be taking account of what metaphysics, ideology, or consciousness has forgotten or hidden, is indeed a task that is necessarily located at the margins of that which dominates (in various modes) and is reluctant to be discarded. It is a short step from there to interpreting this marginality as "heroic" and to uncovering a conspiracy of the powers thus threatened, if we can believe what the philosophists' discourse reveals on this subject. There is a surprising convergence in Bourdieu defining himself as a "newcomer" to the universe of culture, Derrida situating himself in the "margins of philosophy," Foucault claiming that his task is to exploit the multiple margins created by the imposition of its norms, counter to the modern *ratio*, and even Lacan emphasizing his difference from the psychoanalytic establishment. No doubt the pinnacle of the genre is Althusser's explaining in 1968 in *Lenin and Philosophy* that, by reason of a conspiracy of the dominant classes, the intellectual masses have been "subjugated to bourgeois and petit-bourgeois ideology"; fortunately, there are a few "exceptions," which he discusses in his lecture "On the Relation of Marx to Hegel" (February 1968), claiming that during a period when petit-bourgeois ideas are "in power" one must be able to accept the fate of "intellectual pariahs," which was the fate of "Marx, Lenin, and Freud." Beyond what differentiates them, then, the various components of '68 philosophy can be grouped around a *pathos* of "victimization," which was still so typical of the "Estates General of Philosophy" in June 1979, in their odd revelation that philosophy

has been repressed by "nonphilosophical barbarianism":[17] identifying the barbarians as "the heads of industry" whom philosophy keeps from "sleeping peacefully,"[18] or as the agents of this "technopolitics" surrounding modernism,[19] all of which was far less important, to tell the truth, than the manifestation of the law by which "evaluative critical abilities" in our time, selectively incarnated in the philosopher, of course, are found to be "isolated and marginalized."[20]

So representative of our philosophical and, more generally, our intellectual history for the last two decades, these effects of style need to be mentioned as such. Beyond what is merely bothersome or ridiculous in these idiosyncrasies of a generation, it is still important that one not be led to believe that the entire phenomenon of the emergence and resurgence of '68 philosophy is itself ridiculous and of no great (or serious) import. Leaving these surface effects aside, we will now take up the question of effects of the properly intellectual content of the intelligible structure whose component parts we have isolated.

The Subject on Trial

Let us attempt, then, to analyze the common element that groups certain characteristics together, philosophical currents that derive from orientations as different as Marxism, on the one hand, and the Nietzschean/Heideggerian/Freudian deconstruction of rationality on the other.[21] The basic theme is clearly in the project of carrying out a radical critique of subjectivity: This project easily unites the forces concerned, since subjectivity is assimilated by

17. J. Derrida, opening lecture, *Etats généraux de la philosophie*, Flammarion, 1979, p. 31.
18. V. Jankelevitch, ibid., p. 25.
19. Derrida, ibid., p. 32.
20. Derrida, ibid., p. 41.
21. Here one might analyze the links between '68 philosophy and the multiform mode of "structuralism." Cf. on this point V. Descombes, *Le Même et l'autre: Quarante-cinq ans de philosophie française (1933–1978)*, Ed. de Minuit, 1979, particularly pp. 96 ff.

them either to monadic bourgeois egoism or to a concept of man developed by modern metaphysics (as a metaphysics of subjectivity, which posits man as foundation and evaluative limit for all of reality). They are unified in their proclamation of *the death of man as subject*, a theme Foucault made famous: "Where 'ça parle'[22] man no longer exists."[23]

Let us look once more at the practice of genealogy. It clearly challenges again the idea of the subject as consciousness. Moreover, using methods that may appear to be intrinsically terroristic, it is concerned not with what someone said (since there is no signified) but with where he speaks from and with whom he is to say what he said. Let us listen to Foucault: "From now on interpretation will always be interpretation through the 'Who?'; one does not interpret what is in the signified; instead, one ultimately interprets: Who postulated the interpretation?"[24]

This will to reification (in the sense that the conscious subject for genealogy thus becomes a pure object which cannot defend itself in any way against the action brought against it *a priori*, and without recourse) is found in all the currents of French philosophy during the '68 period. So we find Althusser drawing up this indictment against philosophers, which is understood to be without opportunity for an appeal: "Philosophy teachers are teachers, that is, intellectuals employed in a given education system and subject to that system, performing, as a mass, the social function of inculcating the 'values of the ruling ideology.' . . . Philosophers are intellectuals and therefore petty bourgeois, subject as a mass to bourgeois and petty bourgeois ideology."[25] Having stripped those in question of any ability to think and to question their socially determinant origins (thus *reified*), Althusser can then use these phrases of Le-

22. *Translator's note:* The reference here is to the id: "Where the id speaks . . ."
23. M. Foucault, "L'Homme est-il mort?," *Arts*, June 15, 1966.
24. Foucault, "Nietzsche, Freud, Marx," p. 189.
25. Althusser, *Lenin and Philosophy*, pp. 68–69. We note that Bourdieu, interviewed in the *Nouvel Observateur* on the occasion of the publication of his *Homo Academicus* (Nov. 2–8, 1984), still says the same thing: "I see them [philosophers] as the most profligate defenders of intellectual narcissism. . . . I am thinking of all those professional prejudices which are never, or only rarely, questioned."

nin's: "And good riddance to these scoundrels! The party is purging itself from this petty-bourgeois pross!"[26] Althusser gave this lecture, it should be remembered, in February 1968, without this statement threatening in the least, apparently, his position as one of the figureheads of the Parisian intelligentsia. Today our distance in time allows us to wonder at the orientation of what was then the spirit of the times. Althusser responded in advance to the criticism he foresaw that he himself was a philosopher, after all: "This situation, shared by those petty-bourgeois intellectuals, the philosophy teachers, and by the philosophy they teach or reproduce in their own individual form, does not mean that it is impossible for certain intellectuals to escape the constraints that dominate the mass of intellectuals and, if philosophers, to adhere to a materialist philosophy and a revolutionary theory." We admire the discretion of that litotes—*does not mean that it is impossible*—and confess that, in view of the above operations of reification, it is difficult to see which surviving margin of autonomy might be the place where the possibility of these sublime exceptions (those making up the "intellectual pariahs") can take root.[27]

One final example of the reifying effect of genealogical analyses is enough to remind us just how far the "philosophists" took the annihilation of subjectivity. In *L'Economie libidinale*, Lyotard devotes several pages to analyzing in depth the figure of the writer-as-masturbator, using an admirably refined genealogical approach: All writing being sublimation, since writing consists of obtaining pleasure for oneself, it is (barely) sublimated masturbation. The question that arises at this point, if it were answered, ought to be a great help in penetrating the difficulties of *Capital:* "What was Marx's left hand doing while he wrote *Capital?*"[28] We consider it fortunate that, in spite of the marginalization of philosophical activity by the

26. Althusser, *Lenin and Philosophy*, p. 69.
27. Here again, Bourdieu reproduces an analogous inconsistency in answer to a question concerning what authorizes him (as a professor himself) to write *Homo Academicus*. He responded that if the point of view of all the others is not impartial "[his] point of view is that of true scientific gain" (*Nouvel Observateur*, Nov. 2–8, 1984). We will return to this point.
28. J.-F. Lyotard, *L'Economie libidinale*, Ed. de Minuit, 1974, p. 174.

ambient technopolitics of the '68 period, the discovery of these traces of what passed for thought at the time means that the need for historians to try to reconstruct texts that would otherwise have been regarded as caricature can be permanently avoided.

More seriously, it is important to emphasize that the practice of genealogy extended this negation of subjectivity (as finite consciousness) into a formidable destruction of the very idea of humanity as *intersubjectivity*. From the point of view of this type of reification of consciousness, communication (for example, philosophical discussion) must necessarily appear not as free debate among subjects responsible for what they say but simply as the sublimation of relations of force or, if you wish, as a euphemistic form of war (class struggle, intermittent conflicts, clashes of desires for power, etc.).[29] More importantly, the historicism that carries genealogical practice with it, as we have seen, leads inevitably to questioning once again the assumption of the constitutive unity of mankind as profoundly metaphysical. If all the contents of thought, all human spiritual characteristics, are indeed historicized in order to put an end to the illusion of universality that has characterized philosophical discourse, it must be admitted that a radical break between philosophical periods has in fact occurred. If, consequently, this break (for example, the break between the Ancients and the Moderns) is historicized, how can we imagine any meaning for the idea of the unity of the human species? Under these conditions, antihumanism can only take on a particularly radical form, that of hatred for the universal, such as Foucault expresses right up through his last writings: "The search for a moral form acceptable to everyone, in the sense that everyone must submit to it, seems catastrophic to me."[30] Obviously, we have to wonder how, from this point of view, the significance of a theme such as the rights of man can be saved, a

29. For example, the reduction of intellectual positions to class positions gives rise to a similar notion of "communication" in Althusser: Since only the working classes have "a class instinct that paves the way to taking working-class positions," the only "dialogue" that is possible with "intellectuals" who are "petit bourgeois" will consist of subjecting them to "long, painful, and difficult re-education" (*Positions*, Ed. sociales, 1976, p. 37.)

30. M. Foucault, in *Les Nouvelles littéraires*, June 28, 1984.

theme Foucault took up militantly in the last years of his life. Similarly, what happens to the values of the "republic" in its etymological sense, as the *res publica*, when, along with the disappearance of communication behind pure relations of force, the very possibility of intersubjectivity and thus of a real "public space" seems to be called into question?

A number of consequences appear on the horizon of these various efforts to eliminate what Lyotard calls "the humanist obstacle" from philosophy and to "make philosophy inhuman."[31] Their apparent acceptance by '68 philosophers is surprising, which inevitably leads to questioning the *logic* of the establishment of a philosophy leading to such developments. The record would be even clearer if the processes that forged such a radical accusation against subjectivity could be explained. Thus we will try, from this point of view, to cast at least some light on the *intellectual genesis* of '68 philosophy, which may help us understand several aspects of it. But our intention is not to perform a genealogy of the genealogists.

French Philosophy, Hyperbolic Repetition (of German Philosophy?)

At least one tenacious misperception has to be refuted.[32] Far from being a purely indigenous product, '68 philosophy is in fact the use of themes and theses borrowed, in more or less complex combinations, from German philosophers, for example, Marx, Nietzsche, Freud, and Heidegger, to mention the fundamental ones. This exploitation of German philosophical terrain cannot be reduced to mere repetition, and we do not intend to reproach French philosophy for it; rather, our intention is to pose the problem of its originality. French philosophy seems to take up the themes it borrows

31. J.-F. Lyotard, *Le Tombeau de l'intellectuel, et autres papiers*, Galilée, 1984, p. 65.
32. Cf. this fine demand for French originality from Lyotard: "Today when German or American philosophers talk about neoirrationalism in French philosophy, when Habermas is giving Derrida and Foucault progressivist lessons in the name of the cause of modernism, they are gravely mistaken about what the issues are in modernism" (ibid., p. 81).

from German philosophy in order to *radicalize* them, and it is this radicalization that is the source of its antihumanism, the thing peculiar to it. In this regard, it is interesting to analyze two significant examples of how the German heritage was handled on this particular point (the questioning of humanism), in order to show from which kind of work on German philosophy French antihumanism derived.

1. From Heidegger to Derrida In *Letter on Humanism* (1946) Heidegger explained that, if philosophy can no longer "be characterized as humanism," it is "to the extent that humanism thinks from a metaphysical point of view"[33] or, more precisely, that it corresponds to the truly modern side of metaphysics, that is, the metaphysics of subjectivity. Here we will recall only that in Heidegger's view metaphysics, as the search for a supreme reality (a "primary being") who is the foundation and model for all of reality, has been realized since Descartes in the form of an "anthropo-logy" or, in other words, in the form of a philosophy in which it is man as "master and possessor of nature" who confers on every being its real substance and assigns it its real place in a world he organizes for his own purposes. With the modern advent of man as subject, every being, "brought before man in its quality as an object, is established and held in the domain assigned to it and available for it"; in other words, "beings in their totality . . . are understood in such a way that they really are beings only to the extent that man situates them in representation and in production."[34] For humanism, the appreciation of the value of a thing is subject to its capacity to help fulfill man's essence in his destiny as the "Lord of beings." In this way, humanism is inseparable from the modern metaphysics for which the technological period, dominated by calculation and the organization of everything for the purpose of "mastery," is in turn only the highest pinnacle or, if you wish, the "world-to-be": On the horizon of humanism there appears, in Heidegger, the period when man,

33. *Lettre sur l'humanisme*, trans. R. Munier, Ed. Aubier, 1964, p. 85 (*Brief über den Humanismus*, in *Collected Works*, vol. 9, p. 334).
34. *Chemins qui ne mènent nulle part*, trans. W. Brokmeier, Gallimard, pp. 81–82 (*Holzwege*, in *Collected Works*, vol. 5, Frankfurt/M., 1978, p. 89).

having become "*the rational animal,* which today means the working man, can only wander on the deserts of the ravaged earth."[35] The questioning of humanism and subjectivity logically belongs within the framework of this deconstruction of modernity: In view of this "devastation of the earth, a result of metaphysics," where man becomes a "beast of labor . . . , abandoned to the vertigo of his fabrications,"[36] the temptation is certainly great to break away from this approach, the foundation of the metaphysics of subjectivity and so also of humanism, where man has "led his life as *subjectum* at the center of every relation."[37] So the philosophy inaugurated in 1927 by *Being and Time* would attempt to accomplish a sort of decentering of the world from man's point of view: It follows that it would be "against humanism," without, however, being oriented "opposite to what is human" in order to "depreciate man's dignity"; instead, it would be a matter of grasping what this "dignity proper to man" is that the "highest humanist efforts have not yet investigated."[38] As we know, Heidegger would situate it in the opening onto the true revelation of things, in this "illumination of Being" which it is man's to "shepherd," thinking himself as "*Da-sein,*" that is, as the "there" of Being, as the place where Being (the coming forth of things) comes to be gathered in and sheltered in a gaze.

Can the philosophy of man that developed from this decentering still be called "humanist"? Heidegger himself takes exception to the word, on the basis of the interpretation of humanism we have just recalled. However, Derrida, in *The Ends of Man,* analyzes this sustained desire to grasp "the dignity that is proper to man" as a remnant of humanism as a philosophy of the "proper" or of the "as such" ("man as such"). What seems like a bidding up, then, follows a rather simple logic: The values of identity or proximity to self that inspire the research into the "proper" have also inspired not only humanism but also the whole of Western metaphysics as a philosophy of essence, as a search for "the presence of the thing itself in its

35. *Essais et conférences,* trans. A. Préau, Gallimard, p. 81 (*Vorträge und Aufsätze,* Pfullingen, 1959, p. 72).
36. Ibid., pp. 82–83 (pp. 72 ff.).
37. *Chemins,* pp. 84–85 (*Holzwege,* p. 94).
38. *Lettre sur l'humanisme,* p. 75 (*Brief über den Humanismus,* p. 330).

essence."[39] So if the deconstruction of metaphysics is going through
an upheaval of this philosophy of the being of beings as presence
(presence/identity to self, presence as an object for a subject in a
representation) as Derrida, following Heidegger, believes, it is the
questioning of metaphysics itself that is involved when any philosophy of the "proper" is rejected, including the "proper" of man.

We will return at the appropriate moment to this Derridean
"critique" of Heidegger. However, it is already clear enough that it
plays a part in this desire to carry the Heideggerian project beyond
the point Heidegger would have taken it. As far as antihumanism is
concerned, this bidding up will mean eventually disputing not only
the definition of man in his essence as the subject or foundation of
all reality, as Heidegger had done, but indeed any search for an
essence ("the properly human"), which in order to be preserved
would have to be defined as "values." Discovering whether this
attempted higher bid is in fact practicable, and what the theoretical
and practical consequences of such a sharp disqualification of
values might be, will ultimately have to be the subject of a closer
analysis. Nevertheless, from Heidegger to Derrida, the gesture of
radicalizing the critique of humanism is what constitutes French
philosophy of the sixties (in this case what we call French Heideggerianism). It began with the relationship between humanism and
the (modern) metaphysics of subjectivity established by Heidegger
and became a hyperbolic antihumanism that, twenty years later, can
be seen to have had some difficulty accommodating itself to the
newly rediscovered reference to human rights.

2. From Marx to Althusser   In this very different register, an
analogous gesture is nevertheless repeated, with this important
difference, namely, that the antihumanist radicalization characteristic of Althusserian Marxism is presented here as the accomplishment of Marx himself in his break (here again is the notorious
theme of "rupture") with what would have to be called his youthful
errors, errors his followers have often fallen back into and which

39. J. Derrida, in *Margins*, trans. Alan Bass, University of Chicago Press, Chicago, 1982, pp. 131.

have necessitated today a renewal of theoretical activity in the heart of Marxism in order to construct that for which Marx himself only laid the cornerstone. Althusser locates these youthful errors in precisely what he calls "Marx's humanist period," "dominated by a liberal rationalist humanism closer to Kant and Fichte than to Hegel"[40] and later by a "communalist humanism" inspired by Feuerbach.[41] In both cases the young Marx criticizes the historical forms of the state only in the name of an essence of man—man as freedom–reason, man as the being who can only be fulfilled through "universal human relations"; so it is the need to fulfill this essence that establishes history as the movement through which man, overcoming the alienation of his being, becomes what he (properly) is. On the other hand, after 1845 Marx broke with every theory of history based on the essence of man: Criticizing even the idea of a "universal essence of man," Marx questioned the traditional problematic of humanism and founded a "new problematic," which no longer defined the conditions in which "each single individual" can become the "real subject" of an "essence of man," a problematic that from then on would study how the true subject (Subject) of history unfolds, something he located in the complex structuration where forces of production, relations of production, superstructures, and ideologies meet, in the heart of a "social formation."[42] Of course, the young Marx had already criticized the humanism of the Declaration of the Rights of Man, most notably in 1843 in *The Jewish Question*, but only for the purpose of demonstrating the opposition between the abstract man of the Declaration, "an imaginary member of an imaginary realm," and the "real individual" who, suffering and active, does not care about proclamations of "political emancipation" that ignore "human emancipation" as "real emancipation," that is, as "practical emancipation."[43] So for Althusser, the (abstract) critique of humanism remained pro-

---

40. L. Althusser, *For Marx*, trans. Ben Brewster, Verso, London, 1979, p. 223.
41. Ibid., p. 225.
42. Ibid., p. 227.
43. K. Marx, *La Question juive*, "10/18," p. 26 (*Zur Judenfrage*, in MEGA, I, vol. 1, p. 576).

foundly humanistic, because it was motivated by a valorization of the "real individual," thus by a "concrete" or "real" humanism.[44] Marx's true theoretical revolution consisted from that time on of a break with *any* humanism, abstract or concrete, so that, here again, a sort of decentering of the gaze might result. What is in question is, in fact, rejecting any idea of basing history on an essence of man, in any mode whatsoever, and therefore objecting to man as the *subject* of history and to history as the history of man's alienation from his essence and subsequent return to self. This is true to such an extent that Heidegger's formula, "It is precisely no longer man taken solely as such who matters," could also apply here (and it is not a philosophically narrow paradox), even though this time the decentering leads not to the illumination of Being but to the self-development of the social formation with a complex structure.

In any case, it is clear why French Marxism of the '68 period denounced all humanism as dangerously ideological: On the one hand, it reactivated (against the mature Marx) concepts used by the young Marx which were later destroyed by "the newness of the concepts of dialectical materialism," as a result of which, "any philosophy which would depend, in one way or another, on Marx for the restoration of theoretical anthropology or humanism would theoretically be nothing but *ashes*"; and on the other hand, "in practice, it could erect a monument of pre-Marxist ideology that would weigh on real history and be in danger of leading it to an impasse" by hiding the true subject of history and the true scope of progress (one might think that progress, which has been led astray by humanism, as Althusser calmly explains, is played out on the level of "problems that pertain to the domain of the superstructure," such as, for example, "the problems of law and the person").[45] In short, renewing that theoretical activity, which French Marxism would claim was its proper work, will consist of fully learning the lesson of Marx's approach and of expurgating any trace of humanism from the concepts of the Marxist tradition, accepting to the end the "philosophical antihumanism" founded by Marx but too often hidden by the

44. On the critique of "real humanism," cf. "A Complementary Note on Real Humanism," in *For Marx*, pp. 242 ff.
45. *For Marx*, p. 241.

contamination of the workers' movement with bourgeois ideology. Here again, French antihumanism grows out of the will to radicalize a gesture inherited from the German tradition, by finally achieving the rejection of a humanism that Marx himself was freed from only progressively and that a fair number of his heirs did not protect themselves from well enough.

From Heidegger to Derrida, from Marx (or Marxism) to Althusser, the analogy between these constitutive acts of French antihumanism is striking. As we will see, things are not so different on the part of the Freudian component of '68 philosophy either, where Lacan will reproach one type of analytic orthodoxy for preserving a role for the traditional (humanist) ideal of a consciousness that is self-transparent and master of itself, when it should have excluded it from the theory and practice of psychoanalysis instead. We will also see how Foucault devoted his fundamental efforts to extending into new fields (notably that of cultural history) a critique of subjectivity that Nietzsche limited himself to formulating on the strictly philosophical plane. So Foucault explains, also in terms of the formula of the higher bid, that it is a matter of seeing "with the help of Nietzsche's texts—but also with anti-Nietzschean theses (which are all the same Nietzschean!)—what can be done in one area or another."[46] More Nietzschean than Nietzsche himself, then, and again by means of hyperbolic repetition.

So it was that, by taking what it had inherited from German philosophy, French philosophy came to the point of denouncing any form of thought where man in his essence (or the essence of man) was the basis or the *subject* of reality (historical, psychic, or cultural). Various German philosophers, then, were the chief prosecutors who drew up the case against the subject brought by the '68 philosophers, and it may well be that this is the statement that leads us to what this dimension of contemporary French philosophy has basically been: not so much an original and creative moment in intellectual history as simply a secondary growth. It may also be that, through this desire to radicalize a gesture that had already

---

46. M. Foucault, interview of May 29, 1984, which appeared in *Les Nouvelles littéraires*, from June 28 to July 5, 1984.

been a ritual of German philosophy for almost a century, '68 philosophy found itself even more naively and more seriously exposed to difficulties that today require, as we attempt to take account of them, a reexamination of the interminable case that has been endlessly made against the subject for two decades.

The Subject's Appeal

The destruction of subjectivity, rallying cry for the philosophers of the sixties, raises at least two kinds of problems, corresponding to two major figures in the sought-for settlement of the case.

When the prosecution develops its case in terms of Heidegger's deconstruction of the "metaphysics of subjectivity," two traditional characteristics of the modern subject quite logically come under attack: *will* and *consciousness*. When, within this tradition, Lyotard describes the task of "making philosophy inhuman" and, for that purpose, demonstrating, for example, that "man is not the user of language," with the understanding that "there no more exists a subject than there does a language," to *whom* is he addressing the definition of the task and the call to assume it? If today we must "see to it" that "form is given" to the question of the end or ends of man,[47] on *whom* is the effort of this vigilance to be imposed, and what will the status of this effort be? Heidegger had already confronted this problem, as we have shown elsewhere, so when he indicated in the 1943 Postscript to *What Is Metaphysics?* that "we must prepare ourselves to be available solely to experience nothingness" and that for this reason "we [must] not hide from anguish" and must know how to demonstrate "great courage," to *whom*, if not a subject, is the demand for what must be called an effort of *will* addressed? The hyper-Heideggerian higher bid, which is one of the essential components '68 thought, will find in these texts the indication that the early Heidegger had not yet overcome in a radical enough manner the basis of what comes about through the activity of the subject as

---

47. J.-L. Nancy and P. Lacoue-Labarthe, opening of the colloquium *Les Fins de l'homme*, p. 15.

will. But when the later Heidegger, in a text like *Serenity* where he is thought to have gone farthest toward overcoming the will, writes that "we should (*sollen*) do nothing, only wait,"[48] and that to accomplish this we must "break the habit of will" and "stay alert, prepared for serenity," is it not with an excess of *will* that this emptying of the will is pursued? To go beyond even the point Heidegger arrived at in this respect would be *to will*, in this case, too, and to demonstrate in practice that subjectivity as will decidedly and stubbornly resists its own disappearance. The internal difficulty such efforts are exposed to increases if one considers that they call for greater *consciousness* as well. Through this effort of will, we are asked to think "the barely thinkable" if not the "unthinkable,"[49] which metaphysics has always forgotten or hidden: that the thing that has to be thought, be it only as an absence or a retreat (in the sense of the hidden side of the cube that disappears behind any appearance), does not displace the difficulty by a single inch, since one must become conscious *as such* of this concealing (of this *différance*). Consequently, here we have the intrinsically inconsistent search for consciousness and increased mastery or, if you like, the reappearance of the idea of a more encompassing second coming, even if it is quite obviously out of the question to attribute to these efforts the intention to abolish concealment, to overcome withdrawal, or to erase *différance*. To make forgetting itself (the withdrawal of Being, the hiding of meaning, etc.) known (and thus represent it) is nevertheless still to seek greater consciousness, even though it is the consciousness of a lack (the representation of an absence). And if will and consciousness (effort and representation) are still at the heart of these approaches, the beyond of this man or this subject whose death is being declared strangely evokes a *cogito* which is, after all, quite Cartesian. Far be it from us to complain of the subject's resistance to its own extermination; nevertheless, if it is reassuring, the presence of a subjectivity in this context poses a number of questions, everything behaving as though, *ipso facto*, the subject were appealing the charges brought against it.

48. M. Heidegger, *Questions III*, Gallimard, p. 188 ("Zur Erorterung der Gelassenheit," in *Gelassenheit*, Pfullingen 1959, p. 34).
49. Ibid., p. 217 (p. 64).

It can be easily shown that analogous difficulties exist for the other major attempt to eradicate subjectivity, that is, in the context of Marxism. In Althusser's lecture "On the Relation of Marx to Hegel,"[50] he claims, as one result of the "rupture" that characterized Marxism as a science of history, "the elimination of the category of subject (transcendental or otherwise), the disappearance of the notion of subject." History must be conceived of as "process without a subject," that is, as a pure unfolding of structures or relations. However, if the subject may no longer be defined as the source of history, as Althusser states in "Lenin before Hegel,"[51] it is somewhat surprising to read some pages later: "It is the masses . . . who make history."[52] It would be easy to believe that in spite of everything there is still a (practical and collective) subject of history. Of course these "masses" only make history without understanding the history they are making, no doubt penetrated by relations that are expressed through them. All the same, let us look at what Althusser claims is, in his opinion, the status of the experience of the masses.

"No revolutionary perspective is possible unless political struggle has priority over mere economic struggle,"[53] that is, without the deliberate transformation of the masses themselves and of their demands in the struggle to take over the power of the state. In this respect, then, historical process depends entirely on a practical initiative of the collective subject, which is the proletariat. At this point, of course, Althusser appropriates one of Lenin's famous phrases—that there is no effective practice unless there is theory to orient it. This is the basis on which Althusser gives such importance to theoretical practice, which in his view is necessary if the workers' movement is to be revitalized. But a revolutionary perspective appears to be closely linked to the idea of *action* informed by *knowledge!* The subject's disappearance under these circumstances has become oddly hypothetical.

50. Althusser, "Sur le rapport de Marx et de Hegel," in *Lenine et la philosophie*, pp. 84–86. (This lecture was not included in Brewster's translation.)
51. "Lenin before Hegel," in *Lenin and Philosophy*, p. 121.
52. Ibid., p. 124.
53. *Positions*, p. 56.

So we are less surprised to read: "Everything depends, *in the last instance,* not on techniques but on militants, on their class *consciousness,* on their devotion, and on their *courage."*[54] In this final foundation of history on consciousness and courage or, in other words, on the classical attributes of the metaphysical subject—representation and will—"the elimination of the category of subject" seems again most decidedly at an abrupt standstill.

Let us be clear: It is not a matter of accusing '68 philosophy of not going far enough in its antihumanism and in its emptying of the subject, nor is there any question of celebrating too soon, given the reassuring signs of these persistent traces of a philosophy of the subject, or of believing that the dangers inherent in the intellectual structure of the philosophical discourses of the sixties were not so serious after all and no cause for concern. The philosophists of the sixties could not thematize in their own discourses the resistance of subjectivity to its own "vanishing," due to the nature of their fundamental theoretical opinions. They could never confer any status on this residual subjectivity unless it were precisely the status of a persistent residue of a former discourse—in Heidegger's sense when he says, "one cannot strip oneself of metaphysics as of an opinion," and in Derrida's sense when he suggests that "the simple practice of language" (and we know how much, since Nietzsche, grammar serves as a sandbag at the dike of metaphysics) runs the risk of always reinstating "the 'new' terrain on the oldest ground."[55]

In short, if it is not thematized, this survival of subjectivity necessarily tends to be thought of in terms of its future disappearance. Let us make no mistake: Even though subjectivity may find, here and there, some space to survive in within the philosophies included by the ideal type proposed here, this does not imply that the case brought by them against the subject has ended and the charges dropped. The conviction was and is, up through the most recent texts, a radical one. If an appeal of the sentence were to be made, it would be through an equally radical critique of this constellation of philosophies. We at least know as of now that this

54. Ibid., p. 46; the italics are ours—L.F. and A.R.
55. Derrida, in *Margins,* p. 135.

appeal could be argued on the basis of inconsistencies in the discourse of the prosecutors.

Three observations will suffice to make clear what appears to us to be the result of this philosophical typology of the sixties. First, we must clarify that by emphasizing, as we have in this chapter, the dangers and difficulties of contemporary antihumanism we do not mean that we intend to give up our own critique of the metaphysics of subjectivity: It would be absurd today, as we have emphasized, to attempt philosophically to restore figures of subjectivity whose deconstruction dates not to the sixties, or even to Marx, Nietzsche, Freud, or Heidegger, but at least as far back as Kant's *Transcendental Dialectics* in *Critique of Pure Reason*, where his chapter on paralogisms already sketches out the limits of rational psychology. If a certain conception of subjectivity, a "metaphysical" one if you wish, can and even must be the object of interrogation, it is, after all, a classical *topos* of philosophy. What we are arguing, on the other hand, in the way the philosophy discussed here in terms of its ideal type has performed this interrogation, is the massive, brutal, and unsubtle identification it makes between the *philosophy of subjectivity* and *metaphysics* (or, in the Marxist context, *bourgeois philosophy*). This simplistic identification, insofar as it was inspired by various contemporary critiques of metaphysics, was in fact what led '68 philosophy into committing itself to the very costly (perhaps ruinous) antihumanist route. It also prevented any possibility of thematizing this survival of subjectivity after the critique of metaphysics, when by chance, and in spite of itself, the subject sprang back into its discourses. The point is truly decisive. The very possibility, for a philosophy like Kant's (where the least one can say is that it takes subjectivity as its point of departure, by way of the "Copernican revolution"), that a systematic critique of the illusions relative to the subject has been conducted, through the analysis of the paralogisms of pure reason, means that things have to be considered here with more care and thought. However far from the idea of subjectivity straight "metaphysics" may seem to be, one must nevertheless learn to distinguish *several* figures of subjectivity, of which only certain ones are ultimately "metaphysical" or even—why not?—"petit-bourgeois." We consider this perspective to be indispensable for anyone who wants to defend today, nonnaively and nonmetaphysically, *some* humanism, within which *some* reference to the idea of subjectivity seems to be the obvious condition of possibility. Thus, at the horizon of our thoughts (and particularly in our last chapter) can be found our intention to analyze the various forms of subjectivity in modern philosophy in order to bring out, with precision, the error or illusion shared by all the philosophical currents to which the ideal type of the sixties can be applied, the error of assimilating these forms of subjectivity and of believing it could massively denounce *all* subjectivity or *all* humanism.

A second observation may avoid another possible error. It would be easy to ridicule the theme of the "death of man" by merely observing the incontestable fact that today the values of individualism are on the rise on every side and that, in terms of this sign of the times, '68 philosophy seems rather obsolete. The return of individualism is indeed equally as obvious on what is commonly called the Right, the neoliberal wave, as it is on the Left through the promotion of the "new ethics" of the eighties. However, we felt it necessary to avoid the easiest solution, which would have been to rely in some way on this culturally favorable context to send the themes of antihumanism back to the prop room. To exploit a somewhat suspicious horizon of expectations demagogically, as J.-P. Aron so freely did in *The Moderns,* would reduce the critique itself to an effect of fashion, thus seriously weakening it and simultaneously reinforcing what it is attempting to question. Thus the critique we have elaborated here and pursued in the succeeding chapters was intended to be *philosophical,* not *ideological:* It does not appeal to fashionable categories but is limited to giving evidence of internal difficulties within the philosophies it criticizes and to illuminating those consequences that are most difficult to accept.

Finally, we have to return to how the ideal type described in this chapter can be applied to the intellectual currents borne along by or accompanying May 1968 viewed as a historical phenomenon. Here again, things are quite complex: As we recalled at the start, the May movement did not seem at first to be intellectually dominated by the search for the "inhuman" (in Lyotard's sense, when he talks about the necessity of making philosophy "inhuman"). Far from simply being included with other evidence in the history of the eradication of subjectivity, May '68 seems, from several points of view, to be a rebellion of subjects against a system that negated them as such (reification). Are, then, the rebellion of May '68 and the philosophical thought of the sixties really so different, so incompatible? That would be truly surprising. The numerous statements of the philosophers of the '68 period, in which they see themselves as within the movement and its themes, would then be an instance of rather unlikely blindness, to such an extent that to stay with the most immediate content of the May rebellion might easily lead one to suspect that the ideal type we propose here only very imperfectly accounts for French philosophy of the sixties, even though it was so close (chronologically and sympathetically) to the 1968 movement. In short, the appearance of May became an obstacle to the interpretation of '68 philosophy sketched at the most general level in this chapter and specified through its major components in the subsequent chapters. So it became necessary, before addressing the specifics, to raise the problem of the cultural significance of May 1968. This we have tried to do in the following chapter.

2 /
Interpretations of
May 1968

It would have been beyond the reach of this study to review exhaustively the numerous interpretations inspired by the crisis of 1968; nor could we have suddenly claimed to produce a new interpretation. It seemed to us more credible and more effective, in view of the apparently irreducible diversity of the existing interpretations, to search for a guiding principle or thread that might allow us to structure this diversity and, on that basis, understand it. Discovering what motivates the diversity and what is in play, we would then be better able to orient ourselves to it and to pose more thoughtfully the problem of choice among possible interpretations. These days we are well aware that the interpretation of any historical phenomenon poses complex problems, traditionally summarized as the question of objectivity in interpretation: If the historian's work is no longer believed to consist of merely recording a brute fact and "reproducing the reality of the past as it happened," as in the naively positivist view, the objectivity intended requires that the point of view or perspective from which the research will be conducted first be objectified. The theory of these points of view or perspectives can be called the *logic of interpretations*. In view of the amazing diversity of the interpretations of May '68, which have produced absolutely antithetical descriptions of the events, it seemed particularly desirable to propose a logic of our interpretative field at the start.

The Logic of Interpretations

The presentation of such a logic presupposes the existence of a primary material. In this case it is furnished in part by a valuable inventory of interpretations of the May movement by P. Bénéton and

34

J. Touchard, dating from 1970.[1] Though still to be completed
through the inclusion of more recent interpretations, this work is
valuable for the record of a great many studies it provides and for its
attempt to classify them at least *minimally*. The authors did not try
to define a structuration for the interpretative field based on certain
principles but instead limited themselves to grouping together em-
pirically or inductively works that derive from analogous hypotheses
about the causes of the May crisis. For this reason, their analysis
gives us readily accessible material from which to begin formulating
the question of a logic that might possibly organize the interpretative
field cleared in this way. The classification proposed by Bénéton and
Touchard brings into view eight possible readings of the event:

1. *May '68 as a conspiracy.* The thesis of subversive intentions (on
the part of leftist groups or the Communist party, which could ma-
neuver them at will) was at the time developed by de Gaulle and
Pompidou and was later refined by various interpreters according to
more or less surprising hypotheses about the instigators of the conspiracy.[2]

2. *May '68 as a university crisis.* This interpretation evoked the rig-
idity of the old university system, its problems adapting to the new
requirements of higher education "for the masses,"[3] and its "bureaucratic" resistance to change.[4] In point of fact, during the
1960s the *content* of the student population had profoundly
changed in direct relation to the substantial growth in the number
of students, rapidly transforming the old bourgeois university into a
middle-class one. So the crisis was interpreted in reference to the

1. P. Bénéton and J. Touchard, "Les Interprétations de la crise de mai–juin
1968," *Revue française de science politique*, June 1970.
2. Cf. F. Duprat, *Les Journées de Mai 1968: Les dessous d'une révolution*, Paris,
1968, where the conspiracy is described as being radio-controlled from East
Germany.
3. For example, in a study entitled "Quelques causes de la révolte éstudiant-
ine," *La Table ronde*, Dec. 1968–Jan. 1969, R. Boudon points out that between
1961 and 1968 the number of students in the law schools increased 300 percent
and in the humanities departments, 250 percent.
4. Cf. M. Crozier, "Révolution libérale ou révolte petite-bourgeoise," *Communication*, no. 12.

.1ew problems raised for these new students, who were less well prepared for their studies by their social surroundings and less sure than their predecessors had been of acquiring upon leaving, the social status corresponding to the image their studies provided them. From this perspective, the social marginalization of the students is viewed as the major cause of the crisis.[5] It is clear that this interpretation could successfully account for everything in the discourses of May that involved criticizing the examinations as reproducing a social differentiation left intact by the supposedly fictional democratization of the university.[6]

3. *May as an outbreak of adolescent rebellion and fever.* The positive reading views the rebellion as an outburst of play, a celebration of life, or even as "parricide"—"a kind of socioadolescent 1789 that made youth into a sociopolitical force";[7] the critical reading views the rebellion as a "psychodrama," an imitation, or a more or less ridiculous parody of revolution.[8]

4. *May as a crisis of civilization.* In this interpretation, the target of the movement is claimed to have been "not a regime so much as a so-called civilization,"[9] the "consumer society" being the primary object of attack. This theme was developed by Malraux in particular in various lectures during 1968–69: "We are faced not with the need for reform but with one of civilization's most profound crises" (June 20, 1968), as the return of the "old nihilism . . . with its black flag and no other desire than destruction" demonstrates.

---

5. In 1984 in *Homo Academicus,* Ed. de Minuit, p. 211, P. Bourdieu again takes up this interpretation, considering this "structural *déclassement*" as "producing a type of collective tendency for revolt."
6. The discourse of May was considerably nourished in this respect by P. Bourdieu and J.-C. Passeron's *Héritiers,* which E. Faure also heavily relied on in his last statements when, for example, he condemned "the transmitting of privileges that the traditional regimen of examinations and *oonoours* merely infinitely perpetuates, in spite of the appearance" (February 15, 1969).
7. E. Morin, *La Brèche: Premières réflexions sur les événements,* Fayard, 1968, p. 26.
8. This is, in part, the interpretation R. Aron developed in *La Révolution introuvable,* Fayard, 1968 (*The Elusive Revolution: Anatomy of a Student Revolt,* trans. Gordon Clough, Praeger, New York, 1969).
9. J.-M. Domenach, *Esprit,* June–July 1968.

Fundamentally, the crisis of May blames the collapse of the values of progress, the ideas of the Enlightenment which had promised something other than the infinite development of consumerism in a technological society.

5. *May as a new type of class conflict.* Developed primarily by A. Touraine,[10] this interpretation sees "a new form of class struggle" in the 1968 crisis, not a directly economic struggle (owners against employees) but a "social, cultural, and political" struggle, more against domination and integration (against technocracy) than against exploitation (professionals, from whom any real decision-making power has been withdrawn, against the "technocrats" who dominate the important sectors of social activity).

6. *May as a social conflict of a traditional type.* In this perspective, which is of course the orthodox communist one,[11] the core of the crisis is found not so much in the student groups, viewed as mere chance detonators, as in the support of the workers' strikes (specific to France) for "legitimate material demands." The roots of the crisis and its spread are ultimately located in social and economic facts; after a phase of uninterrupted growth since the end of the war, by July 1966 the situation was in a process of reversal with a slowdown in production and sharply rising unemployment that by 1968 had reached a level four times higher than in 1964 (a level that seems fairly modest in retrospect: 245 million people were estimated to be out of work in 1968). Moreover, the interpretation proposed from this viewpoint had the advantage of accounting for the sudden eruption of the crisis: If the situation was disturbing, at least it was not revolutionary.

7. *May as a political crisis,* blamed on the institutions of the Fifth Republic and on the absence of a real political alternative. The major cause of the rebellion (which is described here as focused on the theme "Ten years is enough") would be sought in the growing unpopularity of de Gaulle and his prime minister at a time when the safety valve that a possible change of government represents

10. A. Touraine, *Le Mouvement de Mai ou le communisme utopique,* Ed. du Seuil, 1968, and *La Société post-industrielle,* Denoël, 1969.
11. Cf. R. Andrieu, *Les Communistes et la Révolution,* Julliard, 1968.

had been eliminated by the institutional system. A number of analyses pointed out that in the framework of the Third or Fourth Republic dissatisfactions and weariness of a similar kind would have resulted merely in the fall of the cabinet, most likely during the first incidents at Nanterre. The government's stability, however, guaranteed by the institutions of 1958, had had the perverse effect of creating a rise of extremism, and a ministerial crisis was transformed into a crisis of the regime.[12]

8. *May as a chain of circumstantial events.* This position, which evidently attracted Bénéton and Touchard, should not be rejected out of hand, however superficial it may seem. Within this perspective, it was not inevitable that there happened to be a university at Nanterre cut off from the outside world, that plans to reform the university were so long deferred by Minister Peyrefitte, that the police were called into the Sorbonne on May 3, that the prime minister was absent from France at the time and the president of the Republic was on an official visit to Romania, and so on. These are regarded as a number of chance happenings, each of which played a role and without which nothing would have happened in the same way. This interpretation invites considerable thought, at any rate, about the importance the other interpretations give to various causes of the crisis they regard as fundamental.

This inventory of the interpretations is undoubtedly interesting. Nevertheless, the proposed classification is strictly empirical, and in the absence of any classifying principle nothing prevents our imagining either another structure for this diversity or other conceptions for interpreting it. Without ignoring the diversity but instead taking it as the thing to be questioned, it seems necessary to look for conditions (or at least for some of them) that make this diversity possible, so to speak. If it is our aim to produce a systematic classification rather than a complete list, we have to describe the precise guidelines we will follow to orient ourselves through the maze of this interpretative field toward the discovery of a logic in this diversity.

12. This analysis was developed, for example, in an article by P. Avril, "L'Amplificateur de la crise," published in *France-Forum.*

The guideline we propose here arises from a simple consideration: In the process of an analysis of a historical movement, which is regarded as an overthrowing or even a revolution, the major problem for the interpreter is to determine how much importance and what status to give to the point of view of the participants in the events. They always define themselves more or less by the conviction that they are "making history," that they are opening up a radically new future through their actions. The difficulty is to determine, retrospectively, to what extent this conviction continued to correspond to factual reality. Different types of interpretations will inevitably appear, depending on whether (1) the interpreter espouses the viewpoint of the participants, therefore finding that the meaning of the episode resides in what they themselves intended, or (2) the interpreter considers the participants' point of view illusory or misguided, in which case he will consider that they were making history without knowing the history they were making, duped in some way by a rationality at work in history that is not grounded in the conscious project of any particular subject. At this point we already have two great types of interpretation before us, which depend on the definition of the historical subject: The interpretation espousing the participants' viewpoint defines the subject of history as the active freedom of practical subjects; the interpretation that involves a process developing "behind the participants' backs," so to speak, rather than defining the subject of history as a finite subject, explains the future through the self-unfolding of an immanent logic (and *in this sense* history is conceived of as "a process without a subject").

If we accept this duality, we can accept, in principle, a possible third type of interpretation, one that refuses to attribute events either to the initiatives of participating subjects or to the immanent logic of whatever System is thought to be the true Subject of history. Instead, this third type of interpretation (deconstructing the rationality both of intentions and of an immanent logic to overcome them) foregrounds the absolute indeductibility of what the ultimate truth would be in order to be an Event proper, a pure uprising, a break with all continuity, a radical irruption of newness. As we know, the philosophical model provided by Heidegger's deconstruction of the various figures of subjectivity, the reference here, is one of the major components of '68 philosophy. Indeed, one of the best guidelines for orienting oneself through the interpretations of a crisis whose meaning, for various reasons, poses the problem of the subject (i.e., the content of '68 philosophy, the nature of the link between the ideology of 1968 and the individualism of the 1980s) might well be sought in the idea of the subject (the subject of history) that inspires the interpreters' work: the (finite) practical subject, the (absolute) Subject as immanent System in history, and the disappearance of all subjectivity (Heideggerian *Dasein*)—the vanishing point of the critique of these two sides of the metaphysical subject. For this reason, the problems raised by the interpretations of May 1968 should seem strangely homogeneous with what is, in fact, the deepest intellectual stake in these events: the trial of the subject. Even if it were only for this reason, the guideline we propose is worth developing here.

The Participants' Point of View

In terms of the first type of interpretation, May 1968 should be read as freedom (the practical subject) rebelling against state oppression. This is the fundamental content of all the interpretations that take the most immediate appearance of the crisis and consider it in relation to a revolutionary aim. We will limit ourselves here to describing some important examples.

In an interview with the editors of *Spiegel*,[13] Sartre maintained that in May the "social (that is, true) Left" arose against the limits imposed on its actions both by repression from the powers that be and by resistance from the "political Left": This social Left, he wrote, "went as far as it could and was finally defeated because it was betrayed by its own representatives." An uprising on the part of freedom against the jointly exercised oppression of the state and its instruments, the meaning of the crisis was exhausted in what Sartre called demand itself (thus, conscious and mastered intention itself)

13. J.-P. Sartre, *Les communistes ont peur de la révolution*, Ed. J. Didier, 1968, pp. 7–32.

on the part of those who were rising up: "a new demand for dignity, for authority, for power," in short, for "freedom," thus a revolution made by, and for, freedom. This is essentially the same point of view (that of the participants) espoused and developed by C. Castoriadis (J.-M. Coudray) and E. Morin in *La Brèche*. Castoriadis pointed out that the "most radical revolutionary statement" was made in an unprecedented way in 1968, proceeding from a desire for "a radical break with the bureaucratic capitalist world" and for "a revolutionary rebuilding of society."[14] Here, too, it is affirmed that the driving force and aim of the movement coincide in revolutionary freedom: "The revolutionary nature of the present movement is just as apparent in its aims as in its modes of action, its modes of being, and in the indissoluble unity of all of them."[15] Morin repeats the same thing: Youth seems to him to be "the new revolutionary avant-garde in society." Not yet socially integrated, young people are the most likely to be able to answer the question that "history asks of man's creativity," namely, the indispensable question of renewing or of overthrowing institutions, indispensable in a society that wants to survive, that is, be transformed. Consequently, when the students wanted to transform professor/student relations, the content of the subjects taught, and the relations between society and the university, their intentions were well in line with the real meaning of their actions: At least for the most part, "they knew what they were doing."[16] This is Morin's meaning when he concludes that "the objectives of the student movement are already drawing the lines of force for the historical period that is beginning." In short, the choice and conscious pursuit of revolutionary objectives are what creates a course of history that will conform to such objectives.

What should we think of this type of interpretation? The reader today, benefiting from a certain distance, might ask whether the participants' point of view adopted by these interpretations really is the clearest and most appropriate for framing the meaning of events

14. *La Brèche*, p. 92.
15. Ibid., p. 93.
16. Cf., on this point, ibid., p. 141.

that the participants were caught up in. Thus Sartre, for example, hardly glows with clairvoyance when, in the interview quoted above, he realized that, for the moment, the "bourgeoisie" had won and that it would take back from the "workers" once again, through higher prices, what they had gained through the Grenelle Agreements, though as he points out, "the workers are going to realize this. . . . they will not easily accept it, and it is likely that we will then see a resurgence of the violence of true social forces below the false political picture the elections have just drawn." It must be admitted that the relevance of this prognosis has since been shown to be quite doubtful, as we will see later: To the extent that the history of "after-May" raises the problem of how much integrative power the crisis really exercised, to see it as an irreversible turning point seems particularly blind. And to do full justice to the matter of blindness we might add that Sartre stated that he was "convinced that the present leaders of the Left will represent nothing at all in ten years' time," whereas G. Mollet, the leaders of the Communist party, and . . . Mitterand are all members of this group.

Castoriadis himself, who was nevertheless one of the first to analyze the totalitarian potential of certain revolutions, claimed to believe that "whatever its outcome, May '68 has opened a new period in world history" and that posterity would hail the imperishable greatness of the heroes of this world history that had been launched by the events of May:

> Gifted, poetic words spring up from the anonymous crowd. Educators are quickly educated: university professors and *lycée* principals do not soon recover from the shock of their students' intelligence, as opposed to the absurdity and uselessness of what they had been teaching them. In a matter of days, young people twenty years old reach an understanding and political wisdom that hardworking revolutionaries have not been able to achieve in thirty years of militancy. During the March 22 Movement, at U.N.E.F., at SNESup [Syndicat National D'Education Supérieure], leaders appeared whose clairvoyance and effectiveness are second to none of the leaders of earlier times.[17]

17. C. Castoriadis, in ibid., pp. 92–93.

Reading these lines today, one is forced to conclude at the least that the point of view of the participants lacks critical distance and tends to magnify the event inordinately.

A critical distance no doubt requires time to pass with respect to the event, but also, and perhaps most importantly, it requires that another point of view on the event from that of the participants themselves be adopted. In view of the development of the 1968 generation, we might hypothesize that this so-called break did in fact exercise strong powers of social integration. We might be tempted to ask whether the May movement served, without the participants' knowledge, certain ends that entirely escaped them. In this case the interpretation would have to adopt an entirely different principle: that the meaning of the episode is accessible only to those who can read it from the point of view of a logic that is immanent to the social system and to those who could see that the events of May merely constituted a moment that is necessary for the realization of this logic. Beyond apparent discontinuity lies a deeper continuity; beyond an apparent burst of freedom are the workings of a hidden necessity. These are interpretative principles that are strictly antithetical to the previous ones, the problem being to discover whether a reversal from for to against is enough for light to banish this blindness.

May as Pseudorevolution; or, Change within Continuity

The second type of interpretation can be illustrated by two analyses. In spite of vastly different sources of inspiration (Marxist on the one hand, Tocquevillean on the other), they join at the point where they see the May crisis as a stage in the development of bourgeois individualism, an effect of the capitalist system.

1. The interpretation of R. Debray   May '68 as "Cradle of the New Bourgeois Society." Debray's method is the prototype of the interpretation that claims the viewpoint of the participants to be the least likely to reveal the real meaning of the event: "The game is played behind the participants' backs."[18] Debray is convinced that the same interpretative schema that the Marxist historiographer uses to account for the French Revolution can be applied to the "revolution" of May '68: Just as the "bourgeois republic celebrated its birth by taking the Bastille, it will one day celebrate its rebirth by taking the language of 1968." Not to be limited to the superficial effect of rupture emphasized in the participants' discourse, the historian must work to uncover a hidden continuity between the society that produced May and the movement itself, a hidden continuity that escaped the participants but that might be found, according to Marxist orthodoxy, in the development of the forces of production. According to Debray, the need for increased industrialization imposed a real "cultural revolution" on French society that transformed the values that were still those of a strongly rural society: The rapid development of the forces of production, the great concentration of capital, in other words, the "overthrowing of the infrastructure" in favor of a more complete realization of capitalism—all these required the death of "the France of stone and rye, of a drink with the boys and all that traditional stuff, of yes-dad, yes-sir, yes-dear," so that the "France of software and supermarket, of news and planning . . . could finally take over and display its goods."[19] If May was merely a "spring cleaning," then, and if the real revolution that took place was a revolution in the means of production, May was "the most rational of social movements, the sad victory of productivist reason over romantic unreason, the most mournful demonstration of the Marxist thesis of determination in the last instance by the economic sphere."[20]

Having stated the thesis, do we need any proof that the historic role the movement was to play would be to "teach industrialization some manners"? Debray supplies an impressive amount of it: "The rapid feminization of the work force called for a reconsideration of

18. R. Debray, *Modeste Contribution aux cérémonies officielles du dixième anniversaire*, Maspero, 1978, p. 57.
19. Ibid., p. 13.
20. Ibid.

the status of women; the negative performances of the central state called for a new articulation between metropolis and region; the expansion of the judicial machinery called for a new relationship between the judged and the judgment machine," and so on.[21] Thus it has to be acknowledged that everything presented as a demand for identity, or as an affirmation of the right to be different, in fact merely "anticipated the demands of the system of exploitation for functionality." The participants in the events of May thought they were struggling against "constraints on individual existence," but while believing they were liberating individuality, they contributed to the disappearance of the last "constraints" that had slowed down the "extension of merchandizing across the whole social field." So, if May seemed to confirm the rights of subjectivity against the System, in reality "the only thing that could impose the law of the market on those who refused it was setting fire to subjectivity," and through the sudden liberation and circulation of these ideas, it was in fact "capital [that] wanted to circulate" and that victoriously succeeding in doing so.

We need not dwell on this any further. This interpretative structure here at least has the advantage of clarity, and the author himself explains it as the revelation or a "ruse of Capital," that "old mole," which made use of the aspirations of the young to produce a certain "result,"[22] "against the will of its agents," namely, the opening of the French route to America."[23] In this reading of the May crisis, as we have just seen, it is quite important to be alert to what the content of the ruse is said to be, since it involves the question of subjectivity. Thus interpreted, May '68 could indeed insure *subjectivity* as *individuality*, but only to the extent that French society, in its march toward neocapitalism, was held to be curbed by two "rather embarrassing collective values": that of the *nation* (and

21. Ibid., p. 14.
22. Ibid., pp. 25–26. On the "ruse of reason" at work in the 1968 crisis, cf. pp. 15, 17, 19. We find the same structure today in the analysis outlined by P. Bourdieu (*Homo Academicus*, p. 230): May 1968 as a "multiplicity of simultaneous but independent inventions, although objectively orchestrated." Cf. also p. 256, his critique of the "illusion of spontaneity."
23. Debray, *Modeste Contribution*, p. 39.

thus of national independence), an obstacle to the internationalization of capital, and that of the *working class* (and thus of revolution), an obvious obstacle to the development of bourgeois society. These two collective values had to be destroyed so that nothing would come between the individual/consumer/worker and Capital. Conclusion: May was an individualist revolution, necessary for the elimination of "the two linked and concurrent religions of *nation* and of *proletariat*,"[24] to allow for "the free flowering of capitalist ideology."[25] As for whether May '68, or, more generally, the '68 period, assured the victory of the subject or contributed to its death, this interpretation would answer unequivocally: May was the victory of the (bad) individual subject, of which theoretical humanism gave us only "pale variations," as Althusser has said,[26] over the collective subjects (nations, classes), which were ideological obstacles to the expansion of Capital. Logically, this attempt bogs down when it describes how "the private has been devouring the public"[27] since 1968. Extending the individualism of May, the contemporary cult of private pleasure derives from the conviction that one can "change life without changing the State"—thanks to which the "petit-bourgeois that was ashamed of it in 1968, was effectively 'revolutionized' ten years later into a petit-bourgeois that was proud of itself, triumphant and preacherly,"[28] a clear confirmation that there was indeed a "natural but not preestablished harmony between the individualist rebellions of May and the political and economic needs of great liberal capitalism": "The communion of egos on the barricades [became] generalized egocentrism, the gift of self became the cult of me, . . . the exaltation of liberties confirming inequalities."[29]

This interpretation has undeniable merits, or at least a not negligible seductive power. Like all analyses that adopt a similar

24. Ibid., p. 41.
25. Ibid., p. 48.
26. L. Althusser, "Sur le rapport de Marx à Hegel," in *Lénine et la philosophie*, p. 65. (This lecture was not included in Brewster's translation.)
27. Debray, *Modeste Contribution*, p. 56.
28. Ibid., p. 57.
29. Ibid., p. 88.

structure (that of an interpretation based on a "ruse of reason"), in its favor it has the degree of intelligibility produced by it, or the effect of meaning for the object obtained by it: Suddenly relieved of what has become a matter of simple appearances (with mystifying excesses), the crisis finally seems able to be understood. If one resists this seduction, however, one can observe that this interpretation of May is made possible, quite explicitly, by one of the major components of '68 philosophy itself, namely, the Marxist deconstruction (*in its Althusserian version*) of the idea of subjectivity as an ideological instrument of bourgeois (or petit-bourgeois) domination. Thus, in a certain way, it is still one of the components of '68 philosophy that is being used to interpret May here. For this reason it is not clear that such an interpretation *fully* overcomes the participants' point of view and the limitations inherent in it, even if the participant becomes a merciless judge. Evidence that this is the case can be found in Debray: Convinced that everything—both during and since May—that was presented as emancipating was only a ruse of the domination of Capital, he points out, in his conclusion, that in his view Capital (the real Subject of our history) has extended its ruses today in yet another direction, that of international relations, by reviving the individualist ideology of human rights. The return of judicial humanism for him is merely the latest avatar of the ideology of the sixties, and one of the best manifestations of the real scope of what he calls a pseudorevolution.[30] For those who are convinced that ritually denouncing the discourse of human rights as being intrinsically linked with the interests of the bourgeoisie is both a blunder and a mistake in view of its practical consequences, there is material here for grave doubt as to the overall clarity of the interpretation: Prisoner of its object by virtue of its theoretical presuppositions, this analysis seems destined to repeat certain of the most characteristic and at the same time most problematic intellectual themes.

   2. The Interpretation of G. Lipovetsky   Though structurally analogous to Debray's interpretation (here, again, opposed to the

---

30. Ibid., p. 89.

participants' point of view, it is an attempt to reestablish May '68 in a continuous process), Lipovetsky's method guarantees an adequate distance from the intellectual components of the sixties.[31] The general principles guiding the interpreter's work here are in fact quite different.

One of the most interesting aspects of this interpretation is based on its taking up, right from the start, the fundamental problem arising from the paradoxical nature of "after-May": Following upon the extraordinary emphasis during May on public/political values and on social/associative projects, the eighties seem to be characterized by a return to the private sphere. We have already seen that Debray regards this as a confirmation of his interpretation of the crisis as the "cradle of the new bourgeois society." Even though the time has gone when raising sheep in the Cévennes could be taken for the "simplest of revolutionary acts," what does remain is the deadening of "the *res publica* . . . the great 'philosophical,' economic, political, and military questions arousing about as much interest as a random news item, the 'heights' crumbling little by little, brought, as they have been, into the vast operation of social neutralization and banalization."[32] In view of the new narcissism, where the main concern is taking care of one's body and avoiding "depression," thanks to the combined virtues of jogging, body building, and tennis, one is forced to wonder what has become of the political activity of the sixties: Is there really a break, as everything seems to indicate, or should we once again look for a hidden continuity? The answer Lipovetsky proposes rests on two closely linked general principles of interpretation.

On the one hand, Lipovetsky's interpretation, deliberately situated outside Marxism, adopts a Tocquevillean perspective. Even though it refers to more recent works (Christopher Lasch, Richard Sennett, and above all Daniel Bell), the analysis basically consists of demonstrating that the various cultural movements typical of modernity and postmodernity should be understood as being within the

31. G. Lipovetsky, *L'Ere du vide: Essai sur l'individualisme contemporain*, Gallimard, 1983.
32. Ibid., p. 57.

dynamics of *individualism* in the Tocquevillean sense of the word. We know that Tocqueville defines individualism as "a thoughtful and peaceful feeling that disposes each citizen to isolate himself from the mass of his peers and to retire to a distance from his family and friends, in such way that, after thus creating a little society for himself, he willingly leaves the larger society to itself."[33] Understood in this way, individualism is clearly linked to the democratic process of equalizing conditions or, if one prefers the language of B. Constant, to the "freedom of the Moderns," defined as that private freedom which is always at risk of foundering in political apathy and leading to social fragmentation. Paradoxically, Lipovetsky sees a branch of this individualism at work not just in the neonarcissism of the eighties but even in the rebellions of the sixties.

As a result he must demonstrate that the participants of May are in fact the unconscious agents of a process that encompasses them and moves beyond them. What is more, like Debray, he must show that they have produced precisely the opposite of what they intended. We have, here again, an analysis conducted in terms of a "ruse of reason:" The participants had the public sphere in mind but "privatized" existence; they criticized the desire for consumerism but developed and consolidated the process of consumerism, and so on. In short, they did make history but did not understand the history they were making.[34]

We will return later to the problems raised by the structural analogy between Lipovetsky's *liberal* interpretation and Debray's *Marxist* one. For the moment, however, we will examine the content of the analysis developed from such principles. It is impossible to grasp it precisely, however, without illustrating how Lipovetsky in large part uses the theses established by Bell in his *Cultural Contradictions of Capitalism*,[35] while attempting to derive different conclusions from them. So first we must recall that in Bell's analysis (as Lipovetsky reads it) three ages of capitalism can be distinguished:

33. Tocqueville, *De la démocratie en Amérique*, vol. 2, Gallimard, 1961, p. 104.
34. Cf. esp. Lipovetsky, *L'Ere du vide*, pp. 48, 114.
35. Daniel Bell, *The Cultural Contradictions of Capitalism*, Basic Books, New York, 1976.

Classical capitalism, described by M. Weber as characterized at
the cultural and intellectual level by the *asceticism* of the Protestant ethic and the valorization of work, discipline, and effort.

Between 1880 and 1930, the appearance at the cultural level of
what Bell called *modernism,* or *modern art* in the broadest sense,
characterized by an exaggerated ideology of breaking with tradition
through the cult of the new and the unheard of and through the rejection of any conceivable form of transcendental norm;[36] novelistic discourse was freed from the constraints of chronology and
psychology, music from the constraints of tonality, painting from
the constraints of perspective and objectivity, and so on.

After 1930, the modernist movement of rupture was exhausted,
and the *postmodern* phase began, which basically consisted of the
hyperbolic repetition of the modernist gesture. Having exhausted
the possibilities for renewing the contents, there now appeared the
culture of adopting the principle of renewal itself, as an end in itself, of endlessly aiming at generating the absolutely new. In this
way it became embedded in a contradiction that could not be overcome since in time the production of newness itself appeared to
lack newness.[37]

Bell's primary effort is to interpret the birth of these postmodern movements, having recognized that they brought the asceticism
of protocapitalism to an end, thus opening the way to a *hedonist
culture.* His interpretative work consists mainly of attracting attention to a fact regarded as fundamental in view of its consequences:
the birth of the credit system in the 1930s. In keeping with Marcuse's idea of "repressive nonsublimation," he argues that the credit
system in fact ushered in a new age of consumerism, which had
demands that were no longer compatible with Protestant asceticism
and which produced the new hedonist culture. The obvious result,
in Bell's view, is that modernism has to be considered an agent of
Capital, which would dig its own grave through the infinite development of consumerism: "The Protestant ethic was undermined not by

36. Cf. C. Lipovetsky, *L'Ere du vide,* p. 91.
37. Ibid., p. 92.

modernism but by capitalism itself. The greatest engine of destruction of the Protestant ethic was the invention of the installment plan, or instant credit. Previously, in order to buy, one first had to save. But with credit cards one could indulge in instant gratification."[38] According to Bell (and Lipovetsky will not follow him to this ultimate conclusion), it is precisely the development of a hedonist culture that would lead the capitalist system into contradiction. Although it was created by capitalism itself, the demand for efficiency, which is what drives it from the technological-scientific point of view, and the cultural demand for the satisfaction of desires illustrate their incompatibility: "On the one hand, the corporation requires the individual to work hard, to delay compensation and gratification, in short, to be a cog in the wheel of the organization, and on the other, it encourages fun, relaxation, leisure. One has to be conscientious by day, and a carouser by night."[39] In Bell's view, this first contradiction risks creating a second one, between the cultural (hedonist) order and the politicojudicial one, theoretically dominated by the principles of democracy. If the need for efficiency is seriously disturbed by the demand for pleasure, the risk of economic recession appears, creating the frustration of the satisfaction of desires that can favor resorting to a seemingly capable, heaven-sent someone to correct the situation, even at the sacrifice of democracy. This is the source of Bell's political pessimism in predicting the inevitable decline of the principle of democratic legitimacy.

L'Ere du vide primarily provides both a deviation from and a complement to these analyses. Lipovetsky's Tocquevillean inspiration translates as a reinforcement of the continuity between the different phases in the history of capitalism: For him, modernism indicates less a break with traditional capitalism than "one aspect of the vast secular process leading to the creation of democratic societies founded on the sovereignty of the individual and the people, societies freed from submission to the gods, hereditary hierarchies, and the hold of tradition."[40] As a result, what modernism (hedo-

38. Bell, *Cultural Contradictions*, p. 21.
39. Ibid., p. 66.
40. Lipovetsky, *L'Ere du vide*, p. 97.

nism) introduces and postmodernism completes does not contradict the egalitarian order; as "a vector of individualization," modernism is in fact a "figure of equality." This is particularly evident on the aesthetic plane, where by separating art from the established canons "it sets in motion the process of legitimizing all subjects."[41] In this sense, modernism and postmodernism are merely "the continuation of the democratic revolution by other means."[42]

At the same time, the 1968 crisis seems a key moment in the transition from modernism to postmodernism as a consequence of the rise of consumerism in the postwar period: "During the sixties, postmodernism revealed its true colors: through its cultural and political radicalism, its exaggerated hedonism, student rebellions, the counterculture, the marijuana and LSD fads, sexual liberation and porno-pop films and publications, the increase in violence and cruelty in the theater, ordinary culture gave rise to liberation, pleasure, and sex."[43] More precisely still, the May crisis marked the transition between what was still the offensive phase of the break with the last remnants of traditional values and the phase that defined the postmodern age: The tension of rupture no longer being necessary, it "would be founded in the programmed cool register."[44] Modernism and postmodernism are thus linked during the '68 period, as the *hot* moment and the *cool* moment in a single process: "The end of modernism, the 1960s are the ultimate manifestation of the offensive launched against puritan and utilitarian values, the ultimate movement of cultural revolt, this time from the masses. But they are also the beginning of a postmodern culture, albeit one lacking innovation and real audacity, one that was satisfied merely to democratize hedonist logic."[45] This historical role of the late sixties is confirmed by the personal itineraries of those who were

41. Ibid., p. 99.
42. Ibid., p. 98. For postmodernism, cf. pp. 138–39: "Postmodernism is only a surface rupture. It perfects the democratic recycling of art, it furthers the reabsorption function of artistic distance, it pushes the personalization process of the open work to the limit by cannibalizing every style, by authorizing the most disparate constructions, by destabilizing the definition of modern art."
43. Ibid., p. 118.
44. Ibid., p. 116.
45. Ibid., p. 119.

first regarded as leaders of a revolutionary protest: "Even the hard cases (especially those) among the ex-leaders of the protest succumbed to the charms of self-examination: While Rennie Davis abandoned radical combat to follow the Maharaj Ji, Jerry Rubin has reported that between 1971 and 1975 he was happily involved in gestalt therapy, bioenergy, rolfing, massages, jogging, tai-chi, Esalen, hypnotism, modern dance, meditation, Silva Mind Control, Arica, acupuncture, and Reichian therapy."[46] Borrowing from Lasch,[47] we can readily find their French counterparts in, for example, the direction taken by such publications as *Actuel* or *Libération*. Far from marking a break, a point of departure toward a truly new future, May '68 should be remembered as a "revolution with no outcome, . . . no program, no victim or betrayer, no political framework, . . . a lax and relaxed movement, the first indifferent revolution, the proof that we need not despair in the desert."[48]

Lipovetsky's refined and original analyses are worth recalling once again at a number of points where they are shown to be relevant, for example, when they explain the revalorization of virtues such as "authenticity" or "sincerity," once again the "cardinal virtues" in "an intimist society where everything is measured in the mirror of psychology,"[49] or when they bring out the political importance of the postmodern end of democratic logic: "Essentially, it can be found in the ultimate fulfillment of the secular aim of modern societies, which is the total control of society and, on the other hand, greater and greater freedom in the private sector, which is then turned into generalized self-service."[50] In this way quite an effective critique can be drawn of different attempts to reduce individualism to the ideology of competition which arose on the Marxist horizon, most notably in the sociology of Bourdieu, for example: Here, far from being worn out by the search for objects of distinction, which have the purpose of announcing social difference, individualism is "the historic force which has devalued tradi-

46. Ibid., p. 60.
47. Christopher Lasch, *The Culture of Narcissism*, Norton, New York, 1978.
48. Lipovetsky, *L'Ere du vide*, p. 51.
49. Ibid., p. 72.
50. Ibid., pp. 119–20.

tion and the forms of heteronomy" and which has, correlatively, promulgated the modern figure of "the free individual, inventor of himself," a figure fundamental to the democratic social space, who is understood to be intrinsically "the same as everyone else" in the exercise of his rights and duties.[51] It should be added that at this point Lipovetsky's thoughts do not necessarily lead to a pessimistic prognosis for the future of democracy, as they do in Bell's work: "the excessive privatization of individuals" is only the indication of a "mass reinforcement of democratic legitimacy."[52] Consequently, the longing for the old values, which have disappeared through the logic of democracy, should not appear on the horizon of a work demonstrating how "these individualist values of liberty, equality, revolution" happened to converge in the postmodern age.

All that being the case, this interpretation nevertheless seems problematical to us in spite of its merits, for at least three reasons.

First, as we have seen, the structure of the interpretation is such that the reading of the 1968 crisis is conducted in terms of a "ruse of reason," so that, beyond the detail and finesse of the analysis, ultimately it is difficult to see how this interpretation is fundamentally different from a Marxist interpretation as traditional as Debray's. Here too it is Capital that carries out the "revolution" through its "postmodern" consequences: "Instead of representing a major crisis of a system announcing sooner or later its failure, abandonment of the social sphere is merely its ultimate fulfillment, its fundamental logic, as if capitalism owes it to itself to make men as equally indistinguishable as things."[53] It is not surprising that culture reappears here as a reflection and an effect of infrastructure, as on Marxist terrain: "One of the defining phenomena is the fact that from here on culture is found to be subject to the prevalent administrative (managerial) norms of the infrastructure."[54] Hedonism is also described explicitly as a product of capitalism, "a condition of its very functioning and expansion."[55] This reinsertion

51. Ibid., p. 108.
52. Ibid., p. 144.
53. Ibid., p. 48.
54. Ibid.
55. Ibid., p. 143.

into an interpretative schema, which is very close to an intellectual tradition denounced elsewhere through the radically "continuist" representation of history it induces, is already troubling in itself and raises a series of difficulties.

From this perspective, the norms of the Protestant ethic are crumbling because they are undermined by the advance of that "old mole" Capital, which has to create another culture in order to be realized. When read in this way, the result is that the true scope of the history of the decline of these norms remains external to the norms themselves: Their value is not encroached upon by the process of their decay. On the one hand, this representation of our recent cultural history seems at least debatable: If we think of the state of certain institutions at the end of the 1960s, for example, of what the *lycée* had become, we have to confess that we hardly feel that these cultural norms, respectable in themselves, had to be violently overthrown to allow for the development of the consumer society. Did we have before us an intact Protestant ethic under attack as if from outside, or dead norms, devoid of any life? On the other hand, this representation of the process of decay only indicates a tendency that is hardly compatible with the overall inspiration of the analysis, which mourns the crumbling of the old norms that had not in themselves "broken faith." Like it or not, however, to refer to the contemporary period as the "age of emptiness" is not without its critical or pessimistic connotations. Thus the discourse is often ambiguous: The "process of personalization" the narcissistic society performs is described, against Bell, as the sign of good health for democratic principles,[56] but in describing the main characteristics of such a society, "the indifference and lack of motivation of the masses" are mentioned, as are "the rise of existential emptiness," "numbing" or "the elimination of periodic spontaneity," and, to conclude, even "the dispossession, desubstantialization of the individual."[57]

Moreover, the continuist bias motivating the entire analysis

56. Ibid., pp. 144 ff.
57. Ibid., pp. 164–65. Cf. also p. 164: "The personalization process results in the zombiesque individual, sometimes cool and apathetic, sometimes emptied of any feeling of existence."

leads to erasing from history, when it is interpreted in this way, any dimension of newness. Various interpretations are then possible. For example, is it so obvious that modern art is entirely *reducible* to the logic of individualism requiring the suppression of norms? Is it not also more and perhaps worse than that, namely, the effort to create a new representation of the world that leads to negating the very basis of individualism, which the idea of subjectivity is? Do the attempts to destroy the notion of point of view in painting, to question the linearity of the story and the omniscience of the narrator who organizes it in the contemporary novel, really play a role in achieving a "culture of the free individual, pure organizing activity, whose ideal is to create without a Master"?[58] Or are they stages in the destruction of this culture, like figures of the "dissolution of the Ego"?[59] There is no question of solving this complex problem, which would require extensive development, here. But it is an example of what one type of interpretation that categorically denies the appearance of discontinuity risks in the way of oversimplification and mutilation.

This argument could be repeated in relation to every interpretation that adopts a viewpoint that is absolutely opposed to that of the participants, necessarily reducing their feeling of having inaugurated a new age to just an illusion. Does this mean we have to go one better than the point of view of the participants themselves in order to be more faithful to the object and regard the events at the time of the 1968 crisis as the emergence of an unexpected newness? In any case, this type of one-upmanship has already been practiced among those interpreters of May '68 whose interpretative horizon is phenomenology.

May as Event

C. Lefort's contribution in *La Brèche*, no doubt significantly entitled "Le Désordre nouveau," is the most representative of the readings that appeal to the virtues of "shock": "Everyone is trying to

58. Ibid., p. 105.
59. Ibid., p. 63.

name the event that shook French society, attempting to relate it to what is known, trying to foresee the consequences. Interpretations are hastily being erected, people want to reestablish order, if not in the facts, in thought. People want to forget their surprise. . . . People would like to fill in the breach right on the spot. In vain."[60] In advance, we have to take exception to the multiform efforts, two examples of which we have just analyzed, that had to be made in order to reestablish a continuity and reinsert May into a process: "Specialists in retrospective rationality, Marxo-geologists or Marxo-seismologists, are going to spread out their cards and reel off their calculations to show that the relative decrease in buying power, the growth in the number of unemployed, the slowing of public investment, or industry's handicaps on the eve of new competition from the Common Market created the conditions of a crisis. But is there anyone who still remains to be convinced?"[61] Counter to all these reinsertions of the event into the texture of a history that might explain it, it is important to think of the crisis as an "extraordinary initiative, inconceivable some weeks earlier,"[62] in order to turn this unforeseeability into the truth itself rather than the appearance of the event. The initiative here no longer refers to some design, or some rationality immanent to history, or to leaders, since "those who are taking the initiative in participating are not members of a union or of one of the factions, nor do they belong to the numerous *groupuscules* that usually dominate political struggle in the university: They are *nowhere*."[63] In short, initiative is initiation/absolute inauguration, pure beginning; the revolution arises from nothingness, from this "nowhere" that defies any explanation that searches for an origin armed with the principle of reason.

It is not very difficult to see, judging from the evidence, that the type of representation of history that gives an interpretation of May '68 as "Event" is related to the phenomenological theoretical horizon that attempts to establish historicity (or, if you prefer, "historicality") in the register of "no reason." And if the event can

60. C. Lefort, in *La Brèche*, p. 37.
61. Ibid., p. 38.
62. Ibid., p. 40.
63. Ibid., p. 46.

be found to tally with the "action" of the "revolutionaries," the action in question is nothing like philosophy as an effect of thoughtful decision, oriented by an intention, or, in other words, like the action of a conscious and willing subject. The action is, rather, understood as a creative fulguration, the emergence of a freedom that suddenly establishes new possibilities, as Hannah Arendt has explained it:

> In a society saturated with discourses and organizations, where work and action are assigned their home, where one must take one's place, refuse one's identity in order to have the right to act or to speak, these people are creating a new space. One might better say that they are digging out a nonplace. The possible is being re-created, an indeterminate possible that will start all over again and modify from event to event.[64]

Action, the foundation that breaks the flow of temporal continuity and opens up what Arendt too calls a "breach," (*Gap*)[65] has the virtue of "audacity."[66] Thus the revolutionaries of May '68 were to be described in terms immediately inspired by Heidegger's terms for the authenticity of "resolute *Dasein*": "They gather outside any organization, they liberate themselves from their tutelage as well as from that of established authority. A new mode of action arises from this practice of assembling. Still, it has to be understood that a small group, meeting far away from organizations, is only useful if it recognizes that the possibility of intervening in a concrete situation, *here and now*, is open to it."[67] Nor is it surprising that the goal of the movement is not interpreted here as the substitution of a "better power" for the power being fought against: "the illusion of a *good society*" should still proceed from the desire to establish a "system" seeking to "chain itself to its trap," in the very place where real revolutionary action, which is not the fabrication of a future by

64. Ibid., p. 49.
65. Cf. esp. *La Vie de l'esprit*, vol. 1, *La Pensée*, trans. L. Lotringer, P.U.F., 1981, pp. 227 ff (*The Life of the Mind*, vol. 1, *Thinking*, Harcourt Brace, New York, 1977–78).
66. Lefort, in *La Brèche*, p. 50.
67. Ibid.

virtue of a preconceived design, consists solely of "disturbing projects," of "bringing down the walls," and of "making things move"; in short, the movement is an end in itself, its meaning used up by what it is, which is the opening of a gap.[68]

Nevertheless, in view of this analysis, which does have the advantage of not blunting the emotional charge of the newness (novelty) that accompanies any event with the allure of revolution, one can only express a certain disappointment. If the mystery of the "Event" has to account for everything without anything ever taking account of it, here, as well as for Arendt, the true hermeneutic importance of this thematics, clearly linked philosophically to the Heideggerian philosophy of *Ereignis* or the "ages of Being," seems a bit thin. Can one be satisfied to have the event end up as an "enigma"? We have no difficulty agreeing that maintaining some of the originality and unpredictability of the event is necessary to counter the excesses of these interpretations made in terms of the "ruse of reason." If this also means renouncing any explanatory perspective (any use of the principle of causality) as well, that is much more problematic. Do we really have a choice only between interpretations that *explain everything but nothing* (of the irreducibly unique newness of the episode), that deduct the crisis from a very long process that it consummates, and interpretations that *understand everything* (about this uniqueness) *but explain nothing* (about the causes that created the crisis)? We would add that the phenomenological interpretation, careful to preserve the original character of the revolutionary event, paradoxically risks dissolving this originality, in some sense. This is because, in the logic of this position, the element of the "miraculous" is at work in every historical reality, as Arendt describes it, and we do not see, in this regard, what would make a revolutionary crisis like the one of May a better place (or a nonplace if you like) for assembling the "miracle of Being" than would be the case for any event, the humblest or the greatest. So the interpretation dissolves the originality of the crisis into the everyday banality of events: All events are Events, and it is only through an unjustifiable begging of the question that, from such

68. Ibid., p. 62.

a point of view, paying a greater share of attention (or surprise) to a moment like May '68 can be justified.

An interpretation that uncritically exposes the participants' perspective, as well as one that unreservedly disqualifies this perspective, entirely reducing the apparent break to a hidden continuity, and even an interpretation that radically accentuates the unpredictable newness of the crisis encounter serious difficulties. If we are not satisfied to turn May into a tissue of enigma, there is still the possibility of seeing whether integrating the approaches, which is too often done in a unilateral way, might not shed a more satisfying light on the 1968 rebellion.

For Interpretative Pluralism

The difficulties each of the three types of interpretation encounter, in terms of a methodology of historical knowledge, demonstrate the serious drawbacks encountered when one of the three representations of history that underlie these interpretations is unilaterally and dogmatically administered.[69] Avoiding these difficulties no doubt requires an attempt to integrate the unimpeachable aspects of the participants' point of view (a certain feeling of a break) with the requirement for intelligibility—or, if you will, an attempt to integrate understanding and explanation—while taking contingency into account, that is, the dimension of chance that gives a degree of unpredictability to what happened.

All things being equal, in terms of the need for such an integration, we can find the least reductive of these analyses of the 1968 crisis in Aron. Chapter 18 of the *Mémoires*,[70] which uses the essence of what had been previously elaborated in *The Elusive Revolution*, is an example of the concrete implementation of Weberian methodology, whose entire framework is devoted to the principle of interpretative pluralism. So, for example, there is space for

69. On the philosophical foundation of this rejection of unilaterality, cf. L. Ferry, "Le Système des philosophies de l'histoire," in *Philosophie politique*, vol. 2, P.U.F., 1984.
70. R. Aron, *Mémoires*, Julliard, 1981, pp. 471–97. One must also note *Le Spectateur engagé*, Julliard, 1981, pp. 247–63.

sociological explanations: worker dissatisfaction with the distribution of goods and with the persistent growth of the progressively less
acceptable rigid hierarchy in French society; the crisis in a university in the process of evolving toward higher education for the
"masses," and so on. But the sociological approach, which privileges gneral causalities that can be reproduced in analogous circumstances, has a twofold originality that forms a contrast with more
usual practice. On the one hand, the "sociological effort to establish
laws (or at least regularities or generalities),"[71] is not presented in
these texts as a single structure that claims to be omniexplanatory
(in the sense that in Debray, for example, the whole crisis is
understood as deduced from the logic of Capital alone and, in
Lipovetsky, from the logic of democracy alone). If general laws are
expressed in the birth and development of the May revolt, the fact
that "no single one can claim to be exclusive and total"[72] is made
clear. On the other hand, the originality of this approach is also due
to the fact that it coexists with the awareness of true historical
causality, acted out at the level of unique sequences, irreducible to
any laws, bringing into play facts that cannot be reproduced (so de
Gaulle's role is measured, as is the effect of Pompidou's decisions
and, sometimes, mistakes—for example, the decision to reopen the
Sorbonne), individual facts that Aron attempts to understand while
evaluating their consequences through considering what might have
happened if these various initiatives had been otherwise.

There is no need to reproduce here, in detail, these well-
known analyses. On the other hand, to avoid a misunderstanding,
we should clarify that interpretative pluralism is not a relativism. It
does not mean that in some way a concern for truth had been abandoned. It implies only—and here Aron is opposed to the monists
from the start—that it is absolutely impossible to give an unequivocal response to the Weberian question: "Would May have been the
same if such or such event had not taken place?" In this sense,
Aron's texts can seem deceptive, if only to the extent that *one* inter-

71. R. Aron, *Introduction à la philosophie de l'histoire*, Gallimard, "Tel,"
p. 235.
72. Aron, *Mémoires*, p. 483.

pretation of the crisis cannot be isolated: A plurality of "causes, motifs, and ideologies"[73] is invoked to interpret each level, each aspect, or each sequence of the event (the student revolt, its spread, the workers' strike, its ebb). By comparison with the undeniable appearance of meaning the interpretations of the second type produce, this approach might seem rather poor, leaving desirable intelligibility at an even greater distance. Yet we should ask if it was not precisely this aim to produce total intelligibility that led the "continuist" interpretations themselves to become overly reductive and, in the end, impoverishing through excessive systematization. When there is an attempt to reduce historical temporality to a hidden rationality through which everything in history rationally unfolds, reabsorbing difference into the identical is inevitable, for example, when all aspects of the sixties (notably, contemporary art) are explained solely in relation to the individualist logic of democracy. The fact that this logic is at work in all modernity does not imply that all aspects of all phases of modernity can be deduced from it. Aron's criticism of historical reason certainly proscribes this type of hope; it also prevents this type of illusion.

We should add, for the rest, that the attractive features of the "continuist" interpretations described above, which no doubt contain their share of truth, are also there in Aron's analysis, but together with other explanatory hypotheses that take other causalities into consideration, each in a nonunilateral way. Debray and Lipovetsky, whose perspectives are otherwise very different, both call the fundamental element of the crisis a development of individualism, though they arrive at opposing conclusions about it. This hypothesis explains many aspects of the end of the sixties, and the degree of intelligibility it produces gives these works much of their persuasive force. However, rereading *The Elusive Revolution* today—a book that was misunderstood, whose humor is generally the only thing remembered about it, and whose severe look at a movement it was still too close to mortgaged its chances for being understood—one finds that it includes, along with other explanations, the establishment of an important relationship between the

73. Ibid., p. 479.

62

intellectual climate of the '68 period, the May crisis, and what were regarded as its predictable consequences at the time. "The god of the intellectuals of the sixties," Aron wrote, "was no longer the Sartre who had dominated the postwar period but a mixture of Lévi-Strauss, Foucault, Althusser and Lacan."[74] Their very different approaches nevertheless produced two common effects:

> They brought the formulation "there are no facts" into favor in Parisian milieux, thus contributing to the disintegration of the commonsense belief that "every society is subject to the constraints of fact—the need for production, for organization, for a technical hierarchy, the need for a techno-bureaucracy and so on."[75] Because of this dissolution of facts and thus the constraints of facts, the idea that everything could be represented as valid, and that no norms need be imposed institutionally on the play of desire, for example, was gradually developing.

> From the disintegration of norms to the rise of neonihilism was but a single step, which, when taken, rather easily undermined the fragile order of existing society: "to reject one social order without having any notion of which order might be erected in its place" *demonstrates* "one of the reasons for the decomposition we saw in May."[76]

The relationship between the 1968 crisis as a critique of norms ("It is forbidden to forbid") and the critical work on normativity itself by French philosophers of the sixties should not necessarily be regarded in a simplistic and caricatural way as the establishment of a cause/effect relationship: Neither cause nor effect, '68 philosophy is part of a meaningful whole whose importance it illuminates while being illuminated by it. With this in mind, the observations outlined in *The Elusive Revolution* are all the more interesting when Aron (anticipating Debray's and Lipovetsky's analyses) adds this description of the future of the "'68 generation": The lucky ones, Aron

74. Aron, *Elusive Revolution*, p. 125.
75. Ibid., pp. 110–11.
76. Ibid., p. 126.

concluded, will escape from this situation where the cultural norms (norms defining a collective ideal) are crumbling, not by joining an "order that might replace it" (through political action) but "by withdrawal and apathy, by retiring to their country cottages."[77] As early as the summer of 1968 there were in fact intimations from the recent "elusive revolution": desertion of the political sphere, a return to private life, the rise of hedonistic individualism through which the great public debates that had enlivened the preceding decades would be "neutralized." Through the articulation of the philosophical discourse of the sixties, the nihilism of 1968 (the rejection of one order without a vision of an order that could replace it), and subsequent individualism, as we have outlined it here, interpretative pluralism reveals that it can easily accommodate the best of what is to be found in the unilateral interpretations: The essence of their contents is transformed into one hypothesis among others, into one explanatory element among a variety of other possibilities. If adopting this hypothesis preserves most of the intelligibility produced by the exclusively "continuist" analyses, its integration into a bundle of "causes, motifs, and ideologies" saves it from the reductive excesses inherent in dogmatism. The pluralist approach leaves the task of emphasizing one level of interpretation rather than another to future interpreters, with the understanding, of course, that the choice of one of these levels over another is a methodological abstraction, that they are all closely embedded in concrete historical reality. Given these conditions, nothing prevents using a method that licenses a reading centered on the problem of individualism: As one guideline for historians' reflections on the sixties, the logic of individualism would no longer be the omniexplanatory infrastructure it has been for the last decades; in its possible (and necessary) coexistence with other approaches, it could define the angle of the particular reading of any given question about May 1968, as, for example, the one we focus on here, approached solely from the point of view of recent intellectual and cultural history.

77. Ibid.

64

May '68 and the Death of the Subject

Once its status has been redefined (and *limited*), the reinsertion of May '68 into the vast development of individualism again becomes a fruitful direction to take. However, one fundamental problem remains to be resolved. By constructing the ideal type for '68 philosophy, we were able to see the insistence with which the various themes and motifs of this philosophy converge on an accusation against subjectivity: In this case, how can we view the coexistence of this philosophy (and the relationships it recognizes) with a historical movement where the claims of the Ego against the System are at the most basic level of conviction? We have already encountered this apparent paradox, and it may be resolved by using individualism itself as a guideline for clarifying the logic of the '68 period. In the process, Lipovetsky's analyses may be usefully reinvested in the research, under the condition that one has a keener awareness of their limitations.

In one sense, May was indeed a revolt of subjects against the norms, in the sense that *individualism* was being defended against any claims for the *universality* of norms. But at the same time, the hyperbolic affirmation of individuality set in motion a process that led quite predictably in the direction of the disintegration of the Ego as autonomous will, the destruction of the classical idea of the subject. Lipovetsky grasped this subtle mechanism perfectly, emphasizing that, for the new permissive and hedonistic ethics inherited from the '68 era, "effort is no longer in style, constraint or strict discipline has been devalued in favor of the cult of the immediate satisfaction of desire." We deplore this development not because of a personal taste for repressiveness, or nostalgia for the "old," but in order to measure its importance on the level of the genesis of the Ego. In this regard, all we would need is to reproduce Lipovetsky's analysis, which was inspired by Nietzsche's remark that in modern times the desire for a private center of gravity able to organize impulses and tendencies has been weakened, along with the crumbling of values: "Free association, spontaneous creativity, nondirectedness, our culture of expression, and also our ideology of wellbeing, encourage dispersion to the detriment of concentration, the temporary instead of the will, and work toward the crumbling of the Ego and the annihilation of organized and synthetic psychic systems."[78] The whole issue is the discovery of whether the "new *cool* and unconstrained consciousness," "televiewer consciousness, attracted by everything and by nothing, excited and indifferent at the same time, optional, scattered consciousness, polar opposite of willed consciousness," corresponds any better to a death of the Ego as subject than to its affirmation: Pulverized into tendencies no longer seeking integration into an intention constructed by a desire that imposes goals on itself, can this Ego, significantly called "exploded," really make a *person?* The Ego of contemporary narcissism, "a floating space without ties or reference, pure availability, adapted for the acceleration of combinations and the fluidity of our systems,"[79] a purely receptive opening onto unstructured diversity, seems to obey a logic of heteronomy, which, there is no need to explain, is intrinsically contradictory to the very idea of subjectivity irreducible to the status of simple object, precisely because of the ideal of autonomous will.

Correlatively, this Ego that loses self-mastery, no longer tends to regard other people as other subjects, as other willed consciousness with whom (intersubjective) relations can take the form of a reciprocal recognition of freedoms: "The mode for understanding other people is neither that they are equals nor that they are unequals. It is amused curiosity, each of us condemned for a longer or shorter time to seem surprising, eccentric to others' eyes, like 'ectoplasmic jumping-jacks' with instincts/impulses whose truth is no more understood than it is mastered."[80] Thus, in the age of narcissism, the destruction of the representation of Ego as willed consciousness accompanies the transformation of intersubjectivity into a humorous contemplation of the other as a "loony gadget."[81]

That this subtle process, where the other face of the affirmation of individuality is the degradation of the ideal of subjectivity and

78. Lipovetsky, *L'Ere du vide*, pp. 63–64.
79. Ibid., p. 65.
80. Ibid., pp. 186–87.
81. Ibid., p. 187.

this type of transformation in interpersonal relations, is regarded as the ultimate stage of democracy's growth is an assertion we are not obliged to share fully. Nevertheless, it is still the case that in the latter part of the sixties, these analyses largely dissolved the apparent paradox that sustained the coexistence of a philosophically radical critique of subjectivity and of a social movement oriented toward the promotion of individuality: *The subject dies with the birth of the individual.* In this regard, the roles of the various figures of the philosophy of '68 are understandable: From Lacanian psychoanalysis to Nietzschean/Marxian derivatives, the philosophy of '68 philosophically legitimizes the heterogeneity that emptied the fluid Ego of substance. Criticizing the goal of self-mastery and truth as "metaphysical" or "ideological," an integral part of the traditional notion of subjectivity, and multiplying the variations on the theme "Je est un autre," the philosophical sixties both initiated and accompanied this process of the disintegration of the Ego, which led to the "*cool* and *laid-back* consciousness" of the eighties. When Deleuze and Guattari in 1976 drew up, so to speak, the balance sheet of the critiques of the subject of the previous two decades, it was the birth of this kind of consciousness that they saluted: To get "not just to the place where one no longer says I but to the place where it no longer matters whether one says I or not. We are no longer ourselves."[82] And, among other monuments of '68 philosophy, their *Anti-Oedipus* in fact contributed greatly to the methodical divestment of the "I": "desiring-machines," pure points of departure for "detachments on every hand that are valuable in and of themselves and above all must not be filled in," "continuous fluxes" where "everything functions at the same time, but amid hiatuses and ruptures, breakdowns and failures, stalling and short-circuits, distances and fragmentations, within a sum that never succeeds in bringing its various parts together so as to form a whole,"[83] describing in every case the figure of the pulverized or disintegrated Ego that appeared on the horizon of the rise of individualism.

82. G. Deleuze and F. Guattari, *Rhizome*, Ed. de Minuit, 1976, p. 7.
83. G. Deleuze and F. Guattari, *L'Anti-Oedipe*, Ed. de Minuit, 1972, pp. 47–50 (*Anti-Oedipus*, trans. Robert Hurley, Mark Seem, and Helen Lane, University of Minnesota Press, Minneapolis, 1983, pp. 39–42).

As a result, by denouncing the illusions inherent in the ideal of a "willed consciousness," which carried with it the classical notion of subjectivity, the philosophies of 1968, like their contemporary movement, participated in a no doubt unprecedented promotion of the values of individualism, which at least some of the intellectually dominant figures of the sixties believed they were combating.[84] If there is a "ruse of reason" that can be brought in here, it would have to be located at this level: Agents of an individualism they often denounced, the major representatives of '68 philosophy made history without knowing the history they were making.

So one enigma has been removed from the domain of our inquiry, albeit only an apparent one. The "philosophists" of the '68 period inscribe their critiques of the idea of subject within an intellectual horizon that the principal inspirations of the May movement also evince. The subsequent chapters will be largely concerned with clarifying the various philosophical modalities of this disappearance of subjectivity. With reference to four German models for French philosophy (Nietzsche, Heidegger, Marx, Freud), they will analyze the trial of the subject advanced by these philosophies, a trial where an acquittal seems to be, by definition, out of the question. For each of the four major components of '68 philosophy, we have chosen to concentrate on a particularly significant figure. Our intention was not to write a history of French philosophy from 1960 to the present, so it was necessary above all to aim for completeness in the analyses. We intended to demonstrate how the ideal type described in the first chapter could be applied to the various philosophical currents at issue here, so that in each case what might emerge is the working of an intellectual structure and also, especially through reference to the model, the originality of the use of this structure in the specific problematics that creates effects not entirely reducible to the structure. Thus conceived, the investigation does not intend to be all-inclusive so much as it does to be representative.

84. We need only recall, for example, Althusser's constant denunciation of individualism as intrinsically "bourgeois."

3 /
French Nietzscheanism
(Foucault)

We have chosen to examine the Nietzschean component of '68 philosophy through the work of Michel Foucault for three reasons. 1. Foucault always acknowledged that he was a Nietzschean. Thus, in an interview published on May 29, 1984, in *Les Nouvelles littéraires*, just after his death,[1] he explained that for him there had been two essential philosophers, Heidegger and Nietzsche, the latter ultimately dominating: "Heidegger has always been for me the essential philosopher. . . . My whole philosophical development was determined by my reading of Heidegger. But I recognize that Nietzsche won out," to such an extent that one can even speak, he claims, of his "fundamental Nietzscheanism": "I am simply Nietzschean and I try as well as I can, in a number of areas, to see with the help of Nietzsche's texts—but also with anti-Nietzschean theses (which are all the same Nietzschean!)—what can be done in one area or another. I seek nothing else, but I seek it with care." This, then, is the clear profession of a radical Nietzscheanism, even in a form that makes use of a paradox ("anti-Nietzschean theses" that "are all the same Nietzschean"), with a corresponding acknowledgment of the Heideggerian background. The mention of Heidegger should be emphasized, since that background is so important that it plays a decisive role in most of the French philosophies of the 1960s, if we leave aside the Marxist component of '68 philosophy: This is so for Foucault, but also, as we will see, for Lacan and of course for Derrida. Within an overall Heideggerian context, it may well be possible to define philosophical practice by reference to Nietzsche (Foucault) or to Freud (Lacan), but Heidegger remains the

1. *Les Nouvelles littéraires*, June 28–July 5, 1984.

"essential philosopher," the one who makes a new reading of Nietzsche or of Freud possible, a fertile reading that is the basis of these various protagonists' originality.

2. If Foucault professes to be a Nietzschean, he is nevertheless not the only one to so clearly acknowledge his ancestry, and from this point of view this chapter might just as well have been based on the work of Deleuze. V. Descombes has shown that, although "the vocabulary of *Anti-Oedipus* is sometimes Marxist, sometimes Freudian, the guiding thread from beginning to end is Nietzschean":[2] The distinction between "active forces" and "reactive forces" (will to ascendant power/will to decadent power), analyzed in *Nietzsche and Philosophy* (1962), was renewed ten years later in the opposition between "revolutionary desire" as a true "force of production" and "repressive desire" as a "reactive" turning of desire back on itself. And the whole *Anti-Oedipus* consisted of reinterpreting this *mal du siècle* that Nietzsche had found in "nihilism" in terms of schizophrenia, with the same aim of converting the "passive" (the annihilation of will) into the "active" (the will to annihilation). Schizophrenia not only has to be understood as flight, meaning a "distancing from the social" and, in the search for marginality (passively) allowing the social to survive: "It causes the social to take flight through the multiplicity of holes that eat away at it and penetrate it, always coupled directly to it, everywhere setting the molecular charges that will explode what must explode, make fall what must fall, make escape what must escape, at each point ensuring the conversion of schizophrenia as a process into an effective revolutionary force."[3] In terms of its "fundamental Nietzscheanism," Deleuze's itinerary is not far behind Foucault's. If we preferred to turn to Foucault for our analysis of "French Nietzscheanism," it is primarily because of the extent to which he has the undeniable advantage of being less limited to merely repeating the Nietzschean approach (which Deleuze always did, albeit with talent, in *Différence and répétition* as in

2. V. Descombes, *Le Même et l'autre: Quarante-cinq ans de philosophie française (1933–1978)*, Ed. de Minuit, 1979, pp. 202 ff.
3. G. Deleuze and F. Guattari, *L'Anti-Oedipe*, Ed. de Minuit, 1972, p. 408 (*Anti-Oedipus*, trans. Robert Hurley, Mark Seem, and Helen Lane, University of Minnesota Press, Minneapolis, 1983, p. 341).

Logique du sens). [4] From *Madness and Civilization* (1961) on, Foucault always attempted, as he recalls in the interview quoted above, to put this approach to the test "in this or that area," in the form of broad studies of the history of cultural and institutional phenomena. This attempt, which is very representative of the belief shared by the various components of '68 philosophy—that philosophy is closed and has to be revived by work of different style—also has the advantage of permitting an evaluation of the real resources of a philosophy based on the formula *Heidegger plus Nietzsche.* The potential of this option, or, on the other hand, the difficulties it may confront, should be measured in an "experimental" way, so to speak, depending on whether the areas investigated from the starting point of this option do or do not resist what the interpretation being attempted intends to do. By exposing his conclusions to refutation, Foucault's work can be "tested," a resource that work which is merely a rewriting of the major moments in Nietzsche's discourse, however attractive it may be, does not offer.

3. In terms of antihumanism, the central issue of our inquiry, Foucault's writings have an additional interest: Though based on a single philosophical approach, they reveal an apparent evolution precisely in the area of the problematics of subjectivity. From his first works (*Madness and Civilization, The Order of Things, The Archaeology of Knowledge,* etc.), which gave rise to a kind of Foucauldian "Vulgate" based on the theme of the "death of man," through his last published works (*The History of Sexuality*), important displacements were produced, since at the end of the journey the conditions for the emergence and preservation of an ethical subject had come into question. By choosing to analyze Foucault's work, we are approaching the Nietzschean component of '68 philosophy from what is apparently the least favorable angle for confirming what we have been suggesting up to now: What had become of the destruction of subjectivity in French philosophy during the last two decades if one of its most important representatives returned to raise the question of the subject once again, and in terms that are not

4. Cf., for example, the conclusion of *Différence et répétition,* P.U.F., 1968, pp. 337–89.

entirely negative? On this matter, the taste for the practice of the *lectio difficilior* indeed also suggested the choice of Foucault.

Defense and Illustration of Foucault's Vulgate: The Example of *Madness and Civilization*

In a 1977 interview,[5] Foucault expressed his reservations about what the intellectual fashion of 1968 had taken from his works, which had resulted in the birth of a type of Vulgate centered around the idea of dismantling the mechanisms of power (asylums, prisons, schools, etc.). These were, he explained, necessary simplifications, but they nevertheless formed the "*doxa* of the Left," namely, "the refrain of the antirepressive tune," merely repeating that "beneath power things themselves in their primitive vividness should be discernible" ("under the pavement is the beach," if you wish): "Behind the walls of the asylum, the spontaneity of madness; throughout the penal system, the generous fever of delinquency; under sexual taboo, the freshness of desire"—in short, a group of "simple hurrahs (long live madness, long live delinquency, long live sex)," sustained by the belief that "power is bad, ugly, poor, sterile, monotonous, dead" and that "what power is exercised over is good, fine, rich." This ironic view of his own Vulgate, which came late to Foucault, raises a question that has to be answered prior to a study of the work itself: Is Foucault's questioning of his own thought an invitation to return to the early works in order to derive more complex or more subtle themes from them than the fashion of the day had? Or is it an indication of the turning of a corner, indicating that from then on (1977) there would be a greater distance (and we will have to question how great that distance is) from the early thematics? In order to raise this preliminary question, the simplest (and most efficient) thing would seem to be to begin by turning to the work that truly inaugurated Foucault's itinerary, a work that requires only a brief discussion for its tone to be grasped since it is perhaps the best known and most celebrated of his works.

5. Interview with J. Rancière, *Le Nouvel Observateur*, March 12, 1977.

72

A consideration of *Madness and Civilization*[6] requires first of
all emphasizing the perspective it effectuates between the Middle
Ages and what Foucault called at the time the "classical age,"
which is the period that extended from the end of the Renaissance to
the Revolution.[7] His entire purpose is to demonstrate that, with
respect to the attitude toward madness, the arrival of the humanist
or human attitude of the classical age (and later the modern period)
is only apparently a progress and is really a regression that took the
form of a repression. The emergence of classical reason is interpreted as coinciding with the rejection of the irrational (and thus of
the madman) in the name of rationality, which became the norm.
The major direction of the argument is well known: During the Middle Ages, lepers were isolated and set apart from society, whereas
during the classical age the object of this social segregation was
displaced to the madman, who replaced the leper, and with entirely
new meaning. In order to measure carefully how this analysis
devalues the classical and modern rise of reason, it has to be
pointed out that, for Foucault, the substitution of the madman for
the leper is accompanied by a more radical exclusion. In the Middle
Ages, lepers were indeed considered dangerous but were nevertheless not the objects of a radical rejection, as the location of leper
colonies at the gates of the cities—outside them, indeed, but within
sight of the community—demonstrates: They continued to play a
socially recognizable role, their nearness a reminder to everyone of
the obligations of Christian charity. Everything had changed, on the
other hand, by the time leper colonies had been transformed into
houses of confinement, the date 1656 marking, according to Foucault, what must be considered the real "break," when in Paris
during any given month one inhabitant in a hundred was confined in
an institution. Independently of the displacement that resulted from

6. M. Foucault, *Histoire de la folie à l'âge classique*, Gallimard, 1961, reedited
and augmented, 1972 (our references are to this reedition—L.F. and A.R.);
Madness and Civilization: A History of Insanity in the Age of Reason, trans.
Richard Howard, Vintage Books, New York, 1973 (this is the translation of an
earlier edition, thus only certain citations to the English can be given—trans.).
7. In his later works, the classical age denoted classical antiquity, as opposed to
Christianity and modernity, which began with Descartes, as we shall see.

this incarnation of evil (from the morbid to the irrational), from then on everything possible was done to make the madman *disappear* from the social space. We recall that at this point Foucault opposed the preclassical image of the ship of fools to later representations of confinement: Instead of being locked away, during the Renaissance the "circulation" of the mad was guaranteed through representations of the madman as the symbol of the human condition, a "passenger," passing through: "The head that will become a skull is already empty. Madness is the *déja-là* of death."[8] So madness retained a place and a role in the sociocultural world and would not be negated as such until the end of the Renaissance. On the other hand, the arrival of classicism, rather than merely advancing the values of humanity, would be translated through the absolute negation of madness.

First, madness lost its self-consistency when it was defined no longer in terms of itself but in reference to reason: "Madness became a form relative to reason," reason postulating madness as its other (or what it perceives as its other), that is, as the annihilation of the human condition.[9]

As a result of this "conceptual" negation (madness reduced to unreason), reason could no longer learn from the madman, no longer needed the simultaneously disquieting and fascinating presence/absence of madness that had characterized earlier periods in terms of where it was positioned: Having become nothing other than reason's shadow, madness deserved only the shadow of the cell, where it could be ignored and forgotten.[10]

The intention behind this reconstruction of the history of madness is clear. It is to encourage a rereading of the apparent "progress" to modernity in order to reveal its obverse: a genuine reversal in thinking about madness and the openness to difference the madman represents. From this results the work's extensive development of the various barbarisms accompanying the exclusion of the madman during the classical period: If the madman is nothing but

8. *Histoire de la folie*, p. 26 (*Madness and Civilization*, p. 16).
9. *Histoire de la folie*, p. 41; cf. also p. 44: "Madness no longer has an absolute existence in the night of the world; it exists only in relation to reason."
10. *Histoire de la folie*, pp. 58 ff. *Madness and Civilization*, pp. 40 ff.).

74

the negation of man as reason, he is nothing but a monster or an animal who should be treated as such.[11]

Having recalled Foucault's aim (to disturb the ideology of progress), we should also note his emphasis on the classical and modern mode of production of the madman: In the light of this reconstruction, madness seems purely a product of reason, which, as we have seen, means to designate as "mad" anything that does not seem to correspond to its image of itself. Madness, then, was created by the normalizing function granted to reason. This thesis, essential to Foucault's strategy, is repeated in relation to the way the modern period approaches the treatment of the madman, that is, in the form of *medication*. Here again, a development of the beginning of the nineteenth century, regarded as a form of progress in the sense of a humanization (considering the madman not as a monster but as a person who is ill), is revealed as a subtler, more equivocal, and even more pernicious form of repression: The idea of "mental illness as an object created by medicine for itself"[12] permitted the notion of a "legally incapacitated subject" to be created, "a mythical notion" that provided the means for gathering everyone who could be regarded as a "disturber of the group" into a single false unit. So, when a type of psychiatry appeared for the first time "that claimed to treat the madman as a human being," it was in fact nothing other than a continuation of the experience of classicism: "a normative and dichotomizing social experiment that revolved entirely around incarceration." Here again, Foucault demonstrates that normality produces madness, now understood as an illness: Now decisions would be made as to whether an individual was "inoffensive or dangerous," "suitable or not for incarceration," based on the norm of a *homo natura*, an idea that preexists "any experience of the illness." The logic of exclusion would continue to be the key to the process of medicating, the only difference being that alienation, as the dispossession of rights, has become the specifically modern figure of exclusion: Having become "mentally ill," the madman was then excluded from the community of men as a subject of the law.[13]

11. Ibid., pp. 168 ff. (pp. 70 ff.).
12. *Histoire de la folie*, p. 146.
13. Ibid., pp. 177, 495–96, 529–30 (concerning psychoanalysis), 533.

In short, from classical incarceration to modern medication has been a mere variation in the way that the norms have created and resolved the problem of madness since the end of the Middle Ages, first through incarceration/animalization and then through medication/rehumanization (Foucault emphasizes that in the modern period treatment often includes a dimension of education or reeducation to the norms, which is supposed to lead the madman back to humanity, to make him "normal").

This thesis that madness is a product of normality requires at least two comments:

> On the one hand, its relationship to the antinormative ideology of 1968 is striking: In both cases, it is considered obvious that it is enough simply to abolish the norms in order for the problems they create to disappear.

> On the other hand, in time such an analysis simply denies the problem of madness: If madness is a creation of reason, the norms of reason merely have to be negated in order for the madman to return to society. Unfortunately, it is not clear that the concrete reality of madness permits such a simple and idyllic view.

Already problematic in its principle, the main thesis of *Madness and Civilization* suffers from a carefully managed ambiguity concerning the identification of what motivates the process of exclusion. Sometimes, in line with Foucault's acknowledged philosophical ancestry (Heidegger plus Nietzsche), the history of the exclusion of madness appears to be sustained by the unfolding of reason itself from its emergence during the age of reason to its modern fulfillment in the triumph of technology (in this case, medical technology).[14] The history of madness, from this perspective, results in what he calls "rationalism"[15] or "Western culture," which has been focused for two thousand years on defining man as a rational being.[16] Sometimes, abandoning the Nietzschean/Heideggerian register, Foucault suggests that the motivation of the exclusion of madness is

14. See esp. pp. 191 ff: medicating as the desire to achieve a better "understanding" of madness through knowledge of its causes.
15. Ibid., p. 100.
16. Ibid., p. 169.

none other than the development of the forces of production or, in other words, the rise of capitalism: In explaining the birth of the general hospitals in the eighteenth century, he speaks of "the conspiracy between the power of the monarchy and the bourgeoisie";[17] he identifies "bourgeois concern for putting the world of poverty in order"[18] as a key to the apparently heterogeneous gathering of the insane, the unemployed and the indigent in these hospitals. From this second perspective, the origins of the "break" introduced into the history of madness during the classical age are to be found in an economic "crisis" that began at the end of the sixteenth century and was intensified by the wars of religion: Thus incarceration was "the last great measure to end unemployment, or at least begging."[19] And if incarceration survived even beyond the period of the crisis, it was because "It was no longer merely a question of confining those out of work, but of giving work to those who had been confined and thus making them contribute to the prosperity of all." The economic function of incarceration is therefore clear: "Cheap manpower in the periods of full employment and high salaries; and in periods of unemployment, reabsorption of the idle, and social protection against agitation and uprisings."[20] Medicating the mad in modern times is seen in a new light here: When from the end of the eighteenth century "industry's need for manpower" began to develop, it was no longer enough simply to exile the madman; now he had to be reintegrated *in one way* "into the body of the nation," in terms of his productive capacity; in short, he had to be reeducated in how to work. It is in this context that the end of incarceration during the classical age must be seen, as an "economic mistake" that the asylum would try to repair through the "alienating figure" of the doctor.[21] The "cure," whose motive can be found only in the rise of

17. Ibid., p. 42.
18. Ibid., p. 65. Cf. also his debate with Chomsky (ed. Fons Elders, London, 1974): "The idea of justice in itself is an idea which in effect has been invented and put to work in different societies as an instrument of a certain political and economic power" (p. 184). This text could be readily endorsed by the most modest of our Marxist philosophers.
19. *Histoire de la folie*, p. 75.
20. *Histoire de la folie*, p. 79 (*Madness and Civilization*, p. 51).
21. *Histoire de la folie*, p. 530.

"the liberal economy,"[22] seemed to liberate the "alienated" but was only a ruse of real alienation.

We do not have to try to discover here which of these two registers of Foucault's history of madness is the most relevant. On the contrary, it is more useful to demonstrate that there are certain advantages to permanently playing on both of them, although this poses serious problems of philosophical coherence. At the level of the horizon of the proposition, the difficulties encountered are undeniable.

When the history of madness is written from a perspective borrowed from the Nietzschean or Heideggerian deconstruction of the modern *ratio*, the "natural" horizon of the topic is an excuse for the irrational, to which the last pages of this work are unrestrainedly devoted. Passionately describing the great figures of madness (Goya, Sade, Nietzsche), Foucault praises their "sovereign affirmation of subjectivity" (we will question Foucault's use of this word in what follows), their "rejection of natural freedom and equality," their "excessive expression of violence" as "free exercise of sovereignty over and against nature."[23] Through such lightning flashes, the truth of madness returns, a truth reason tries to disguise, the truth of a "power to annihilate" that suddenly rediscovers its own power; with Sade or Goya, "the Western world acquired the possibility of overcoming the violence of reason."[24] Overcoming reason: the horizon of the interpretation is thus clearly traced, and thus is it entirely logical that the book should end with an homage to Nietzsche, in whom the irrationality of madness triumphed over what was believed to have negated it.

On the other hand, when the history of madness is seen in the light of the history of the internal contradictions in a liberal economy, with its alternate crises and phases of growth, the horizon should be exactly the same as from a Marxian perspective, for example, whose analyses Foucault's seem particularly to resemble. For this reason it is difficult to see how his approach could lead to

22. Ibid., p. 510.
23. Ibid., pp. 552–53.
24. Ibid., p. 554.

praising the irrational and to calling for overcoming reason. The adopted register can in fact easily accommodate a critique of technoeconomic rationality that bourgeois society seeks, although in this case a pseudorationality disguised as a fuller form of rationality conceived as truly emancipating would have to be revealed; what is implied is excessive rationality, not a release of the violence of the irrational. The history of madness viewed as a superstructural reflection of the accumulation of capital would not, it seems, be able to enter a new (postmodern) phase until the alternation between periods of growth and periods of crisis, which define the *absurd* logic of bourgeois society, is over.

Two details: (1) Foucault never explains this second horizon of his analyses, and for good reason: The incompatibility between the two registers of his history of madness would then become clear; yet the line of this horizon is indeed a potentiality or a virtuality of his discourse, or at least of one aspect of it. (2) This aspect, rather than being abandoned in the later works, continues to coexist with the first. For example, the "birth of the prison" will be directly linked, in *Discipline and Punish*, to the "process by which the bourgeoisie in the course of the eighteenth century became the politically dominant class," that is, ultimately, through the "accumulation of capital."[25] Those of his followers who most often emphasized this second guideline in Foucault's reconstructed histories were not wrong. For example, P. Nemo, who would not discover until some years later the virtues of Hayek's kind of hyperliberalism, in January 1972, at the time Foucault was elaborating what would become *Discipline and Punish* in his courses, wrote: "The truth is, Michel Foucault has yet to do a book on prisons. As a matter of fact, his work concerns the world of incarcerations in the broadest sense, rather than prisons, the whole group of 'imprisonments' that marked the political arrival of the bourgeoisie at the beginning of the nineteenth century, which have the names factory, prison, lycée, school, barracks, psychiatric hospital—precisely the places where,

25. *Surveiller et punir: Naissance de la prison*, Gallimard, 1975, p. 223 (*Discipline and Punish: The Birth of the Prison*, trans. Alan Sheridan, Vintage Books, New York, 1979, pp. 231 ff.).

since 1968, nothing works any more." As a result, whoever reads *Madness and Civilization* carefully will see that what Foucault says about the "great confinement" of the classical age is clearly about the domination of the bourgeoisie, since "the classical age is the period of transition between feudalism and capitalism." Having reviewed the various modes of "the decline of the bourgeoisie" through "the rotting away of the institutions that were the armor of its reign," the author then concludes: "Thus Foucault, who before May 1968 had never been particularly notable for his positions on leftist political activities, found himself side by side with leftists in the work of undermining the structures of capitalist oppression. The remote cause of this oppression is indeed the economic domination of one class by another."[26] This type of reception of his works, though it may *look* like caricature, was in fact broadly authorized by Foucault himself, as though it were testimony to his own ambiguity about the ultimate influence of his research.

The fact that ambiguity is maintained and reinforced permits us to suppose that this double game, in spite of and perhaps because of the flux it introduces into its own importance, has certain advantages. One might even wonder whether practicing this double game did not contribute in large part to Foucault's success and to his ability to please. More generally: in the management and care of this ambiguity, we perceive one of the most significant characteristics of recent French philosophy, *Madness and Civilization* from this point of view being the matrix. Playing constantly across two surfaces (a Nietzschean/Heideggerian critique of reason in the name of "unreason," if not in fact irrationality, and a critique of bourgeois rationality in the name of another rationality, if only a potential one) maintains the possibility of an "objective alliance," beyond the surface polemics, between Foucault and Bourdieu, or between Derrida and Althusser.[27] In fact, grouping together profoundly hetero-

26. P. Nemo, in *Le Nouvel Observateur*, Jan. 1972.
27. So Althusser would at times borrow from Derrida even the verbal tics of his writing style and refer to the history of philosophy as "the history of the displacement of the indefinite repetition of a zero trace." So Derrida, at the opening of the "Estates General of Philosophy," would denounce the conspiracies of international capitalism. Althusser would regard Lacan's support as essential, etc.

geneous and ultimately incompatible tendencies made the birth and survival of a "'68 philosophy" possible in spite of the divisions, a philosophy whose *intrinsically antinomical* component parts could coexist in receptive publications such as "Cahiers pour l'analyse" and, today, the "Collège international de philosophie." The minimal common goal of denouncing reason as an instrument of power allowed them to walk some way down the road together, even though their critiques of reason are effected from definitively antithetical perspectives.[28]

In a late text published by H. Dreyfus and P. Rabinow, Foucault poses the question: "Do we have to bring reason to trial?" He proposes a clever answer: "In my opinion, nothing could be more sterile. First, because the field concerned has nothing to do with guilt or innocence. Second, because it is absurd to refer to reason as the entity which is the opposite of nonreason. Finally, because such a trial would condemn us to playing the boring and arbitrary role of either rationalists or irrationalists."[29] Wholly removed from Heidegger, for whom, as we know, irrationality was the bitter enemy of rationality and was rejected as such, the answer still has to be completed: If it had been necessary to accept choosing one of these two roles, which the slightest degree of seriousness shows are mutually exclusive, the development of a Vulgate from *Madness and Civilization* would not have been so easy. This double game allowed him to "cast his net wide" and controlled the possibility of what was then being presented, with somewhat bad grace, as "simplifications": The "refrain of the antirepressive tune" might have been

---

28. J. Lefranc, in a recent article in the *Revue de l'enseignement philosophique* (Oct.–Nov. 1984, pp. 95–104), blames us for combining (in "Philosopher après la fin de la philosophie?," *Le Débat*, Jan. 1984) various profoundly heterogeneous currents under the heading "1960s generation." It goes without saying that one would have to be blind not to have noticed this heterogeneity. On the other hand, what our critique did not in fact see is that it is precisely this "strange combination" that is the basis of '68 philosophy and that this is what makes possible its effects.
29. H. Dreyfus and P. Rabinow, *Michel Foucault: Un parcours philosophique*, with an interview and two essays by M. Foucault, Gallimard, 1984, pp. 299–300.

more easily sung by the chorus[30] if the choir director, limiting himself to the analysis of the "relations between rationality and power," had maintained all the desired ambiguities to the last horizon of this analysis.

Madness and Civilization, the inaugural work of '68 philosophy, thus became the model for a discourse whose relations to the Vulgate, which is said to simplify it, seem very close. The question of why Foucault thought it important later in his itinerary to keep his distance from this Vulgate consequently becomes that much more pointed. Before we attempt to answer it, however, it is important to understand that the theses developed by Foucault in the major part of his work—theses that made him famous and nourished the "antirepressive tune"—were not without serious difficulties—not because of the ambiguous register of the analyses but because of their products or results. Remaining within the territory of *Madness and Civilization*, we will address two of these difficulties, one specific but meaningful and the other more general. In the process, we will have occasion to refer to the debates that flourished around *Madness and Civilization*.

Derrida against Foucault: Reason and Unreason

Incidentally, this fundamental work of 1961 established a parallel between what occurs in the history of society with respect to madness and what occurs in the history of philosophy with respect to the status of the irrational: Corresponding to the creation in 1656 of the general hospital, symbol of the desire to eliminate the mad from society, is the desire to eliminate the irrational from philosophical

30. One example among many: G. Hocquenghem, in a short essay on *Le Désir homosexuel*, Ed. universitaires, 1972, transposed the theses of *Madness and Civilization* word for word, applying them to the problem of homosexuality. Interpreting homosexuality as one type of marginality produced by the norms of a society founded on the family, it is significant that the disciple repeats the ambiguities of the master's discourse, sometimes inputing the process of exclusion to the "social machine" in general and sometimes to "capitalist society." This is one good example of the relationship between the work and its Vulgate, which is less refined but faithful right down to the use of ambiguities.

discourse in Descartes's *Meditations*. Though it occupies only a few pages,[31] this parallel is very important strategically since it contributes to the credibility of the idea that the break in the history of madness indeed does have to be linked to the birth of the classical *ratio*. Now, as it happens, the interpretation of Descartes, outlined in this way, occasioned an instructive polemic between Foucault and Derrida, which, beyond its immediate object, is perfectly representative of the type of theoretical relations maintained by the main proponents of the philosophy of the sixties. Understanding this debate presupposes examining three items from the file.

1. *Madness and Civilization* devotes a short analysis to the passage in the *First Meditation* where Descartes, having put in doubt the existence of the outside world and his own body, raises the objection of madness: Is to deny, he wrote, "that these hands and this body are mine" not to behave like one of "those insane men, whose brain is so troubled and clouded by black vapors of bile that they constantly claim to be kings when they are very poor, say that they are dressed in gold and purple when they are naked, or imagine themselves to be pitchers or to have a body made of glass?" And he adds: "But the fact is, they are madmen (*amentes*), and I would be no less extravagant (*demens*) if I took their example for myself." In the subsequent lines, Descartes confronts the eventuality that he is dreaming: "It may be that I am dreaming and that the world is a dream." This hypothesis of the dream, as we know, was the basis for returning to hyperbolic doubt from which only truths having no basis in the senses (mathematical truths) can escape: True "whether I am awake or dreaming," the certitude of the mathematical sciences can be shaken only when challenged by the artificial hypothesis of the Evil Genius.

Reading this famous text, Foucault invites us to compare how the encounter with madness is effected with how Descartes confronts the hypothesis of the dream: "Descartes does not avoid the peril of madness in the same way that he gets around the possibility that he is dreaming."[32] The two experiences—madness and dream-

31. *Histoire de la folie*, pp. 56–58.
32. Ibid., p. 56.

ing—will in fact be considered as situated differently with respect to the truth. Descartes, according to Foucault, eliminates the hypothesis of madness from the start without seriously considering it: The extravagance of believing that my body is made of glass is not even a serious possibility, *because I think*. If the fact of thought and reason eliminates madness from the start, the hypothesis of the dream, on the other hand, has to be examined carefully, as a radicalization of the hypothesis that states that the senses can sometimes deceive: In a dream, all my sense images become deceptive, and consequently the case of the dream requires careful examination since it allows me to imagine, at the level of hyperbolic exaggeration, the problem of sense error. If the *cogito* seems to Descartes to be compatible with the hypothesis of the dream, it is not compatible with the hypothesis of madness, *by definition*, and for this reason it is dismissed without further explanation. The lesson Foucault takes from his reading is predictable: This declaration of the exclusion of madness by the Cartesian *cogito* foretells the political declaration of the great confinement, which he must be said to agree with in this way. Descartes's gesture marks the beginning of the *ratio*'s repression of its "other" that characterizes the entire classical period.

2. In a 1963 address to the "Philosophical College" of J. Wahl, which was published in 1964 in the *Revue de Métaphysique et de Morale* and later reprinted in 1967 in *Writing and Difference*,[33] Derrida, while praising *Madness and Civilization* highly,[34] argues against the possibility of understanding the *First Meditation* as an early exclusion of the discourse of madness as being radically outside the *cogito*. Rereading the passage, he concludes that madness, the hypothesis of extravagance, does not receive any specific

33. J. Derrida, "Cogito et histoire de la folie," in *L'Ecriture et la différence*, coll. "Points," pp. 51–97 ("Cogito and the History of Madness," in *Writing and Difference*, trans. Alan Bass, University of Chicago Press, Chicago, 1978, pp. 31–64).
34. *Writing and Difference*, p. 31: "A book that is admirable in so many respects, powerful in its breadth and style, is even more intimidating for me in that, having formerly had the good fortune to study under Michel Foucault, I retain the consciousness of an admiring and grateful disciple."

84

treatment at this point in the development of the *Meditations* and is
subject to no particular exclusion. It can in fact be shown that the
incriminating lines—between those that implicate the senses (we
must never "rely entirely on what has sometimes deceived us") and
those that refute the hypothesis of the dream—keep silent on the
treatment of the hypothesis of madness. And in fact Foucault interpreted this silence as the sign that madness is absolutely outside
reason. Since I think, there is no need even to refute the hypothesis
of madness: "*I* who think, I cannot be mad."[35] On the other hand,
Derrida attempts to demonstrate that Descartes's silence is preparatory to the broader reprieve, hyperbolizing the hypothesis of madness in the form of the fiction of the Evil Genius: The hypothesis of
the Evil Genius allows us to imagine total madness, "total distrac-
tion," so that any exception is removed from what is only the
possibility of partial extravagance (I think that my body is made of
glass, but my other perceptions are not necessarily "distracted").
My entire relations with the real would then be such that, Descartes
would say, "the sky, the air, the earth, the colors, the figures, the
sounds, and everything outside us that we see would be only illusions and deceptions" that the Evil Genius abuses me with; and as a
result I have to consider myself "as having no hands, no eyes, no
flesh, no blood, as having no senses, but falsely believing I have all
these things." For Derrida, the repetition of the same examples in
the context of a generalized extravagance is the sign that madness
does not take time off, contrary to what Foucault suggests: It is in the
context of the hypothesis of the Evil Genius, thus in the context of
the possibility of an extended madness, that Descartes establishes
the *cogito, sum*. The method of the *Second Meditation* consists of
demonstrating that the *cogito, sum* is still true even if I am "distracted" by the Evil Genius: "Whether I am mad or not, *cogito,
sum*."[36] And as a result the *cogito* precedes the break between
reason and madness: "The act of the *cogito* is valid even if I am mad,
even if my thought is mad here and there. *Cogito* has value and
meaning that escape the alternative of madness and of determined

35. *Histoire de la folie*, p. 57.
36. Derrida, "Cogito," p. 87.

reasons."[37] Thus the certainty of existence is not protected from an isolated madness in Descartes; rather, it is touched and affirmed *by madness itself:* The *cogito* is valid even for the madman, the thing differentiating the madman at this point being that he cannot think and express the *cogito.*

It is easy to see the stake Derrida could have in this restatement: Cartesian reason, rather than excluding what was different from it, recognized the presence of madness, the potentially threatening, unnatural black light surrounding and even incorporated into it. With Descartes, reason discovered its other in itself, discovered the rupture that constitutes madness inside of reason—a clear indication for Derrida of a crisis within reason at the very beginning of its reign: the trace of *difference* at the very moment that the figure of *self-identity* was being imposed.

3. Foucault undertook an answer to Derrida in an appendix to the second edition of *Madness and Civilization.*[38] A careful analysis of this response, which addresses line by line Descartes's text and Derrida's interpretation of it, would require a detailed analysis of the two readings, which does not seem to us to be particularly important here. Foucault's purpose is to win the argument with Derrida, and his approach is of little importance if one is convinced that they are both, in a sense, fundamentally wrong, as we will suggest. For our purposes here, then, only Foucault's main point need concern us. His response severely questions Derrida's "narrow, historically determined pedagogical technique," which "teaches the student that there is nothing beyond the text," that it has to be interpreted from the point of departure of itself, and that interpretation has to be limited to the search for *its* unsaids (even if it is in "words as erasures"), refusing to "look elsewhere." Foucault's position, on the other hand, is that Descartes's text would be incomprehensible without "replacing its discursive practices in the field of transformation where they occur." This is what, since the time of *The Order of Things* (1966), he has called the *épistéme,* or the universal system knowledge of the period (its cultural/scientific structure). Closed off

37. Ibid., p. 85.
38. *Histoire de la folie* (ed. cited), pp. 583–603.

from the outside from where the text speaks, Derrida can only miss its real import.

The circular reasoning underlying Foucault's response is perhaps surprising. The analysis of the passage on madness in the *Meditations* was intended to describe the prevailing attitude toward the irrational at the time of Descartes; if we read the *Meditations* from the starting point of the characteristic *episteme* of the period, the meaning of Descartes's text would be clear only now! No doubt this is an example of one of those subtle, so-called dialectical, interactions favored by the philosophical discourse of the sixties. But no matter: the last episode in the debate reveals that to impose the test of genealogy systematically on texts is to be exposed to infinite higher bids. Derrida and Foucault profoundly agree on the matter of reading the "unsaid" of a text, which is assumed, by definition, to say more than what its author intended. They differ only in defining the source of this excess of meaning: Is the source in some way an internal outside, which works on the text from the inside, as Derrida suggests in deconstructing the Cartesian statement on self-identity in order to make the play of difference visible—or is it, as Foucault claims, a more radical outside, that of the period itself? The bidding up, as we see, could no doubt go on, because the *episteme* of the period, in order to be fully understood, would in turn perhaps gain by being interpreted from the point of view of what speaks in it and what constitutes its "unsaid," whether it be the history of the development of the forces of production or some other history for which this particular cultural structure is only one of its moments. The debate that opposes Derrida and Foucault in this way perfectly represents both the resources and the difficulties (which in this case take the form of an uncontrollable regression to the infinite) that characterized the practice of genealogy common to the two protagonists. In this way, we are reassured, the disagreement does not get to the essence of the matter.

That said, what should one think of this polemic as far as the problem it debates is concerned, namely, the problem of the status of madness in Descartes's discourse or, more generally, in the *episteme* of the seventeenth century, a broader approach that Foucault recommends? The problem has to be considered at two levels.

With respect to the relations Descartes's text established between *cogito* and madness, Derrida is undoubtedly right in his assertion that the elimination of madness does not intervene prior to the foundation provided for the philosophical edifice by the *cogito, sum:* The division between reason and madness happens only when the hypothesis of the Evil Genius is refuted. In the *Meditations,* the fact that philosophy is founded before such a division does not necessarily imply that the fissure, which is difference, is at work at the very heart of the constitution of identity: In this respect, Derrida's analysis is typical of a characteristic gesture of French Heideggerianism, the desire to overinterpret marginal texts. But with respect to the relations between *cogito* and madness in the economy of Descartes's text, Derrida's restatement can hardly be disputed and cuts short the effort to turn the *First Meditation* into the expression or reflection of the great confinement, in itself a not negligible accomplishment.

As for the larger question of understanding the seventeenth century's view of madness, on the other hand, Derrida seems as seriously mistaken as Foucault.[39] They both read the *Meditations* with the preconceived idea of madness as hallucination, as the inability to distinguish between sensory information and an image. Now, for all intents and purposes, the idea of madness as hallucination is a nineteenth-century concept. Madness was no more the suppression of perception for Descartes than it was for Pascal.[40] Throughout the seventeenth century, madness was considered to be the balance between *perception* and *judgment:* The madman perfectly perceives his body and the outside world but chooses to believe in his judgment rather than his senses; in his judgment, for example, he might have no body. It is precisely this type of conception of madness that permits a parallel to be drawn between madness and philosophy, which is present in Pascal as well as in Descartes. Like the madman, the philosopher prefers to believe in his judgments rather than his perceptions: Whereas the senses tell him that

39. We remember that this misunderstanding was always emphasized with great clarity by F. Alquié, especially in his teaching.
40. Cf., for example, Pascal, in *Pensées,* ed. L. Lafuma, Paris, 1943, p. 44.

an outside world exists, that he has a body, hands, and so on, he prefers to question these sensory facts since his senses have previously deceived him and he *judges* the content of those perceptions to be doubtful. Consequently, to distinguish philosophy from madness, it has to be demonstrated that there is a difference at the level of judgment that is preferable to the senses, insane judgment in the case of the madman, well-founded judgment in the case of the philosopher. For Descartes this is precisely the function of dreams: to establish that the philosopher's judgment is not insane. The whole of reasoning is, then, the following:

> In the act of hyperbolic doubt, as a philosopher I am comparable to the madman who believes in his judgment rather than his senses.
>
> Dreams are evoked to demonstrate that my judgment, unlike the madman's, has a basis since I have already experienced the feeling of existence in my dreams, even though they are merely a product of imagination. So privileging a judgment that casts doubt on the existence that my senses present as real to me is not mad but philosophically wise: In this case the judgment that disqualifies my perception depends on reasonable arguments.

Within the overall framework of this reasoning, the reference to madness does not in fact mean what both Foucault and Derrida say it does. The possibility of madness ("But after all, they are mad") logically arises as soon as defining philosophy by questioning what one sees becomes an issue. And at this point in the *First Meditation*, when we do not yet have the truth criterion, the possibility that the philosopher may be mad is not easy to overcome: How, without a truth criterion, can we establish that the philosopher, as distinct from the madman, prefers a *well-founded* judgment of what he perceives? From here a higher level is attained where the choice of judgment over the content of perception is no longer the issue so much as disturbing perception is. Conclusion: Descartes does not leave aside the objection of madness ("But after all, they are mad") because classical reasoning excludes madness from the beginning (Foucault) or because it includes madness as its other, as its difference which is at work on it from the inside (Derrida). The objection is left aside more simply and more soberly because, at this moment in the argumentation of the *Meditations*, the means for refuting it are not yet available. So it is necessary to go on in spite of this unresolved objection (by virtue of which doubt might be madness) and to radicalize doubt, which the dream argument invites.

Thus the polemic between Foucault and Derrida is essentially defused. Two main lessons can be drawn from his analysis.

The limits of genealogical hermeneutics, common to the two readings (which are opposed only in the modalities of practice), are revealed: If one allows oneself to be convinced that the text cannot be understood except from the starting point of something other than itself, there is the risk that one will no longer be careful to construct internal coherence within the work in question and that it will be forcibly inserted into a logic that is not its own. If from the theoretical point of view genealogy dispossesses *a priori* the subject of mastery over one's own utterances, clearly participating in the deconstruction of subjectivity that unites the components of '68 philosophy in terms of practice, it also has perverse effects, not the least of which is interpretative delirium. Literary criticism of the sixties also paid its tribute to the systematic adoption of such an approach.

By means of this mistake about the classical conception of madness, which was equally shared by Derrida, a certain fragility in Foucault's reconstruction appears: This reconstruction is false, if only in relation to how the history of madness is expressed in the history of philosophy. What is more, the object of the mistake is not a mere detail, since it is the point of departure for Foucault's effort to demonstrate that classical reasoning is born and develops through the exclusion of madness. Prudence requires, under these conditions, that the question be reformulated in the most general way: From the classical to the modern age, can the development of Western societies be interpreted only at those moments when an exclusionary logic in relation to madness, and to other "margins" as well, can be observed?

Gauchet and Swain against Foucault: The Logic of Democracy

This time the debate took on the entire interpretation of madness proposed by Foucault. M. Gauchet and G. Swain turned their attention first to reestablishing certain facts.[41]

The asylum is an institution that in fact only made its appearance around 1800, or right after the French Revolution, under the aegis of Chaptal, the minister of the interior at the time.

The great confinement Foucault speaks of did in fact happen, but not at the beginning of the classical age (*Madness and Civilization* mentions the year 1656). In fact, the documents show that an estimated two thousand people were incarcerated in 1660. This number rose to about five thousand after the Revolution. It reached 100 thousand in 1914.

These facts suggest a hypothesis: The phenomenon of incarceration has perhaps a closer relation to the implementation and development of a democratic society, in the Tocquevillean sense of the word, than to the dawn of the classical age and to Cartesianism. For the very reason that it is so incongruous in a field widely influenced by the Foucault Vulgate, the regenerating potential of this hypothesis has generally been ignored. Therefore, it seems to us to require particular emphasis.

Three theses aimed directly at Foucault's reconstruction support the hypothesis:

1. Contrary to Foucault's claim, the dynamics of modernity is not essentially that of the *exclusion of otherness*. The logic of modern societies is rather more like the one Tocqueville describes, namely, the logic of *integration* sustained by the proposition of the fundamental *equality* of all mankind.

Let us return to the basic principle of Foucault's analyses as it

41. See esp. M. Gauchet and G. Swain, *La Pratique de l'esprit humain: L'institution asilaire et la révolution démocratique*, Gallimard, 1980. A series of articles by G. Swain for the journal *Esprit*, devoted to the analysis of the birth of specialized educations, should also be mentioned ("La Naissance des éducations spécialisées," *Esprit*, 1982).

appears in *Madness and Civilization* and later, most notably in his study of the penal system. This principle, clearly inspired by his Heideggerianism/Nietzscheanism, consists of locating the domain of modern reason in its inability to consider *difference* (or otherness) and in its tendency to reject it. Applied to the history of madness, this principle produces the following: If the madman is disturbing and inspires fear, it is due to his being the example of the *entirely other.* Correlatively, if the Middle Ages were still able to provide a place for the madman, it was because they were not yet dominated by the intellectual configuration whose outline Foucault borrows directly from Heidegger's analysis of the (modern) metaphysics of subjectivity (the mastery and possession of the real through the reduction of differences, the forgotten/rejected, in favor of identity). The model for this regression in relations between the community and the mad, described by Foucault and situated by him at the beginning of the classical age, is this "decline of philosophy" that Heidegger reconstructed, attributing to it the primary responsibility for the rise of Cartesian reason in the transition to Modern Times.

Gauchet and Swain show that this vision of history depends on a twofold illusion:

> An illusion about preclassical societies: If the madman was toler-
> ated by traditional societies, it was not because those societies
> were "better," more tolerant, or, if you wish, less "metaphysical."
> On the contrary, it was because these societies were fundamentally
> inegalitarian and hierarchical; Radical difference was not a real
> problem yet. The madman was indeed tolerated, but the toleration
> was based on the implicit affirmation of his absolute difference
> from the rest of humanity; sometimes regarded as subhuman,
> sometimes as superhuman (and nearly divine), the madman was
> considered to be outside humanity and outside all possible com-
> munication. In such a cultural framework (defined by the princi-
> ples of inequality and of *natural* hierarchies), absolute difference
> did not prevent familiarity, and the presence of madmen in the
> community could be accommodated.
>
> An illusion about modern societies: If madness began to be a prob-
> lem with the rise of democratic, egalitarian modernity, it was not

because the madman was the Other but because, to the extent that he is an alter ego, he *had* to be thought of as the same, as another *man*.

Nothing better illustrates this mutation than the visible evolution, from traditional to modern societies, in the attitude toward the mad. In traditional societies, the madman is indeed a familiar being who does not necessarily have to be locked up; however, because he is outside humanity and communication, because he does not understand us (and does not suffer *like a man*), one may relate to him through ridicule. So in the cities of the seventeenth century children were allowed to chase madmen through the streets, throw rocks at them, and make fun of them; so, too, until the beginning of the nineteenth century, a visit to see the madmen in the Hôtel-Dieu was still often an end to a Sunday afternoon walk with the family. In short, the madman was accepted into society but in the mode of village idiot, in the same spirit that allowed the public display of ill people at fairs. In modern societies this attitude has gradually disappeared, and where it remains it is criticized. Meetings with the mad occur at a distance rather than on familiar terms. The very reason the madman is disturbing, what prompts us to keep him at a distance, is that he is a fellow man, so that his behavior cannot be regarded as cause for amusement or curiosity. To summarize, *during the Middle Ages there was proximity with the mad in fact but absolute distance in terms of rights; in the modern period, on the other hand, there is similarity of rights and distance only in fact.*

The interpretation that should be made of the phenomenon of incarceration, then, is the opposite of Foucault's from every point of view. Two elements of the logic of the modern state can explain the real nature of incarceration: (1) in *principle*, the modern state is obviously sustained by the dynamics of equality; (2) in *function*, it intervenes, like the policeman, to perform the task of repression and to "protect" the future of the welfare state. Reinscribed into this logic, the meaning of incarceration becomes both obvious and subtle:

From the point of view of equality, the madman is threatening to us because he represents, in legal terms, a man whose humanity vacillates; for the logic of the repressive function of the state, the madman has to be locked up.

Threatening as he may be, the madman is also threatened and feels diminished by being made fun of. The principle of equality requires that he be considered an alter ego, that he become *de jure* what he no longer is *de facto*, a man like any other who deserves the protection of the state like any man. Within the logic of the second function of the state, he must be not only locked up but taken care of.

It is significant in this regard that between 1770 and 1830, in the middle of the democratic movement, specialized education was introduced.[42] It was aimed at the deaf, the blind, the retarded, at precisely those who were regarded in the Middle Ages as *naturally*, and therefore *definitively* (in law), excluded from communication. Since from this time on they were considered men *de jure*, society was obliged to appoint "specialists" to *reintegrate* them into human communication *de facto*.

2. Gauchet and Swain drew an important consequence from this first thesis concerning the overall meaning of the modern history of madness (as a history of integration, not exclusion), which emphasizes another of Foucault's misunderstandings, this time with regard to the introduction of "moral treatment" and its meaning. Before modern democracy, there were attempts to treat insanity. For the most part, however, they were physical treatments (bleeding, hanging by the feet, immersion in cold or warm water depending on the case, etc.). Moreover, these physical or external treatments, which the subject rarely survived, followed a logic: Since the madman was radically excluded from communication, one did not have to understand him, but at least he could be acted upon. On the other hand, the beginning of moral (= psychical) treatment depended on the idea that the madman can still be communicated with since *de jure* he is still, beyond his *de facto* disturbances, the "subject of his own madness," in Swain's words. This mutation, which Gauchet and Swain analyze in the history of psychology (along with d'Aquin,

---

42. Cf. on this point the articles by Swain, "La Naissance des educations spe-cialisées."

Esquirol, Pinel), is clearly linked to the modern democratic notion of "humanity": To see it as Foucault does, merely as the arrival of a softer and more insidious form of exclusion, is to be seriously mistaken.

This mutation can also be noted in the history of philosophy, as Swain has demonstrated with respect to Hegelianism.[43] As we know, Hegel explicitly gave Pinel the credit for "having discovered a bit of reason in insanity and madness, and for having discovered that it was the key for their cure."[44] For Hegel, madness was a provisional moment only, superimposed on a foundation of reason and thus humanity: The madman does not stop being a man *in law*, even if in fact, or in appearance, he keeps his distance from humanity. Using the schema of the "ruse of reason," Hegel even called madness a moment that is integral to the development of the Mind, as Swain describes: "Given what I am as a man, I am exposed to madness, madness is my 'privilege'. . . . One does not escape from the human condition by virtue of insanity. Indeed, something of the human condition is expressed through madness. . . . Reason itself is imbued with madness. Of course, madness is nonetheless reason's other, but it is an other that is somehow inside of it, and whose unexpected arrival is contained in the very logic of its development."[45] The conviction that there is no absolute (*de jure*) difference between madness and reason reappears, then, against the background of democratic modernity—the conviction that contains the germ of the psychoanalytic ideal of eliminating the gap between the normal and the pathological.

One problem remains to be resolved: Why in the modern history of madness has the institution of the asylum grown, given that moral treatment, like psychoanalysis, can most often be given outside a particular institution? In other words, is the asylum an obstacle to the claim that the history of madness has developed in the direction of integration rather than exclusion?

3. The appearance of the asylum as an institution has an

43. G. Swain, "Deux Epoques de la folie," *Libre*, vol. 1, Payot, 1977.
44. Hegel, *Philosophie de l'esprit*, trans. Vera, p. 409 (*Enzyklopadie: Die Philosophie des Geistes*).
45. Swain, p. 194.

importance which, according to Gauchet and Swain's interpretation, justifies including the modern history of madness in the dynamics of democracy. Two factors meet in the appearance of the asylum:

> Once the first enthusiasm for moral treatment had passed, an enthusiasm which had been based on the belief that communication with the mad might be possible, it encountered difficulties that psychoanalysis attempted to describe: Communication does not necessarily lead to a cure, a claim that suggested that institutional treatment could be indispensable. The general hospital became the model for the new institution under the pressure of widespread social demand. But the model was also, and this is crucial, overdetermined by revolutionary utopianism: The French Revolution had profoundly transformed the way society was represented. The model for society, rather than being defined by the outside and the past, as it had been by theological-political schemas, became the representation of a society in terms of a vision of its future. The emergence of this utopian ideal of a future society, producing itself in a wholly constructive way, was to become the framework for the evolution of the idea of the asylum.

The asylum might be regarded as a *democratic utopia* in three ways:

> First, it is an *insular* institution, cut off from the rest of society, thus concretely reproducing the ideology of the *tabula rasa*.

> Second, it represents the effort to produce a new man with the use of scientific knowledge and a regimen of discipline and internalization. To this end, an entire system was put in place, a system organized and directed by the head doctor, a power assumed to be well-meaning, omniscient, omnipresent, who was intended to control the whole experience with the help of an appropriate architecture.

> Third, the utopian aspect of the asylum was understood in the trivial sense of utopia, as a goal that contains within it the suggestion of its own failure—because (and this is an essential point in Gauchet and Swain's analyses that should be emphasized) it is not a question of systematically defending the asylum against Foucault's criticisms of it. There is indeed a "totalitarian" danger

inherent in the practice of institutionalizing, though it is the obverse of what Foucault thinks. This danger (evidence of the utopian nature of the project) is related to a fantastic will for integration and not exclusion: On the one hand, the project for power that is behind the idea of the asylum is unrealistic (today we understand that the panoptic eye sees nothing and that total planning plans nothing) and has dangerous effects; on the other hand, the basic belief underlying this utopia is that by radically transforming the environment man will also be transformed. Now, although there is no doubt that the natural environment conditions the mind, the difficulty arises from the fact that its effects cannot be controlled: Though man is perhaps determined by society, that does not necessarily mean that society knows how to produce him.

Thus reinserted into the dynamics of modern democratic societies, the development of the institution of the asylum continues to raise certain questions concerning its effects. Nevertheless, in spite of its failures, in spite of its dangers, the asylum has a role in representing madness as simply a *factual and temporary* disturbance that interferes in a humanity that is still legally asserted. From this point of view, the history of madness, which includes the appearance of the utopian idea of the asylum, can hardly be interpreted, in spite of everything, in any way other than as a history of progress. Thus Foucault's main theses should seem historically as well as philosophically false, even fallacious: In the course of his inquiry into the history of madness—an approach that would later be applied in his history of punishment—a vast undertaking of the falsification of modern history was unfolding, a history unilaterally represented as a multiform process of repression. This falsification later gave rise to and, through repetition, maintained the antirepressive Vulgate, which seems to have ended up as an embarrassment to a later Foucault. Are we to conclude that the master came to see the limitations of his own presuppositions when faced with his disciples' exaggeration of them? Given that *The History of Sexuality* seems to represent the turning of a corner in this way, Dreyfus and Rabinow have argued that this is already enough to "prove" that Foucault "was one of those exceptional thinkers, like Wittgenstein and Heidegger, whose work demonstrates both an underlying continuity and a striking sudden turn."[46] Even though Heidegger, an expert on these matters, assures us that "whoever thinks on a grand scale must also be wrong on a grand scale," it is not clear that the fact that a theoretical retraction is broad is proof of its depth. More seriously, anyone has the right to be wrong, and if there was a retraction it deserves to be considered with attention and interest. So we have to take note of various statements of Foucault's from 1975 on that no doubt surprised many of his disciples. One example is enough for the moment to suggest the likelihood that they were indeed surprised:

> We will indeed have to rid ourselves of the "Marcusianisms" and "Reichianisms" encumbering us that try to make us believe that sexuality is the most obstinately "repressed" thing in the world, "overrepressed" by our "bourgeois," "capitalist," and "Victorian" society, whereas nothing since the Middle Ages has been more studied, questioned, wrung out, brought into the light of day and discourse, forced to confess, required to express itself, and praised when it finally found the words. No civilization has known a more talkative sexuality than ours.[47]

The retraction that we apparently have to assume in order to account for effects like these seems to go to the essence of his work. Taking into account certain indications furnished by Foucault himself, it seems indispensable to return at this point to the notorious question of the death of man and, more generally, to the status of the subject as it was treated from *The Order of Things* through the last two volumes of *The History of Sexuality*.

The Death of Man

In terms of a first reading—which is ultimately the most important one, as we will see—the notion of the "death of man" as it was introduced in *The Order of Things* is given in terms of a critique

46. Dreyfus and Rabinow, *Michel Foucault*, p. 147.
47. M. Foucault, in *Le Monde*, April 23, 1976.

of humanism as the metaphysics of subjectivity, in terms elaborated by Nietzsche and Heidegger, in a break with the indissolubly humanist and dialectical philosophy of Hegel and even Marx: "Those who are most responsible for contemporary humanism are obviously Hegel and Marx."[48] Thus speaking of the death of man, Foucault explicitly appeals to this "nondialectical" and "thus nonhumanist"[49] culture, which "began with Nietzsche" and "also appeared in Heidegger" before being echoed in the structuralist current, "with linguists and sociologists like Lévi-Strauss," who also practiced the death of the subject in the birth of structures. But in addition to its philosophical thematization, in Foucault's view the death of man is also apparent in all the literature from Mallarmé to Blanchot (required references for the entire French Heideggerian/ Nietzschean current of thought) that has expressed in writing the rupture within metaphysical subjectivity, unveiling self-mastery in all its illusory and imperious pretension:

> Beginning with *Igitur*, Mallarmé's experience (he was Nietzsche's contemporary) demonstrates that the game of autonomous language itself came into being in precisely the place where man had just disappeared. We may say that, since then, literature has been the place where man has never stopped disappearing in favor of language. Where "ça parle," man no longer exists. Works as different as Robbe-Grillet's and Malcolm Lowry's, Borges's and Blanchot's testify to this disappearance of man in favor of language.[50]

Presented in this way, the theme of the death of man consists purely and simply of celebrating the victory of *Dasein* over the consciousness of the self, over *Bewusstsein*, and of recording the dissolution of the metaphysical illusion of a subject's transparency to itself. J.-M. Benoît, who now greets the return of the subject with a great brouhaha, not too long ago heralded Foucault as a voice "that

48. M. Foucault, in *Arts*, June 15, 1966.
49. Through this identification of *dialectics* with *humanism*, Foucault reveals his continuing dependence on Heidegger, for whom dialectics (Hegelian and Marxian) was the culmination of the metaphysics of subjectivity.
50. Foucault, in *Arts*, June 15, 1966.

speaks more and more majestically, urging us to awaken from our humanistic and anthropological sleep":

> Foucault is delivering us from a certain soft, moist, weeping prophesying: Sartre, Merleau-Ponty, *Les Temps Modernes*, the functionaries of "freedom" and of "meaning" . . . the syrupy philosophy of Père Teilhard de Chardin and the sadly academic yawns of Albert Camus. . . . A prophet, he announced in his wonderful book *The Order of Things* the definitive closing of a period in which ideas and scientific disciplines were contaminated by this vague and fluid notion, this philosophical catchall: Man. Foucault offers our culture the clear mirror of a philosophy of the system in which man, a indeterminate entity, is only a moment. . . . On his side he has Sade and Nietzsche, whose Socratic and Dionysian discourse had the highest mission: to be done with humanism and the values of the schoolmaster.[51]

Among other enigmas, we will ignore the strangeness of this representation of a history of philosophy where Socrates would have done battle with this humanism, whose eminently modern character Foucault is first to affirm. Here antihumanism takes on a militant tone in order to recognize in *The Order of Things* the clear definition of a duty—to do away with the inheritance from the metaphysics of subjectivity that still more or less consciously motivates the human sciences.

If we turn again from the Vulgate to the works of Foucault, two problems arise whose solutions are relatively delicate. First, a problem of historical periods: the main thesis of *The Order of Things* is that man is an invention of the nineteenth century, the definitive date being the publication of the *Critique of Pure Reason:*

> It is believed that humanism is a very old notion going back to Montaigne and beyond. . . . All that is of the nature of an illusion. First, the humanist movement dates from the end of the nineteenth century. Second, when one looks rather closely at the culture of

51. J.-M. Benoît, *Sciences Po information*, no. 9, p. 32 (review of M. Foucault, *Les Mots et les choses*).

the sixteenth, seventeenth, and eighteenth centuries, one can see that man literally had no place in it. Culture at the time was busy with God, the world, the resemblance of things, the laws of space, and also of course the body, the passions, the imagination. But man himself was entirely absent.[52]

Formulated in this way, the thesis may at first seem absurd, the primary advantage being that it is easily falsifiable and falsified, if only by reference to the Declaration of the Rights of Man. If we do not want to stay with our first reaction, however, we have to try to comprehend the deliberately provocative nature of this type of characterization. The problem is easily formulated: The theoreticians of the death of man to whom Foucault refers—above all, Heidegger—agree that the philosophical emergence of man is found in Descartes. Foucault is not unaware of this interpretation, and for that reason it is important to question why he displaces it forward to the end of the nineteenth century. Does he have the birth of the human sciences in mind, for example, the rise of man as an object of study? But in that case why not simply say that in the seventeenth century the sciences of man did not yet exist? That might have been less striking than saying that man was entirely absent at the time, but the formulation would have been more accurate.

Even if we adopt the hypothesis that Foucault was referring only to the birth of the human sciences, we confront a second problem. *The Order of Things* explains that the human sciences do not succeed in grasping their object, so that, in the human sciences as well as in antimetaphysical and antihumanist philosophy, man dissolves. *Thus two very different, if not wholly opposite, deaths of man have to be distinguished:*

> The death of man as suggested by the philosophies of Nietzsche and Heidegger: the fragmentation of the subject was discovered, proof of the irreducible opacity of the subject to itself.
>
> The death of man in the sense that results from the sciences that support the remnants of metaphysical humanism and that make

52. Foucault, in *Arts*, June 15, 1966.

man an *object* of study by reifying him, thus allowing his authentic selfhood to escape.

We can now locate the difficulty more precisely. If the human sciences kill man through reification, should we not conclude that nonmetaphysical philosophy saves him? And if this is so, why assign it the task of making man disappear? Reciprocally, if one claims that nonmetaphysical philosophy kills man, dissipating an illusion that is after all quite recent, are not the human sciences the last refuge of metaphysical humanism?[53]

The solution adopted by Foucault consists of stating that man does not exist, that he is in fact neither living nor dead. As Deleuze explains, commenting on Foucault: "From the classical to the modern age we move from a situation where man does not yet exist to one where man has already disappeared."[54] To explain this apparently enigmatic proposition, we have to retrace the four stages of what in fact make up a false birth and, at the same time, a false death of man.

1. *The classical age:* Illustrated by the Meninas of Velázquez, this is the age of representation but not the age of man. This statement, which has an anti-Heideggerian flavor, cannot be understood without reference to Heidegger's interpretation of the *Critique of Pure Reason* as an analysis of finite reason, or an "analysis of *Dasein*." What Foucault wants to suggest is that during the classical age, with Descartes, for example, representation was still taken for granted; or, in other words, representation had not yet been represented. Dreyfus and Rabinow's summary is cogent:

> What is represented are the functions of representation.[55] What is not represented is the unified and unifying subject which postulates these representations. . . . According to Foucault, that sub-

53. M. Foucault, *Les Mots et les choses*, Gallimard, 1966, p. 353 (*The Order of Things*, trans. Tavistock, London, 1970, p. 342).

54. G. Deleuze, "L'Homme, une existence douteuse," *Le Nouvel Observateur*, June 1, 1966.

55. That is, its production by the painter, the represented objects, and the spectators.

ject only appears with the coming of man, with Kant. . . . If the great undertaking of the classical age was composed of organizing representations in a painting, the only thing that could not mark the epoch was representing its activity in the painting thus constructed.[56]

2. *The Kantian moment:*[57] In the *Critique of Pure Reason*, the discovery of man as *Dasein*, that is, simultaneously finite and transcendent (open onto the world) as in Heidegger's interpretation, returns. Kant is not satisfied merely to describe the representations of the subject but questions the possibility conditions of representation, conditions he searches for in the course of an analysis of finite reason: Categories, space, time, and so on, are not representations but the conditions of representation and, as such, the structures of finitude, since only a finite subject can be represented. Foucault returns to the principal themes developed by Heidegger in his *Kant and the Problem of Metaphysics* with a degree of literal fidelity that is even more surprising in that the debt to the German model is not even mentioned.[58]

3. *The birth of man:* Against the background of this radical finitude, the idea of man that appears in the nineteenth century will be defined through four characteristics: "The connection of the positivities with finitude, the reduplication of the empirical and the transcendental, the perpetual relation of the *cogito* to the unthought, the retreat and return of the origin, define for us man's mode of being."[59] Seemingly enigmatic, this definition can be easily clarified merely by referring to Heidegger's *Kantbuch:*

> "The connection of the positivities with finitude": From the perspective inaugurated by Kant, I can have representations (positivities) only if in the opening of transcendence the real is given to me, in other words, if I am *finite*.

56. Dreyfus and Rabinow, *Michel Foucault*, pp. 45–46.
57. *The Order of Things*, pp. 315–17, 318, 337.
58. Ibid., pp. 315 ff: Foucault appropriates Heidegger's notion of the "analysis of finitude." In their commentary, Dreyfus and Rabinow, *Michel Foucault*, pp. 47 ff., are careful to point out this inveigling.
59. *The Order of Things*, p. 335.

"The reduplication of the empirical and the transcendental": Man becomes both a potential object of science and the *transcendental subject* through whose activity representations, including scientific ones, come into being. In other words, man is not only one fact among others, one object of knowledge among others, but also the condition of possibility for all knowledge. From this duality, the ambiguity of anthropology arises, as we will see.

"The perpetual relation of the *cogito* to the unthought": As a finite subject I am immersed in the "non-me," thus in the unthought that conditions me and that I do not control. Logically, the three fundamental sciences develop from this, which correspond to the three fundamental regions of the unthought. *Biology* responds to the fact that I am always already alive, that is, caught in the chain of the living, which always precedes my consciousness, surrounds me, and surpasses me; *philology* takes on language that is also given to me and preexists me, without my being able to do anything other than discover that it is already at work; finally, *economics* corresponds to the field of work that I will be plunged into, which is already organized, already structured by history. These are the three discourses of the unthought that will serve as the model for the human sciences in the fourth phase.

"The retreat and return of the origin": The last figure of finitude, it concerns the fact that "man can uncover his own beginning only against the background of a life which began before him"[60]—so that modern philosophy always comes up against this retreat of the originary: Any preoccupation with the return, with beginning again, expresses this concealment of the origin, inevitable for (finite) beings whose existence is necessarily articulated on "what has already begun."[61]

4. *The birth of the human sciences:* Psychology and sociology are located in this space where the subject, since it is finite, is

60. Ibid., p. 330.
61. In relation to this necessarily aporetic research on the origin, Foucault briefly refers to the example of Heidegger (ibid., p. 334) and his pursuit of the impossible task of restoring the originary. It could be surprising that the figure of Heidegger, always nearby during these analyses, is mentioned explicitly only at a moment of criticism (which is pertinent, by the way).

opened (by being fragmented) to an unthought working in it and defying its control. In imitation of the three sciences of finitude, the human sciences are all sciences of the unconscious, and from this point of view their scope seems to correspond with the definitive moment of the rupture with classicism, the age of representation: "They also permit the dissociation, which is characteristic of all contemporary knowledge about man, of consciousness and representation. They define the manner in which the empiricities can be given to representation but in a form that is not present to the consciousness."[62] But at the same time the human sciences, as distinct from what an authentic philosophy of the split subject would do, reappropriated the classical ideal of representation, thus attempting to produce what they believed man's liberation to be by making the unconscious conscious, by leading it toward representation, in short, by making the unthought an object of knowledge. Attempting to "extend the reign of representation," they did not really succeed in "reshaping the preeminence of representation" that characterized classical science.[63] On this basis one might conclude that what emerged with Kant, a philosophy of man as open to the outside, to representation, which breaks open the classical figure of man as a subject (conscious and master of himself), would soon have been buried: The human sciences complete the death of man who—"constituted only" during that brief moment "when language, having been situated within representation, and, as it were, dissolved in it, freed itself from that situation at the loss of its own fragmentation"[64]—will disappear again.

Structurally subtle, this is the thematics of the death of man that *The Order of Things* made famous. Its internal logic having been clarified, two further observations are now required.

To summarize the meaning, one would say that during the classical age man had not yet been born (the classical period sacrificed man in favor of representation and did not think about "the perpetual relation between the cogito and the unthought"); not

62. Ibid., pp. 362–63.
63. Ibid., p. 364.
64. Ibid., p. 386.

until the *Critique of Pure Reason* did this relation come to light. Man was born with Kant, then, but only to die at the same time, and in two ways: first because the newborn man escapes representation by definition and can only disappear into nothingness, and also (in a "bad" death of man) insofar as the human sciences, in attempting to grasp man, are going to fall once again into the primacy of representation. In other words—and such is the real meaning of this whole thematics—man does not exist and never did.[65] As a result, the discourse on the death of man allows a number of games to be played. If we decide purely conventionally to call the moment when a break was introduced into the ideal of the subject "the death of man," this proposition might seem to be quite far from Heidegger's critique of humanism and the metaphysics of subjectivity; in fact, it is entirely exhausted in this critique. And Foucault, playing off the terms, can claim both that man is dead and that he never existed, depending on the requirements of the moment; he can state that the human sciences kill man while remaining attached to the metaphysical dominance of representation or, on the other hand, that they defend man for the same reason, as they try to reinstate the figure of the classical subject; he can claim that modern philosophy since Kant has saved man or, inversely, that modern philosophy "from Kant to us," having forgotten "the opening that made it possible," has been "the stubborn obstacle standing obstinately in the way of an immanent new form of thought."[66] The strategic potential of such discourse is very great; it seems to defy beforehand any attempt to determine its content, disqualified from the start for attempting to grasp or to formulate a thesis that is "complex" in entirely different ways.

Dismantling what is a question of strategy for the thematics of the death of man nevertheless does permit the "hard core" of the construction to appear. This "new philosophy," which almost came

65. Ibid., p. 322.
66. Ibid., p. 342 (this is to be compared with p. 318: "Our culture crossed the threshold beyond which we recognize our modernity when finitude was conceived in an interminable cross-reference to itself. . . . Modern culture can conceive of man because it conceives of the finite on the basis of itself").

to be but never did, would be defined in direct opposition to the idea of consciousness, by refuting this "self-presence" that constitutes the Cartesian *cogito* as *subject* of its own representations and discourse. Whatever man may be, he is not this subject that "humanism" or "rationalism" wanted to make him.[67] In spite (and perhaps because) of its solicitude for him, humanism both allowed man to disappear and caused him to: It slept "serenely over the threatening rumble of his nonexistence,"[68] rejecting the forces of the unthought by affirming a subjectivity present to itself. In this way, the entire subtlety of the thematics of the death of man is ultimately eliminated by a thesis whose "unexpected and stupefying profundity" Clavel applauded: "The humanism of the last three or four centuries is secretly totalitarian, though less and less so, and man is dying from it."[69] Here again, in spite of all the precautions and the artifices of presentation, Foucault's work rejoins its Vulgate.

One problem still remains: His last work seems to reveal a sudden retraction in relation to these themes, as we have said. During one of his last interviews (May 29, 1984), Foucault's questioners remarked that "the question of the subject" reappears in volumes 2 and 3 of *The History of Sexuality:* "Your previous books seem to destroy the sovereignty of the subject. Is there a return here to the question we will never finish with and which could be the crucible of infinite labor for you?" And Foucault replied unhesitatingly, apparently: "Infinite labor, certainly; that is exactly what I confronted and what I wanted to do," that is, to study "the whole process of the subject's existence with its various problems and obstacles, through forms that are far from being completed." He even admits that "it is a question of reintroducing the problematics of the subject, . . . more or less forgotten in [his] early works, and of trying to follow its pathways or difficulties throughout its history."[70] In a way that at first seems quite strange, the trial of the subject in Foucault seems to have ended through a type of re-

67. Ibid., p. 318.
68. Ibid., p. 322.
69. M. Clavel, in *Le Nouvel Observateur*, Dec. 27, 1976.
70. Interview with G. Barbedette and A. Scala, in *Les Nouvelles littéraires*, June 28–July 5, 1984.

habilitation, to the extent that there is a felt need to reconstruct the history of the subject. If the reality conforms to the appearance, his retraction would be so radical that the possibility would have to be examined with great care.

Return of the Subject?

In the same interview, Foucault dates his project for a "history of the subject" to 1975–76, which he defines elsewhere as the attempt to explain how individuals are led to the recognition of themselves as subjects through their understanding of desire.[71] Since then, he explained, "it has been not power but the subject that constitutes the main theme of my research."[72] And readers of *The History of Sexuality* can note, in the last volumes published, a real inflexibility in his vocabulary, Foucault mentioning from this point on not only the problem of the subject but "ethical problematizations," evoking the "question of ethics," and so on. So he asks, for example, how individuals in classical Greek culture handled problems such as "question[ing] their own conduct, watch[ing] over and giv[ing] shape to it, and shap[ing] themselves as ethical subjects."[73] And if the research on these problems of the subject and of ethics was intended to be historical, at least the perspective was not, since in an interview on January 20, 1984, Foucault is comfortable claiming that "ethical freedom has to be practiced" and defining ethics as "the thoughtful practice of freedom."[74] Ethics, reflection, self-mastery, freedom, defined as the relations of the self to the self, all these themes that seem to renew the enterprise profoundly, converge in a stunning definition of the "critical function of philosophy": "This critical function of philosophy derives, to a certain extent, from Socrates' imperative: 'Know thyself'; that is, base yourself on freedom, through self-mastery."

71. M. Foucault, *L "Usage des plaisirs (Histoire de la sexualité*, vol. 2), Gallimard, 1984, pp. 10 ff. (*The Use of Pleasure [The History of Sexuality*, vol. 2], trans. Robert Hurley, Vintage Books, New York, 1986, pp. 4 ff).
72. "La Question du sujet," in Dreyfus and Rabinow, *Michel Foucault*, p. 298.
73. *The Use of Pleasure*, p. 13.
74. "L'Ethique du souci de soi comme pratique de la liberté," interview with R. Fornet-Betancourt, H. Becker, and A. Gomez-Muller (Jan. 20, 1984).

It is understandable that this last part of Foucault's work has most often been regarded as inaugurating a new phase as maintaining a certain distance from the earlier project of denouncing norms, as the following example illustrates: Foucault "taught us to dismantle the apparatus of power. . . . We had accused him of vacating the subject, and he now shows—for he is always a step ahead—that to remove the prohibitions is not enough and that one cannot dispense with an ethics through which the subject posits the form he gives his life. Designer, aesthete, and moralist—here is Foucault's new look."[75]

One statement, however, requires some moderation of enthusiasm. In his last interviews, according to the interviewers, Foucault seems reluctant to situate his last works with respect to his earlier research. Sometimes he emphasized, as we have seen, that his concern is to reintroduce a problem he had left aside, thus lending credence to the idea that this return to the subject was an about-face for him. Sometimes, however, with respect to his efforts at a "hermeneutics of the subject" he states: "In reality this was always my problem, even though I formulated the framework of the thought in a slightly different way."[76] A fundamental retraction or simply an evolution in the formulation? This visible fluctuation in his self-interpretation requires an adjustment if we are to determine whether one of the principle protagonists of the philosophical scene of the '68 era did or did not end up removing his philosophy from the style of intellectual undertaking whose ideal type suggests organizing it around the theme of the death of the subject. Three questions can be addressed: (1) What does the later Foucault mean by "subject"? (2) How is his "history of the subject" chronologically situated? (3) What lessons for the future does he draw from it?

1. The Ambiguity of the Subject   Deliberately or not, Foucault's late works fluctuate in their use of the notion of subject. The subject intervenes according to two perspectives.

In a metahistorical perspective, subjectivity designates the atemporal, ahistorical structure of the human being, characterized

75. R. Maggiori, in *Libération*, June 15, 1984.
76. Interview of Jan. 20, 1984 ("L'Ethique du souci . . .").

by its relations with itself. Understood in this way, the notion of the subject traditionally denotes consciousness, or the *for oneself* (this is Hegel's fundamental meaning). This is what Foucault means in his interview of January 20, 1984, when he explains that what makes the subject subjective is that it "is not a substance": Through successive appearances of subjectivity, a common "form" remains, that of the relationship to the self. Of course, this form is not "always identical to itself";

> You do not have the same kind of relationship to yourself when you act as a political subject who is going to vote or who stands up in a meeting as when you want to act on your desire in a sexual relationship. There are no doubt relationships and interferences between these different forms of the subject, but we are not in the presence of the same type of subject. In each case, one plays, one establishes with oneself different forms of relationships. And what interests me is precisely the historical constitution of these different forms of the subject, in relation to the games of truth.

Here the idea is clear: Subjectivity is a form or a structure, that of relations to the self, which has various historical forms—the history of the subject being precisely the history of these various figures of the relationship to the self as revealed in successive problematizations of desire (for which reason the history of the subject will be a history of sexuality).

Within a second, more Heideggerian perspective, subjectivity becomes a figure of the relationships with the self, or of the consciousness of self, that can be historically located: a historical form of the structural form of subjectivity according to the first meaning of the word, an electively "modern" form (we will see what it is through a study of the chronology) that has to be examined by reconstructing its genesis. The purpose of a history of the subject has changed meaning then: What is in view first and foremost is the process of subjectivation, that is, the construction of this particular type of relation with the self that makes up subjectivity. Let us listen to Foucault: "I call subjectivity the process through which one obtains the construction of a subject, or more precisely of a subjectivity, which is evidently only one of the possibilities given for the organization of a consciousness of self."[77] Or again, in this same register of accusation against what must be called "bad subjectivity": beginning from a process that can be reconstructed (and where power mechanisms play a certain role), *"individuals* are transformed into *subjects"* in two ways, which necessitates understanding that there are "two meanings to the word *subject"* (read: two faces of bad subjectivity): "the subject subjugated to the other through control and dependence and the subject attached to its own identity through consciousness or self-knowledge. In both cases the word suggests a form of power that subjugates and subdues."[78]

In this register, subjectivity is still a form with variations, but in a historically bound framework where subjectivity is merely *the form of the subjugated individual* (subject in the quasi-political meaning of the word): The different forms of such a subjectivity, Foucault explicitly writes, are "the various forms of submission," the various "forms of subjugation" to power, which is itself considered with its various faces, including the tyranny of self-identity. On this basis, a priority for the history of the subject should be the study of how relationships to the self that constitute individuality ("good subjectivity") became the submission of individuality to a "group of specific mechanisms,"[79] which dispossess the individual of himself ("bad subjectivity" as alienation).

This ambiguity in the notion of the subject allows Foucault to play a double game. Sometimes located in the first register, where subjectivity denotes only relations to the self, Foucault can claim that his problem is subjectivity and that for him it is a question of elaborating new forms of subjectivity, for which the Greeks of classical antiquity will serve, if not as models, at least as a rich reference, as we will see. Sometimes located in the second register, where subjectivity denotes the modern modality of relations with the self, he can continue to practice a deconstruction of modernity as the submission to norms, as the normalization of individuality. Thus the earlier positions are wholly preserved while benefiting from an

77. Interview published in *Les Nouvelles littéraires*, May 29, 1984.
78. Foucault, "La Question du sujet," in Dreyfus and Rabinow, *Michel Foucault*, pp. 302–4.
79. Ibid., p. 306.

effect of language, which both cuases the theme of the search for
new subjectivities to appear and sets in motion the return to the
subject, all the while masking what is profoundly out of date in the
discourse he uses. Another accessory advantage to this operation is
that it masks the contradiction that modernism is to be criticized
(therefore subjectivity, therefore humanism) and that the discourse
of human rights is to be appealed to, as Foucault did, going so far as
to draw up the draft of an embryonic new declaration of human
rights.[80] In this sense, the so-called step ahead that Foucault is said
to have taken by returning to the idea of an "ethics through which
the subject posits the form he gives his life" is instead related to a
desperate attempt to disguise the unbelievable step back he, in fact,
achieved relative to the development of ideas and manners. This can
easily be demonstrated by analyzing the chronology of Foucault's
history of the subject, which testifies to the fact that even until his
last texts the subject is indeed on trial.

2. The History of the Subject   We can distinguish three stages,
of which only the first had been fully examined before the sudden
interruption of the enterprise.

1. *Classical antiquity.* The fourth-century Greeks exhibit what
Foucault called the care of the self. In a very particular way, they
resolved the problem of constructing a "technology of existence" in
order to live as well as possible within the framework of the community. With them, there is indeed a relationship with the self (subjectivity in its broadest meaning), there is indeed ethics (determination
of the principles of existence), but the frame of reference for the
adoption of their style of existence is that of the individual's attempt
to care for himself. Classical ethics does not conern the problem of
universal norms from which individuals determine the conduct of
others but prescribes only caring for oneself by making one's life a
work of art (by designing one's life), with the conviction that by
caring for oneself the individual renders the greatest service to the
community. Without going into the details of the analysis, it appears
that what Foucault discovered in this "care of the self" was the old

80. Cf. the text read during a press conference in Geneva in June 1981 and
published in *Libération* (June 30–July 1, 1984) after Foucault's death.

112

classical ideal of *kalos kaghatos*, the ideal of a cultivation of the self which, while combining the search for pleasures with mastery over appetites one does not want to be enslaved to, proposed creating "an *ethos* that is good, beautiful, honorable, estimable, memorable and that can serve as an example." For this ideal, the essential point is that access to the ethical, far from implying that one be uprooted from oneself, that one renounce individuality, emerges through the cultivation of individuality: Cultivate yourself, create your own beautiful individuality, aestheticize your existence. As for the use of pleasures in classical antiquity, which have to be respected above all, it is not a matter of greater tolerance, Foucault emphasizes,[81] so much as it is a question of the meaning and function of the prohibitions for me: Taboos were not thought of as necessarily leading to self-renunciation, their primary purpose being the aestheticization of the self, that is to say, the *individual's* choosing to "live a beautiful life and leave the memory of an honorable life for others."[82] So thoroughly was this the case that—and here we touch on the value of classical culture—"I do not think one can say that this type of ethics was an attempt to normalize the population," concludes Foucault.[83] Aesthetic and nonnormative, sustained by personal choice and not by legal constraint,[84] relationships with the self that characterized the great Greek age are *differentiated*, then, and belong even less to the search for a *universal* model, which is to be imposed, as such, on everyone.

We understand that the classical relationship to the self structured in this way is not—and this is obviously the essential point for Foucault—to be interpreted in terms of the meaning of *subjectivity* within the second register, where *The History of Sexuality* continues

81. Cf. *The Use of Pleasure*, pp. 249 ff. The analysis emphasizes the austerity and moderation of the Greeks.
82. Interview published in *Le Nouvel Observateur*, June 1, 1984.
83. Ibid.
84. Interview published in *Les Nouvelles littéraires*, May 29, 1984: "First, the ethics of antiquity were addressed to only a small number of people and did not require everyone to obey the same behavioral scheme. It concerned only a small minority of people, and even among free people there were many forms of freedom: The freedom of the head of state or the leader of the army was not the same as that of the wise man."

to use it. The interview of May 29, 1984, very clearly reveals that valorizing the Greek *ethos* has no other meaning than as a continuation of the trial of the subject. Foucault was asked: "Reading you, one has the impression that the Greeks had no theory of the subject. But might they have had a definition which was lost with Christianity?" The answer must be given in its entirety:

I do not believe one must reconstruct an experience of the subject where it was not formulated. I am much closer to things than that. And since no Greek philosopher ever found a definition for the subject, and never looked for one, I will say simply that there is no subject. This does not mean [and this is what makes them great, of course—L.F. and A.R.] that the Greeks did not attempt to define the conditions where *an experience which is not that of the subject but that of the individual, to the extent that he seeks to be constituted as master of himself,* could be provided. Classical antiquity had not problematized the constitution of the self as subject [where one must obviously understand, as we will see in the following lines, that this lack is an opportunity—L.F. and A.R.]: On the other hand, beginning with Christianity morality was confiscated by the theory of the subject. Now *moral experience centered on the subject no longer seems to me to be satisfying today.* And for that reason we are faced with a number of questions today which are posed in the same terms as they were in antiquity.[85]

Finally, we have an unequivocal text: The power of the Greeks was in their having drawn up the design for an *ethics without subjectivity,* a problem now posed again after the metaphysics of subjectivity has been fulfilled (and surpassed). An *ethics of the individual,* not of the subject: from this point of departure, if the history of sexuality (as the history of the subject) is going to demonstrate a fall or a decline of the ethics of freedom into the ethics of law or discipline, it is precisely for the reason that this history is *the one in which, after the Greeks, the subject was born.*

   2. *The birth of the subject.* It coincides with the diffusion of Christianity but was already present in the Greco-Roman world that

85. Ibid.; the italics are ours.

studied *the care of the self.* In fact, from the time of Seneca, and even more markedly from the time of Marcus Aurelius, a new dimension appeared in the ethical register. Though there was no question yet that ethics should be "everyone's obligation," being still "a matter of individual choice," these values, which had been differentiated and reserved for the few during classical antiquity, tended, from then on, to "become ultimately valid for everyone," a universalist conception of the *ethos* that then tended to reject the individualist viewpoint.[86] Through a strange perversion of perspective, what might otherwise seem attractive about imperial Stoicism, that is, the claim that the rules for living well are the same for everyone (slave or emperor), is given the opposite interpretation in Foucault: Progress in degrees of integration (there are no longer certain values for masters and others for slaves) is again interpreted as proceeding from a logic of exclusion. This interpretation, of more dubious philological integrity in relation to Stoic texts, is primarily supported by a point of view that does raise some misgivings on the ethicojuridical level: Because it has to be admitted that, both to denounce the danger of the representation of values that are "potentially valid for everyone" and to defend the tradition of human rights (that is, of every human), one has to give oneself up to a vertiginous intellectual balancing act. The intrinsically most perverse consequences of the fundamental Nietzscheanism motivating the whole enterprise are found here in this conviction that a process which leads to equating the morality of the masters and the slaves could be profoundly catastrophic.

This turn taken by the Stoics, in whom Foucault detects the appearance of a "quasi subject,"[87] is supposed to have been radicalized later by Christianity: The Stoic universalization of values is held therefore to have been "bad luck for ancient philosophy, or in any case it was the historical moment when philosophy gave rise to a

86. Ibid. Cf. on the same topic the interview with Dreyfus and Rabinow, *Michel Foucault*, p. 336: "From the classical period to the Greco-Roman philosophy of the imperial age, one can observe modifications concerning above all the mode of subjugation, with the appearance of this theme of a universal law imposed in the same way on every rational man, a theme that is primarily Stoic."
87. Interview of Jan. 20, 1984 ("L'Ethique du souci . . .").

form of thought that would later be found in Christianity"[88] and would become the cradle for the birth of the subject. The individual would from then on be doubly subjugated, thus "subjectivized." On the one hand, he would no longer be his own source of the free determination of his *ethos* and would be subdued by the ecclesiastical power, which possesses the truth concerning the values that permit *everyone* to achieve salvation. On the other hand, the individual is subjected to this care for "salvation truth," which comes before the care for the self: It is a matter not of making one's own existence beautiful but of turning away from oneself, of overcoming one's individuality in order to subjugate oneself to the common law, the law of the human condition. Caring for the self became a guilty act, an egotistical love of self; the regulated use of pleasures gave way to the denunciation of the flesh; the virtues became self-sacrifice and self-renunciation; individuality had to disappear in the triumph of the universal. Thus the road that leads to modernity was definitively opened.

3. *Modern universalism*. It is Descartes who is rightly credited with opening up the new age. The *Meditations* symbolize the modern figure of the care of the self, characterized by the absolute transformation of the subject through the renunciation of part of himself (the act of doubt, detaching the mind from the senses, is the very image of this self-renunciation) to accede to his real being, "entirely defined by knowledge." Access to the self becomes access to the subject of knowledge, thus the submission of individuality to universal values that define truth and the scientific.[89] In Descartes, subjectivity was constructed by blurring individuality: "To gain the truth, all that is necessary is that I be *any subject at all* capable of seeing what is obvious"[90]—"any subject at all," that is to say, the universal. There is no longer the need under these conditions to work on oneself, no longer any ethics, properly speaking; there is only the emptying of the self. Kant, by distinguishing between the subject of knowledge and the moral subject, apparently resists

88. Interview of May 29, 1984 (*Les Nouvelles littéraires*).
89. Interview of Jan. 20, 1984 ("L'Ethique du souci . . .").
90. Ibid.

abandoning ethics as the cultivation of the self. In fact, Kantianism is also inscribed within the process of self-forgetting, since practical reason requires me to "recognize myself as a universal subject, to constitute myself in each of my actions as a universal subject by comforming to the universal rules."[91] Kant did not return to the path followed by the Greeks, then, but merely opened "another new path in our tradition" where relationships with the self consist of man constituting himself as a subject, as individuality subjugated to the universality of the law.

To follow this history of the subject in its broad outlines to the end we still have to indicate that, according to Foucault, in the modern period the ecclesiastical power of Christianity is gradually secularized by multiplying the centers of power (the family, medicine, psychiatry, the school, employers, etc.), which also subordinate individuality to norms that are predefined by a discourse outside the individual. This is merely a move "from concern that people be led to salvation in another world to the idea of securing it here below."[92] If from then on salvation takes the form of health or well-being or security, individuality continues to be assigned the form of subordination to the norms prescribed by institutions. According to Foucault, a ruse in the process of subjectivation is even produced in that these norms can be perfectly individualized, or "personalized." It is in fact one characteristic of modern powers that they resort to an "individualizing tactic" specifying, for example, the objective of a "correct living standard," depending on the groups of individuals considered, the media presenting different models to different groups. This is a question of a pseudoindividualization able to subordinate individuality even better to norms that can be superficially diversified. Individualization is then one form of subjectivation, a particularly subtle aspect of the process of subjugation. As a result, Foucault concludes, one must not so much "free the individual from the state and its institutions" in order to thwart this process as "free *ourselves* from the state and the type of individualization that attaches us to it." To this end we have to work

91. Interview with Dreyfus and Rabinow, *Michel Foucault*, p. 345.
92. "La Question du sujet," ibid., p. 307.

to encourage (and here the vocabulary of subjectivity in its broadest sense reappears) "new forms of subjectivity that reject the type of individuality that has been imposed on us for many centuries."[93] This skillfully expressed conclusion allows us to see how the intention to reactivate subjectivity came to be attributed to Foucault's last texts. The real tenor of this conclusion would be more apparent if one substituted for the wordplay of the passage something more direct; for example, "We have to encourage new forms of relationship to the self (subjectivity in the broad sense), new forms that correspond to an affirmation of authentic individuality, rejecting the type of relationship to the self that has been imposed on us for several centuries in the form of a normative subjectivity sometimes disguised as pseudoindividuality." To clarify the real importance of this "history of the subject," the particular future it opens onto still remains to be deduced.

3. *The Classics versus the Moderns* What is it, in fact, that is to be re-created today, based on the lessons of history? One clear result of all of the above, even though Foucault (like Heidegger) constantly denies it, is that the framework for the effort should consist of a retreat from subjectivity as the moderns have described it and a return the individuality of classical antiquity. However, the gesture of a simple return to the Greeks is indeed repeatedly refused: "Neither exemplary nor admirable," Greek thought was saturated with contradictions (particularly striking in the Stoics) between the search for the art of living and the effort to "make it universal," between aestheticizing existence and legalizing or "judicializing" ethics.[94] From this point of view, "Antiquity was one long mistake." As for believing that the Greeks "offer an attractive and plausible alternative," Foucault believes he must answer: "No! I am not looking for an alternative solution; the solution to a problem cannot be found in one proposed by other people in other times." What is more, as we know, the Greeks were not faultless; they had slaves, despised women, did not really succeed in accepting homosexuality, were ultimately more interested in health than in plea-

93. Ibid., p. 308.
94. Interview of May 29, 1984 (*Les Nouvelles littéraires*).

sure; in short, "one cannot go back," and there is no *arché* that might be free of all forgetting of concern for the self (just as for Heidegger there is no period in the History of Being where the forgetting of Being is not already at work).

And yet we can still learn something from the Greeks. The parallel with Heidegger is remarkably striking here, too:

HEIDEGGER   To isolate what the task of philosophy is today, we must "put the *Aletheia* to the test *in the Greek mode*, as nonretreat in the heart of Openness, in order then to think of it, through *going beyond the Greek experience itself*, as a glade in the retreat of Openness."[95]

FOUCAULT   "The effort to rethink the Greeks today consists not of valorizing Greek ethics as the moral domain par excellence that we need in order to think about ourselves but of doing it in such a way that European philosophy can *start again from Greek philosophy* as an experience once given, in relation to which we can *be totally free*."[96]

For both thinkers, though there is no question of merely repeating the Greeks, it is nevertheless necessary to return to the ancients in order to go beyond modernism: The postmodern road passes through a preliminary return to the ancients, which is the only consistent basis for a new departure. In terms of Foucault's approach, the Greeks provide three lessons:

They furnish "the example of an ethical experience which includes a very strong link between pleasure and desire," by refusing to make desire a source of later guilt.

Classical ethics is an ethics of freedom (it grows out of personal choice in a style of existence) and not an ethics of law.

The classical age finally allowed an ethics without subjectivity to be conceived of, as we have seen; the question of ethics had not yet been taken over by the theory of the subject.

95. M. Heidegger, *Questions IV*, p. 137 ("Das Ende der Philosophie und die Aufgabe des Denkens," in *Zur Sache des Denkens*, Tübingen, 1969).
96. Interview of May 29, 1984 (*Les Nouvelles littéraires*).

This last lesson is evidently the essence of what the Greeks have to teach us in order for "European philosophy" to "start up again." If a moral experience centered on the subject is no longer satisfying today (since it has been revealed as subjugation), "we are confronted by a certain number of questions posed to us in the same terms used in antiquity." The experience of the subject, Foucault explains, was linked to the definition of universal values based on a religious view of the world, which therefore assumed that religion was the foundation of ethics. Now, however, we are alive in a period when "God is dead." "We no longer believe ethics to be founded on religion." Both because this basis of universal values has disappeared and because "we do not want any legal system to intervene in our private moral and personal lives," "our problem today . . . is . . . somewhat similar" to what it was for t he Greeks: how to base ethics on the rigorously personal choice of a style of existence. This is what we have to relearn from classical antiquity as against modernity: "The search for styles of existence as different as possible from each other," understood today, Foucault concludes, as "the search for a form of morality that would be acceptable to everyone, in the sense that everyone should submit to it," can finally be seen for what it is, namely, "catastrophic."[97]

This is the conclusion and culmination of the last stage in Foucault's thought. We may also believe that here it found its resting place. In this hatred of the universal, by condemning without appeal the idea of values that can be given a common meaning (a public space, if you wish), Foucault certainly affirmed his Nietzschean/ Heideggerian ancestry to the end. At the same time, however, his so-called retraction of the later years appears profoundly problematical. The ultimate "new-look Foucault," who was portrayed as returning after his critique of norms to reflecting on an ethics "through which the subject postulates the form he gives to his life," strikingly resembles the author of *Madness and Civilization* or *Discipline and Punish*, resembles that Foucault who through reference to Nietzsche and Heidegger denounced the tyranny of identity in modernism, the tyranny of the normative or the universal in relation to the individual

97. Ibid.

120

in his difference. From the beginning to the end of his work, Foucault remained consistent with his Vulgate. Until his very last works, he regarded the '68 notion of individuality as the opposite of subjectivity defined as the consciousness of principles that seem universal and at the pole of intersubjectivity. It is highly significant, from this point of view, that in one of his last interviews he admitted to his disagreements with Habermas and denounced as a utopia one of the latter's favorite notions, namely, the idea of a communicational space.

> I am very interested in what Habermas is doing. I know that he does not at all agree with what I say, though I am a little more in agreement with what he says. But still there is something that always gives me problems; that is his giving communication such an important position and specifically a function I would call "utopian."[98]

It is in fact difficult to see how Foucault and, more generally, the French philosophers of '68, dissolving subjectivity into individuality, could appropriate the problematics of communication and of "common sense." The antihumanism of '68 philosophy opens onto "barbarism," not because it leads to unleashing all kinds of violence but insofar as all possibility of a real dialogue between consciousnesses, which had been open to thinking of their differences on the basis of identity, is destroyed by the accusations brought against subjectivity: When only exaggerated individual differences survive, then everyone's other becomes "wholly other," the "barbarian." The link between the critique of subjectivity and the expulsion of the problematics of communication (from the re-public) is so close that we see once again in someone like Lyotard the same hostility and incomprehension toward the question of intersubjectivity: "Consensus obtained through discussion as Habermas believes? It violates the heterogeneity of language games."[99] If we think for a moment of the political implications of this type of statement (in terms of the representation of the community) in

98. Interview of Jan. 20, 1984 ("L'Ethique du souci . . .").
99. J.-F. Lyotard, *La Condition post-moderne*, Paris, 1979, p. 8.

Lyotard, as well as in Foucault, we should logically congratulate ourselves that the authors of these statements have so ardently cultivated inconsistency and have fortunately also been able to defend human rights and the values of the republic, as almost everyone has.

4 /
French Heideggerianism
(Derrida)

First, let us define our object:

1. For our purposes here, the name "French Heideggerianism" does not include those disciples of Heidegger who contributed to introducing the philosophy of the master in France, sometime well before the 1960s (as is the case with J. Beaufret) but claimed no other role than that of the most authoritative interpreters. Beaufret and his disciples openly took up the task of repetition or explanation, making themselves into the translators of a great philosophy, both literally and figuratively. Whatever judgment might be made of their particular way of serving this function, it is clear that their approach was intended to be more faithful than original and that they claimed no desire to introduce new determinations of any kind into the field of problematics opened up by Heidegger which might permit them to be thought of as "French Heideggerians."

It was entirely the opposite for writers like Derrida and Lyotard. In them we do indeed find a celebratory language clearly acknowledging the decisive nature of the inheritance, as for example in this discussion of Derrida's: "What I have attempted to do would not have been possible without the opening of Heidegger's questions, . . . without the attention to what Heidegger calls the difference between Being and beings, the ontico-ontological difference such as, in a way, it remains unthought by philosophy."[1] But, in addition to this type of profession of faith, the statement is accompanied by the will to be distinguished from the model and by the claim of beginning with the Heideggerian "opening," in order to

1. J. Derrida, *Positions*, Ed. de Minuit, 1972, p. 18 (*Positions*, trans. Alan Bass, University of Chicago Press, Chicago, 1981, p. 9). Citations are from the English translation.

pursue an autonomous and original course, irreducible to the "model." Thus, as we will see, Derrida dedicates the entire second half of his key text *Différance* to explaining that his own work is located in the *a* of *différance*, it being understood that "*différance* is not a 'species' of the genus *ontological difference.*"[2] We will of course have to examine the contents of this supposed originality and measure the degree of autonomy it reveals with respect to Heidegger. However, this claim to an approach that starts from Heidegger but obeys its own logic does explain why, if there never were any "Beaufretians," there are indeed "Derrideans," striving to certify that posterity for Heidegger is not limited to the tasks of translation or interpretation but that it has indeed produced a body of work. Presenting itself as an original product, "French Heideggerianism" is exported as such. We will limit our discussion of this component of '68 philosophy exclusively to it.

2. In order to define and delimit this component of sixties philosophy in relation to its other aspects, we have to state precisely its particularity. Why in fact select Derrida's work as the principal manifestation of French Heideggerianism[3] when, as we have already seen with Foucault and will see again with Lacan, the reference to Heidegger is a constant throughout most of '68 philosophy, except for what comes directly from Marxism? For the moment, our answer is merely a declaration, which the following analyses will attempt to justify. If according to the formula we have explained, *Foucault = Heidegger + Nietzsche*, and if, as we will show later, we can say that *Lacan = Heidegger + Freud*, French Heideggerianism can be defined by the formula *Derrida = Heidegger + Derrida's style*. This statement may seem crude, even shocking. Parodying Derrida himself, however, we would suggest that, with respect to the proposed

2. J. Derrida, *La Différance*, lecture to the Société française de philosophie, Jan. 27, 1968, published in *Marges de la philosophie*, Ed. de Minuit, 1972, pp. 24– 28 (*Margins of Philosophy*, trans. Alan Bass, University of Chicago Press, Chicago, 1982, p. 26).
3. We have also mentioned Lyotard's work as a manifestation of French Heideggerianism. We prefer here the example of Derrida because his work is more consistently established within this connection to Heidegger. In Lyotard, this connection becomes fully explicit only with *Le Différend* (Ed. de Minuit, 1983).

formula, it is not so much a matter of being "foolishly precipitate" in criticizing it as of "returning to this proposition its power to provoke."[4]

On the basis of this classification of French Heideggerianism, the work to be done on Derrida seems to respond to a more limited treatment than Foucault's itinerary required. Foucault seems to have followed a complex course, marked by an eventual retraction. Starting from the philosophical model of reference, the works lining his path attempt to contribute to multiple fields of research and, in this sense at least, have the undeniable value of renewing the process of "managing" the model. It must be acknowledged that there is nothing of this kind in Derrida. Beyond the writing, where it seems all originality has gradually been concentrated, the philosophical discourse is in fact quite traditional in terms of its nearly exclusive motivating preoccupation: that of defining a position with respect to objectivity or, if you prefer, a "what is" approach that is summed up in the thematics of *différance*, which Derrida himself claims to be his main contribution. Now, at this level where everything is said to reassemble "in a sheaf,"[5] it seems there is nothing intelligible or sayable in the contents of Derrida's work that is not, purely and simply, a recapitulation of the Heideggerian problematics of ontological difference. If we can verify what we present for the moment as a deliberately provocative statement, we will then need to ask what survives that is "French" in this surprising enterprise of repetition, after first showing the particular jamming effects that produce the illusion of a *philosophically* original work.

Our thesis that Derrida's work is limited to recapitulating the problematics of ontological difference immediately confronts two apparent objections. On the one hand, as we have already indicated, Derrida refuses to make *différance* a simple species of the genus *ontological difference*. On the other hand, the unbiased reader of successive works of Derrida cannot help but be struck by the author's ingeniousness and lexical richness as he multiplies, so it

4. *Margins*, p. 23.
5. Ibid., p. 3. The image is used again by J.-L. Houdebine at the beginning of the first of the interviews in *Positions*, p. 39.

seems, the creation of concepts that have no immediate correlates in the language of Heidegger. In addition to the famous *différance*, numerous links in the "chain" introduced by the 1968 lecture have appeared: trace, writing, archiwriting, architrace, spacing, reserve, supplement, *pharmakon*, hymen, margin, mask, mark, temporizing, and so on. And even after those early works that concern us here, the chain continued to grow: dissemination, "gl," style, gift from the blue, and so on, reinforcing this simultaneously prolific and mysterious appearance, which is able to create the illusion of the progressive birth and development of an original undertaking.

We limit ourselves here to an outline for dismantling this "chain," illustrating through a number of examples how the various links make up just so many repetitions within the Heideggerian "opening" of the problematics of ontological difference. With no difficulty (but also with no pleasure), this exercise, or game, could be indefinitely prolonged by including the links added to the chain in the later works. However, it seemed to us more economical and quite sufficient to produce the rules of the game. No doubt our analysis of the terms is exposed at every stage in the process to the objection that "things are not so simple." Nevertheless, we will question the purpose of the incessant claim to endless complexity, the unflagging demand of a so inexpressible otherness: What of a discourse that feels the need to be immunized through such procedures against not just any objection to it but any presentation of it that might be attempted, perceived, and denounced ahead of time as treasonous?

From Difference to *Différance*

In spite of cleverly maintained appearances, the Derridean notion of *différance* is (dare we say it?) a very simple one. Derrida defined it as "what makes possible the presentation of the being-present" and thus what "is never presented," "never offered to the present," and, "reserving itself, not exposing itself," is thinkable only as what disappears in any appearance, namely, appearance itself, which disappears in the appeared being and retreats in the being-present.[6] Appearance as disappearance: we easily recognize what Heidegger had broadly described, in *Being and Time*, as Unveiling–Hiding, through deepening ontological difference (Being/beings) in the direction of a philosophy of Being as Illumination–Retreat. For example, "Being withdraws while revealing itself in beings themselves";[7] Being must be thought of as "veiling-unveiling Illumination";[8] "Being retires insofar as it unfolds in beings";[9] "the veiled-Being of the being-present rests on the veiling of the distribution of presence."[10] This Heideggerian thematics does not require further recapitulation. It is more instructive to show how Derrida's discourse, establishing itself in this register, could go as far as parody.

Thus Derrida's lecture in January 1968 describing *différance* (and its *a*) announced, in a way that at first seems enigmatic: "In every exposition it would be exposed to disappearing as disappearance."[11] Not only does appearance itself "disappear in every appearance" but the disappearance of this disappearance also needs to be thought. However mysterious in appearance, here this formula takes up again a true *leitmotif* of Heidegger's texts, as for example in the 1949 Prologue to *What Is Metaphysics?*: "At the lifting of disclosure, what deploys its essence in the latter, that is, closure, hides itself everywhere." Or, in other words, the concealment that is the essence of manifestation, or the retreat that is present in the heart of appearance, can only disappear in turn, in favor of a pure philosophy of presence which then never stops forgetting the retreat, never stops exposing the disappearance to disappearance.

6. *Margins*, pp. 5–6.
7. M. Heidegger, *Nietzsche*, trans. P. Klossowski, Gallimard, vol. 2, p. 288 (*Nietzsche*, Pfullingen, 1961, vol. 2, p. 359).
8. M. Heidegger, *Essais et conférences*, trans. A. Préau, Gallimard, p. 336 (*Vorträge und Aufsätze*, Pfullingen, 1959, p. 278).
9. M. Heidegger, *Chemins qui ne mènent nulle part*, trans. W. Brokmeier, Gallimard, p. 274 (*Holzwege*, in *Collected Works*, vol. 5, Frankfurt/M, 1978, p. 354).
10. M. Heidegger, *Contribution à la question de l'être*, trans. G. Granel, in *Questions I*, Gallimard, p. 238 (*Zur Seinsfrage*, in *Collected Works*, vol. 9, p. 416).
11. *Margins*, p. 6.

We will not multiply the comparisons, nor are the linkages disputed by Derrida. The problem is to understand how, under these conditions, Derrida can claim that *différance*, as he proposes to understand it (or rather write it), does not entirely correspond to what Heidegger called "ontological difference." This same lecture proposes a discussion of two moments when this articulation between the two *differences* must be distinguished:

1. The Acknowledgment of the Inheritance   Derrida admits that, with this disappearing appearance/disappearance, "it already appears that the type of question we are redirected to in this way is, shall we say, of the Heideggerian type, and that *différance* seems to bring us back to ontico-ontological difference."[12] In this reminder of the *différance* that is at work in all presence and all self-identity, Derrida is questioning, as Heidegger did, the authority of presence as it has been affirmed throughout the whole history of metaphysics, culminating in the dawn of subjectivity or in modern humanism: The horizon of the "traditional, metaphysical domination by the present"[13] is indeed the mastery of the world through technology, where the manipulation of the real appears that much more easily to be limitless when one is closed to the appearing/disappearing dimension over which no hold is conceivable. Significantly, Derrida also recalls that the very category of *subject* participates in this metaphysical hegemony of presence: Traditionally, what defines the subject as such is "the privilege accorded to consciousness," privilege that a philosophy of *différance* must destabilize. Thus inheriting from Heidegger the intention to think "against subjectivity,"[14] Derrida adds, in describing this process of unsettling one of the constitutive dimensions of subjectivity: "What holds for consciousness holds here for so-called subjective existence in general."[15]

12. Ibid., p. 10.
13. Ibid.
14. *Lettre sur l'humanisme*, trans. R. Munier, Ed. Aubier, 1964, p. 131: "Against the subjectivation that makes beings purely an object, to bring before philosophy the illumination of the truth of Being" (*Brief über den Humanismus*, in *Collected Works*, vol. 5, p. 349: "Gegen die Subjektivierung des Seienden zum blossen Objekt die Lichtung der Wahrheit des Seins vor das Denken bringen").
15. *Margins*, p. 16.

Here again we find in this Derridean inheritance from Heidegger the major theme of the sixties: the trial brought against the "bad subject," all forms of the theoretical survival of which still privilege presence (that is, the forgetting of *différance*), "which is the ether of metaphysics."

2. Calling "Ontological Difference" into Question   As so often, at another moment the heir becomes a parricide when he explains a reservation which until now had only been suggested: "*Différance* seems to bring us back to ontological difference." For, in reality, *différance* goes beyond and completes the unfolding of ontological difference: "The *a* of *différance* marks the movement of this unfolding."[16]

It must be understood that, in fact, Heidegger's return to ontological difference had provided only one, still metaphysical version of *différance*, encouraging thinking about the unfolding not of difference (difference as unfolding) but of its terms, and especially Being conceived as one of the terms. Redirecting meditation back to the difference between beings (present) and Being (disappearing "behind" being-present), Heidegger would induce the representation that there exist two terms *and their difference*—a representation still thick with metaphysical classifications, since for the philosophy of Being it would still be a matter of aspiring to a signified hiding behind the presence of a signifier. Thus the privilege of presence survived even in the return to ontological difference. Whereas it is a question of thinking of presentation itself as disappearance, Heideggerian Being acquired the appearance of a *hidden present* whose hiding one would attempt to reveal, and on this basis Heidegger's contribution is called into question: "Are not the thought of the *meaning* or *truth* of Being, the determination of *différance* as the ontico-ontological difference, difference thought within the horizon of the question of Being, still intrametaphysical effects of *différance*?"[17]

Quite logically from such questioning, there develops with

16. Ibid., p. 22.
17. Ibid.

Derrida a vast effort to track down in Heidegger evidence of a mode
of philosophy and writing that is still metaphysical. Thus, four types
of remnants are run to ground:

> The remnants of a philosophy of presence: against Heidegger
> searching for the *truth* or the *meaning* of Being as a word that had
> disappeared from the (ontic/ontological) relation, it will be claimed
> that appearance/disappearance does not conceal an originary or
> transcendental signified.[18]
>
> The remnants of a philosophy of essence: thus the strongly meta-
> physical connotations of Heidegger's call to seize Being *as such*, in
> its *self*, are emphasized, as if it were a matter of a word one could
> define.[19]
>
> The corresponding remnants of a philosophy of man: Heidegger's
> pursuit of the search for the "proper of man" is related to this con-
> cept of a "meaning of Being," which would require an "exemplary
> being," gifted with a "sixth sense," to grasp it in its original pu-
> rity.[20]
>
> The remnants of a philosophy of transparence: these traits con-
> verge in the direction of defining the "task of philosophy" as con-
> sisting of *unveiling* what one holds as a "truth" or as an ultimate
> "meaning," in short: as an *arché* that must be made manifest. Thus
> Derrida denounces Heidegger's search for a word closer to Being,
> against the concealing *logos* of metaphysics, for a voice that truly
> coincides, in terms of the old idea of adequation, with the tran-
> scendental signified: "the quest for the proper word and for the
> unique name"[21] stills participates in phonologism[22] or in phono-
> centrism,[23] which is proof of the metaphysical obsession with pres-
> ence because of the privileged position granted a spoken word

18. Cf. for example *De la grammatologie*, Ed. de Minuit, 1967, p. 33 (*Of Grammatologie*, trans. Gayatri Spivak, Johns Hopkins University Press, Baltimore,
1976, p. 39).
19. *Margins*, pp. 24–27.
20. Ibid., p. 124.
21. Ibid., p. 29.
22. *Of Grammatology*, p. 29.
23. *Positions*, p. 24.

(claimed to coincide better with pure presence than writing, which is more distant from the signified).[24]

Derrida's strategy consists of attempting to be fundamentally more Heideggerian than Heidegger himself, as this agenda almost explicitly suggests: "Despite this debt to Heidegger's thought, or rather because of it, I attempt to locate in Heidegger's text—which, no more than any other, is not homogeneous, continuous, everywhere equal to the greatest force and to all the consequences of its questions—the signs of a belonging to metaphysics."[25] So it is that, by very reason of the acknowledged inheritance, through fidelity to Heidegger, Derrida seeks in Heidegger the traces of metaphysics, that is, the traces of "ontotheology," which he explains as (1) ontology of presence, (2) theological research for an "archia," for a "principle of all principles."[26]

It is by reference to this strategy, then, that one must understand the substitution of *différance* for "*ontological difference.*" In fact, the operation becomes perfectly clear in the two aspects that characterize it: the transformation of the term and the broadening of its application.

1. The advantage of the term *différance* is twofold: On the one hand, it describes a movement better than the usual noun we are too used to understanding as indicating a relation between two terms, each of which is outside the other. On the other hand, unlike that which the use of the infinitive *differ/defer* suggests,[27] it does not require the operation of referring to some subject or other, which might bothersomely reintroduce the need to interpret difference as the eventual action of a term that in fact might just as well not differ/defer.[28] The superb moment of *negative ontology* comes from these considerations.

24. It is on this basis that Heidegger praises the *word* of the poets, the *word* of Anaximander, and, using Nietzsche's language again, praises Socrates as "the one who did not *write.*"
25. *Positions*, p. 10.
26. Cf. on this point *Margins*, p. 63.
27. *Translator's note:* In French the verb *différer* contains the meanings of both *differ* and *defer* in English.
28. *Margins*, p. 9.

Because it brings us close to the infinitive and active kernel of *différer*, *différance* (with an *a*) neutralizes what the infinitive denotes as simply active, just as *mouvance* in our language does not simply mean the fact of moving, of moving oneself, or of being moved. No more is *resonance* the act of resonating. We must consider that in the usage of our language the ending -*ance* remains undecided between the active and the passive. . . . That which lets itself be designated *différance* is neither simply active nor simply passive, announcing or rather recalling something like the middle voice, saying an operation that is not an operation, an operation that cannot be conceived either as passion or as the action of a subject on an object, or on the basis of the categories of agent or patient, neither on the basis of nor moving toward any of these *terms*.[29]

For the moment, we will not explore the problems posed by the exclusively negative character of these statements. They at least confirm what the term *différance* is supposed to designate. It is, then, pure difference, or, if we decide in spite of everything to borrow for a moment the language of the proper, or of essence, difference as such. It is neither relations between terms nor the action of an active instance but the unfolding of difference.

2. The displacement from "ontological difference" to *différance* also consists of broadening the field of the concept itself, as Derrida stresses: "*Différance* therefore would name provisionally this unfolding of difference, in particular, but not only, or first of all, of the ontico-ontological difference."[30] This specification may be disconcerting, allowing the following thought: that rather than *différance* being "a species of the genus ontological difference," the relationship is fundamentally the reverse. In this case, correspondingly, one would have to consider, of course, not that Derrida constitutes a species of Heideggerian (a "French Heideggerian") but that Heidegger was a sort of pre-Derridean German. Strategically at least, the point is important. What does Derrida's indication that the field of *différance* is broader than that of ontological difference mean? By presenting *différance* as ontological difference,

29. Ibid.
30. *Positions*, p. 10. Cf. also *Margins*, p. 26.

Heidegger would have let it be thought that *différance* as the difference between beings and Being is essentially outside beings or, if
you wish, outside the self-identity of beings: that Being as difference is outside beings.[31] Obviously, this dislocation of Being and
beings would suggest in an unfortunate way a (metaphysical) Plato-
nist split between the intelligible and the sensory. One must learn to
believe, as we have already remarked, that "*différance* is not pre-
ceded by the originary and indivisible unity of a present possibility
that I could reserve."[32] It is a question of thinking not of a secret
dimension that could be outside presence, outside identity, but
rather of the work (or game) of the difference *in the heart of identity*.
Every being whose definition includes identity as its center has a
dimension no concept succeeds in encompassing. This dimension
(precisely that of the "there is," of disappearing appearance) works
in every identity: to present *différance* as the difference between
beings and Being would be to disguise the particular multiform
interference in it every time that the concept necessarily lets "something" escape that it can literally not identify in the process of
defining.

Let us take as an example the set nature/culture.[33] We can
perfectly define the identity of each of these terms and grasp the
identity of their difference and the content of what differentiates
them, which we might identify as the opposition between innate and
acquired, or as some other intelligible opposition we may choose.
But what we cannot succeed in grasping is "the movement of *différance* as it produces differences, as it differentiates them." This
movement that dispenses differences as differences, and is therefore "anterior to" difference that can be identified (defined) between
terms that are themselves identifiable (definable), corresponds to a
strange dimension of *sameness* (since it is a question of the common
root of the differences) that cannot be confused with the *self-identity*

31. We suspect that Heidegger was in fact able to correct in this respect certain
effects of his terminology himself. See on this point the discussion in *Nietzsche*,
vol. 2, pp. 162 ff. (p. 203). Heidegger substitutes *for the same reasons* the word
Austrag for *Differenz*.
32. *Positions*, p. 8.
33. This example is described in *Positions*, p. 9.

of each one of the terms, or with the *identity of their difference*. This *element of sameness* does not fade when the terms are opposed, nor is it reabsorbed into the identity of each one that the term *différance* designates. In this sense, the term *différance* is, then, not just difference between beings and Being, of course, since these other "differences"—nature and culture, sensory and intelligible, man and woman, and so on—are also produced by the "unfolding of difference." With this in mind, it becomes possible to emphasize that, indeed, *différance* designates ontological difference, but not only that and not as first priority. The field of *différance* has in fact become broader than that of ontological difference. Derrida encompasses Heidegger even while surpassing him.

When we consider the question more closely, however, it is not difficult to see that this "element of Sameness" Derrida evokes is obviously what all things that are different, including opposites (nature/culture, sensory/intelligible, etc.), have in common:[34] that is, Being, in the very sense that Heidegger meant when he often said, in reference to Heraclitus, that that is what he calls this dimension of the unifying of the diverse which creates "inapparent harmony" between the most opposite beings, like the bow and the lyre, as they come into being. To define this uniting or this joining, Heidegger also described what Anaximander's *Dike*[35] or the sphericality of the Parmenidiean Oneness[36] seemed to him to have been, in order to emphasize this injunction to think of Being (difference) as an "adjustment" (*Fug*) of the diverse. Given this, it is very difficult to see how "the element of sameness" found all through Derrida's *différance* could broaden by an inch the field of "ontological difference," as Heidegger called it.

At the very least, therefore, it is somewhat unfair to give the impression that Heidegger would have indulged in thinking about Being as a dimension held in reserve outside beings simply in order

---

34. *Translator's note: De comme un* and *de connum* in French. Derrida's play on words is lost in English.
35. Cf. *Chemins,* "La Parole d'Anaximandre" ("Der Spruch des Anaximander," in *Collected Works,* vol. 5, p. 354).
36. *Introduction à la métaphysique,* trans. G. Kahn, Gallimard, p. 166 (*Einführung in die Metaphysik,* vol 40, Frankfurt/M., 1983).

to purchase a degree of originality at a good price. On the one hand, this would not have made much sense, and on the other, the number of defenses against it increased. For example, to avoid substantializing Being (and to posit difference outside of every identity), he not only ultimately renounced the expression "ontological difference" but had recourse to graphics as well: ~~Being~~ When Derrida states: "I also cross out the ✗,"[37] indicating that "différance ✗ what makes possible the presentation of the being-present," we see yet one more indication of a clever management of the inheritance. At this stage of the enterprise, only a somewhat unlikely speculation about the ignorance of his readers could have allowed the hope that this might appear to be original work or to at least renew the problematics opened by Heidegger.[38]

In order to see how French Heideggerianism managed to inaugurate a philosophy that obeys "its own logic," will we, then, have to remove successive concepts like links from the long chain, a chain Derrida claims was constructed in just that way? One concept, at least, deserves particular attention: the concept of writing. Foregrounding it will open up infinite perspectives onto French Heideggerianism, perspectives Heidegger himself never dreamed of.

Writing as the Subversion of Metaphysics

Derrida frequently refers to Aristotle's celebrated text on language at the beginning of *De interpretatione*, presenting it as emblematic of a certain devalorization of writing which would become essential to metaphysics.[39] Here Aristotle defines written words as

37. *Margins*, p. 6.
38. It is true that speculations about ignorance are not always pointless. In *Le Différend*, Lyotard appropriates words for word Heidegger's thematics of ontological difference (cf., for example, p. 114: the dimension of the "there is"; p. 129: being–nothingness; etc.). This, however, does not prevent A. Badiou from praising "Lyotard's ontology" (in a review of his book in *Critique*, 1983, pp. 851–63) as if the discovery of a new philosophical continent were in question. French philosophy has often lived off what can only be called *intellectual provincialism*.
39. Cf. esp., *Margins*, p. 75. On writing, cf. *Of Grammatology*, chap. 1; *Writing and Difference* (particularly the third and seventh essays); *Margins*, particularly "Ousia and Gramme," and "Form and Meaning," etc.

the symbols of spoken words, spoken words themselves being the symbols of states of the soul, which are in turn the images of things. So language appears as the place of a progressive distancing of signifiers in relation to the signified, which is located in the presence of the thing, in its self-identity. From mental states to the word, and from the word to the written word, presence is progressively more concealed. Metaphysics, therefore, has to valorize the word over writing as a direct result of interpreting being as presence, thus becoming inseparable from *phonocentrism* in the process: "Phonocentrism becomes confused, then, with the historical determination of the meaning of being as presence."[40] Or, to be more explicit: the ideal of an absoluteness of presence, and the conception of truth as adequation to a signified located in the originary presence of the thing, requires interpreting the play of meaning as *a secondary effect* and, in this play, devalorizing writing as the signifier of a signifier.

As a result, a philosophy that questions the privileged position of presence once again, emphasizing the working of *différance* in the heart of identity, should no longer regard meaning as a distance from the supposedly transparent presence of an originary signified: All presence conceals something that is hidden in it, the "origin" must be erased, and with it the idea of a primary signified must vanish. This Heideggerian version of the thesis is favored by the "philosophists," for whom there are no facts but only interpretations. The idea that meaning has to be rehabilitated, and thus writing as well, as a redoubling of meaning, is one positive development from this. The voice is not closer to a self-identical signified since all identity is traversed by *différance*. On the contrary, the play of writing as a redoubling of meaning articulates more faithfully the movement of *différance* as retreat or distancing of presence, or even as *spacing* (here, in passing, we find one of the concepts in the "chain" described by Derrida): Every aspect of presence, when considered from the starting point of *différance*, appears in such a way that "an interval must separate the present from what it is not in order for the present to be itself," that is, an interval or spacing that "constitutes

40. *Of Grammatology*, p. 29.

136

it as present."[41] On this basis, *différance*, as such a spacing, can be called writing, like the production of a *trace* (the chain continues to unroll its links) which no longer refers back to the presence of a signified, or originary trace, whose writing is only the deforming trace. Writing that is no longer secondary to a living word will then be called *archiwriting*; a trace that no longer refers back to a primary signified will be an *architrace*. With the understanding, of course, that the *archi* here is no longer a real one, since as trace or writing *archi* already means something other than itself.

Again referring to "what makes the presentation of the being-present possible" (which Heidegger called Being), Derrida can now reassemble the most important moments in the chain: "This constitution of the present . . . I propose to call archiwriting, architrace or *différance*. Which (is) (simultaneously) spacing (and) temporization."[42] So a supplementary link is joined to the others. "Temporization," another name for *différance*—*différance* as the dispensation of presence, being here as in Heidegger the fourth dimension of time (the one that makes past, present, and future come to pass)[43]—also means "temporizing" in the most trivial sense of the word: To temporize is to delay a presence, "calculate a delay, a detour, a slowing, a reservation," in short, *differ/defer*, implying a loss of presence through a gesture (deferring a meeting, for example), therefore *différance*. Derrida also suggests that *différance* from the point of view of temporization as delay or reservation is an economic concept, if not "*the* economical concept":[44] *Différance* refers to the movement that constitutes putting possibility in reserve, as when one defers an expense, except that here the expense deferred is not deferred to a later date, sent to a future when the reservation (the retreat) will finally be abolished, in terms of the absurd perspective of a transformation of presentation in presence (of *différance* in identity). *Différance* is therefore thought of as an infinite temporization, or infinity: a trace which refers back only to another trace,

41. *Margins*, p. 13.
42. Ibid.
43. Ibid., p. 21.
44. *Positions*, p. 8.

writing which refers back only to another writing, pure play of meaning without end.

Establishing this link between *différance* and writing clarifies two additional elements of Derrida's discourse:

It is clear that the term *différance* furnishéd the enterprise its emblem. Unusual, apparently not easy to use (always capable of being badly understood and confused with *difference*), it also has the advantage of being only a written form, which delights Derrida![45] The *a* of *différance* cannot be heard, and *différance* disappears in the spoken word, no doubt the unimpeachable, considerably profound indication that phonocentrism (thus the metaphysics of presence) might be decisively shaken through adopting such a purely visual distinction.

Above all, in this reflection on writing it is clear why Derrida was led to place a very particular importance on linguistics as the theory of the sign.[46] If sign theory as it was established by Saussure is taken up again and deepened in his work, it is in relation to Saussure's focus on the arbitrary nature of the sign; that is, in a given linguistic system, the meaning of a term is based solely on "relations and differences with respect to the other terms of language"[47] and is not assignable to it based on itself or its mimetic relationship to the signified. On the basis of this theory of the sign, one can work out Derrida's use of it, drawing the "conclusion that the signified concept is never present in and of itself, in a sufficient presence that would refer only to itself." The truth of Saussurean linguistics resides in the idea that the field of meaning must be conceived as a chain in which any signifier only signifies through reference to other signifiers, in the absence of any signified that can be grasped in itself. As such, language itself becomes a good paradigm of *différance*, as Derrida very clearly suggests when, in answering a question about what the *a* in *différance* means, he said: "I

---

45. Ibid.
46. V. Descombes has long argued for the importance of the role of the linguistic paradigm in Derrida's work in *Le Même et l'autre*, Ed. de Minuit, 1979, pp. 160 ff.).
47. *Margins*, pp. 10 ff.

138

do not know if it *signifies* at all—perhaps something like the production of what metaphysics calls the sign (signifier/signified)."[48] Beyond the verbal pirouette, the answer that *différance* is pure meaning, the production of signs referring endlessly to each other, simultaneously demonstrates the function and the limitations of the reference to linguistics in Derrida's text, is entirely at the service of and is entirely exhausted in managing the thematics of *différance*.

It would be easy to demonstrate, though not very purposeful, that the sole content of Derrida's discourse derives from extending this conceptual chain. We have already encountered (and exhausted) the figures of trace, architrace, spacing, and temporization or reservation moving from *différance* to writing, which is merely a perceptible presentation of it. Instead, we will limit ourselves, through a few pleasant examples, to suggesting how the reader might pursue the exercise, given the time or taste for it:

1. *The supplement.* If we refer to the study of the *Essay on the Origin of Languages*, as *Of Grammatology* suggests, we find that supplementarity seems to denote the logic of meaning as Derrida reconstructs it starting from Rousseau, for whom the sign was a supplement that kills living presence and veils transparency. We suspect, on the contrary, that for Derrida it is, quite obviously, precisely this supplementarity that needs to be addressed and thought about if the metaphysics of presence is to be subverted and phonocentrism overthrown.

2. *The pharmakon.* In *Plato's Pharmacy*, published in 1968 and again in *Dissemination*, a study dedicated primarily to analyzing the myth of Theuth in *Phaedrus*, the term *pharmakon*, which refers to both the poison and the cure, proves to denote the ambivalence of writing. Plato describes the invention of writing as the search for a cure for forgetfulness, thus for the effacement of presence. But once the cure is discovered, it comes to seem, if not worse than the disease, at least a figure of the disease it was supposed to prevent: Writing in myth is finally seen as damaging to memory and the living word, a "philter of forgetfulness,"[49] because it puts them

48. *Positions*, p. 8.
49. *La Dissémination*, Ed. du Seuil, 1972, p. 126 (*Dissemination*, trans. Barbara Johnson, University of Chicago Press, Chicago, 1981, p. 126).

to sleep and infects their very existence, which would otherwise be intact. Prompting memory to depend on written material, writing is metaphysically interpreted as also having contributed to erasing presence, which the philosopher must struggle against while recalling pure presence, lost from the *eidos*. So Plato's "pharmacy" testifies to the inauguration of the metaphysics of presence, and, counter to Plato, we eventually realize that we should understand the *pharmakon* as *différance* and ultimately refuse to "close the pharmacy." In spite of Socrates, then, "the one who did not write," we have this assertion of the philosopher as polygraph.

3. *The hymen*. As the consummation of marriage, the hymen (as marriage)[50] is the abolition or suspension of differences (fusion in unity). However, this reunion takes place only through the hymen, which is "what is maintained between differences," thus causing them to appear as differences at the very moment of their abolition.[51] So the hymen beomes another name for *différance* itself, fantasizing about this veil—between inside and outside, between desire and its fulfillment, between present and future—which acts (as veil) only "when it does not happen" (as the fulfillment of desire where differences are joined): difference (outside/inside, present/ future, etc.) that makes differences appear as such at the very instant of its withdrawal.

It is not very useful to emphasize this any further. The meditations on the hymen are pursued most notably in *Spurs*, a short essay with a clever subtitle: *The Styles of Nietzsche*. From the question of the *hymen* to that of *style* as *stiletto*, it is easy to see why the spur furnished a new emblem for the enterprise.[52] We can also understand the type of logic Derrida used in his later writings[53] to give a particularly important place to the question of "femininity": Femininity, naturally, leads right back to the *leitmotif* of *différance* as opposed to the "phallogocentrism" of metaphysics, as it must,

---

50. "L'hymen (en tant qu'hyménée)."
51. "The Double Session"; 1969 text published in *Dissémination;* cf. esp. pp. 237 ff.
52. Cf. *Eperons*, Flammarion, 1978, p. 82.
53. See esp. *Glas* and *La Carte postale*.

through the hymen. The end of man liberates the possibility of an affirmation of woman.

If so inclined, anyone with a little ingenuity can prolong the game in relation to a "gift from the blue" [*coup de don*], "sheath," "bunch," or "band." But nowhere in all this will any distance between Derrida and his model other than a rhetorical one be revealed. French Heideggerianism is therefore dedicated exclusively to *symbolizing* ontological difference. It is indeed *French*, even very French, but only by virtue of its taste, talent, and aptitude for producing *literary* variations on a simple, even poor, philosophical theme, and that a borrowed one. Very closely linked to certain French peculiarities in the approach to philosophical discourse (the essay, the *khâgne*, the aggregation), this taste and this aptitude have been put to the service of one of the most stunning exercises in *repetition* that intellectual history has ever known.

The principle of repetition is that nothing be transformed and nothing lost. In this context we have to stress that, if *Derrida* = *Heidegger* + *Derrida's style*, that is not to say that it means *Heidegger minus something*, for instance, minus the philosophical difficulties, even insurmountable aporias, inherent in such a philosophy of ontological difference. The discourse is so adequate to its model that our critical analysis cannot suggest a special treatment of it here. We can merely limit ourselves to mentioning a certain number of problems that reappear in French Heideggerianism which are directly inherited from its eponymous philosophy.

Dead Ends of *Différance*

We believe that simply mentioning these dead ends here in connection with Heidegger is enough since we have analyzed them more extensively elsewhere.[54] We will simply show, therefore, the kind of logic that this approach could only lead to and lose itself in.

As in Heidegger, the intention of Derrida's philosophy of *différance* was to turn the attention of present beings to the fact that

54. Cf. the essays in our collection, *Système et critique*, Ousia, 1985.

there is presence, remind us of that *gift from the blue* that makes things be there for us. [55] This return to the "there is" requires that the "gift" be screened from what Heidegger called the tyranny of the principle of reason, in order that philosophy become faithful to dispensation as such. Subjecting the "there is" to the question "why?," metaphysics as ontotheology has in fact brought presence back not to presentation (to *différance*) but to the founding identity of a primary being, a creator (as understanding and will) of other beings. Thus, overcoming metaphysics as ontotheology [56] requires giving up any foundation of presence, such as a traditionally theological one, which might also have taken the secularized form of a philosophy of history. [57] When various metaphysics of history consider the rise of events through reference to the practical causality of active wills (Fichte), or the theoretical causality of a logic immanent to the historical process (Hegel), they are merely recasting the theological foundation of presence on *reason* (become merely internal to the development) and on *will* (merely transferred from God to man as subject) in a new form. Therefore, the philosophy of *différance* should eliminate everything from its discourse that is intrinsically linked to the double point of view of reason and will, within the logic of this kind of deconstruction of metaphysics. However, the need to eliminate it in turn raises two types of difficulties, for Derrida as well as for Heidegger:

1. *Factual difficulties.* To eliminate from presence the point of view of reason means giving up the basic or merely explanatory approach; [58] to eliminate the point of view of will means rejecting the perspective that requires goals or defines the values by which will must act, or, in other words, it means eliminating any ethical

---

55. It should be remembered that Heidegger always emphasized the necessity of understanding in the "there is" (*es gibt*) a dimension of giving (*Gabe*), which is the very mark of the exemption of Being from presence.
56. Derrida constantly returns to this theme. Cf., for example, *Positions*, pp. 48, 54, etc.
57. We recall how Hegel explicitly presented his philosophy of history as a "theodicy" in his effort to establish that "everything happens rationally" in history.
58. Cf. on this point H. Arendt's condemnation of any use of the principle of causality; "Compréhension et politique," in *Esprit*, June 1980, pp. 66 ff.

142

dimension from philosophy and discourse.[59] Nevertheless, it is undeniable that the vocabulary of foundation and evaluation survives throughout this enterprise, which is supposed to mean something only if it succeeds in escaping what it apparently has in common with this vocabulary.

Heidegger presented the question of Being as the "ground" of the "foundation" where all philosophy is rooted, while refusing any terminology that would reinsert the philosophy of difference into the grasp of the "very powerful principle of reason." Being is rightly called the "ground," and its "withdrawal" is rightly defined as the "ground" of our history, which in this sense is the "history of Being." However, it must be added that such a "ground" is not to be understood in the metaphysical sense of "substructure," that this "ground" is instead a "bottomlessness" or an "abyss" (*Ab-grund*). This gesture of denying the foundation is identically repeated in Derrida: Thus the trace is "neither a ground, nor a foundation, nor an origin"[60] but "the movement of *différance*, as that which produces different things, that which differentiates, is the common root of all the oppositional concepts that mark our language."[61] On this basis, the return of reason still has to be rejected. Having recourse to parentheses to enclose metaphysical connotations, Derrida will write, for example, "This (active) movement of (the production of) *différance* without origin . . .";[62] or, using quotation marks, *différance* is "the playing movement that 'produces' . . . these effects of difference," which is "the nonfull, nonsimple 'origin,' the structured and differentiating origin of differences";[63] or again, practicing the art of italics, "The alterity of the 'unconscious' [obvious figure of *différance*—L.F. and A.R.] makes us concerned . . . with

59. Cf. *Lettre sur l'humanisme*, p. 129: "Any valorization is a subjectivation" and, as such, "the greatest imaginable blasphemy against Being" (*Brief über den Humanismus*, in *Collected Works*, vol. 9, p. 349: "Das Denken in Werten ist hier und sonst die grösste Blasphemie, die sich dem Sein gegenüber denken lasst").
60. *Positions*, p. 52.
61. Ibid., p. 9.
62. *Margins*, p. 13.
63. Ibid., p. 11.

a 'past' whose future to come will never be a *production* or a reproduction in the form of presence."[64]

Similarly, Heidegger, who made "valorization" a blasphemy, called for philosophy to demonstrate "courage" and "bravery" in order to experience Being as difference (as absolute nonbeing) in nothingness, undergoing the ordeal of anguish. Even though Derrida had explicitly reproached Heidegger for these reappearances of an ethical perspective,[65] he himself hardly manages to escape from the point of view of will, when he can say, for example, *just like anyone:* "What has seemed necessary and urgent to me in the historical situation which is our own is a general determination of the conditions for the emergence and the limits of philosophy, of metaphysics, of everything that carries it out and that it carries on."[66] For that matter, the whole inaugural discourse for the "Estates General of Philosophy" is inscribed in a register where we do not see how "ethical preoccupation" and the perspective of valorization could have been excluded.[67] Here again, only negation provides the approach with a minimum of cohesion: The thesis is posited that "the history of truth, of the truth of truth, has always been . . . the abasement of writing and its rejection outside of the full word."[68] but it is specified that "evidently it is not a question—which would be contradictory to the entire context—of raising up writing from what I, myself, considered to be its abasement"[69] and that no "ethical or axiological reversal" had been foreseen.[70]

These denials are significant of what can be problematical, and

64. Ibid., p. 21.
65. Cf. *Positions*, p. 103, n. 25: "Why qualify temporality as authentic—or *proper* (*eigentlich*)—and inauthentic—or improper—when every ethical preoccupation has been suspended?"
66. Ibid., p. 51.
67. See, for example, *Etats généraux de la philosophie*, Flammarion, 1979, p. 32 ("What is, can, or *must* be taught by this name, in this name and in relation to what is presented in this name?"); p. 35 (the demand for the extention of philosophy is "*legitimate, vital, decisive,*" etc.).
68. *Of Grammatology*, p. 12.
69. *Positions*, p. 53.
70. Ibid., p. 13.

at the same time inadequate for an undertaking that intends to be subversive of metaphysics itself, about a language that is still metaphysical. Problematical, as Derrida clearly registers,[71] for there is the risk of "ceaselessly confirming, consolidating or *relifting* [*relever*], at an always more certain depth, that which one allegedly deconstructs." But still inadequate, since again, at this level, the classic aporias of negative theology and the analogical use of language can still be found. When the task of indicating that *différance* is in fact a common root of differences only by analogy (or metaphorically), and that *différance* is in fact a root that is not one, is confined to "the quiet work of italics and quotation marks,"[72] the problem of showing the specific nature of the relations between *différance* and differences still remains. In the work of italics and quotation marks these relations, which are in fact nothing other than the unfolding of *différance*, continue to escape from discourse. Under these conditions, the inadequacy of what must then be called a procedure can only be disguised as well as possible by the *provisory or programmatic* attractions of the discourse:

> We will designate as *différance* the movement according to which language, or any code, any system of referral in general, is constituted "historically" as a weave of differences. "Is constituted," "is produced," "is created," "movement," "historically," etc., necessarily being understood beyond the metaphysical language in which they are retained, along with all their implications. We ought to demonstrate why concepts like *production*, constitution and history remain in complicity with what is at issue here. But this would take me too far today . . . , and I utilize such concepts, like many others, only for their strategic convenience and in order to undertake their deconstruction at the currently most decisive point.[73]

The discourse of *différance* (and perhaps also the philosophy) is yet to come; today it is enough to prepare its coming, or to prepare

71. *Margins*, p. 135.
72. *Positions*, pp. 33–34.
73. *Margins*, p. 12.

oneself for it. The main issue, however, is to discover whether this subtle art of preparatory study, which Heidegger had already practiced with great talent,[74] does not in fact serve the primary function of hiding those aporias that we know to be in principle insurmountable, by delaying their climax to some indeterminable future moment.

2. *Difficulties of right or principle* appear to increase these difficulties of fact. Assume for a moment that the difficulties of fact have been resolved and that *différance* is faithfully spoken and thought, or at least written. It is quite simple to see that such a possibility is in principle radically excluded. The idea of such a philosophy and of such a writing testifies to a desire to try to express *différance* itself, in spite of everything—in spite of the fact that appearance "disappears in every appearance"—or, in other words, to try to make appearance itself appear. Such an idea is both absurd (if the presentation is presented, it is no longer presentation but being-present) and strangely motivated by a desire for a second coming and for mastery, which, suddenly reinstating subjectivity to its rights, seems rigorously incompatible with the principles of the enterprise. This difficulty of principle seems to present the whole approach with a very uncomfortable alternative:

> Either accept the difficulties of fact, renounce the preparatory tone, do not support the illusion of a more accomplished or less deforming approach to *différance*—but also acknowledge that one cannot go beyond the discourse of reason and will and despair of any future for philosophy whatsoever, an unhappy thought.
>
> Or do not see (pretend not to see?) the difficulty of principle and search for a *writing* of *différance* beyond simply the quiet use of italics and quotation marks—but also obviously be exposed to setting out in a direction that is flatly contradictory with the premises of the undertaking.
>
> The dead end in both directions is obvious. The first alternative at least manages the possibility of a clear awareness of its limits, at

74. Cf. "Heidegger en question," in Ferry and Renaut, *Système et critique*, p. 70.

least for French Heideggerianism. However, everything indicates that it was decided to exploit the second alternative.

And All the Rest Is Literature

The option thus chosen was important. Through it, French Heideggerianism acquired what we have called its only originality in relation to its model: to have attempted a *literary* working out of this philosophy of *différance* to which its content is repeatedly reduced.

Dissemination seems to have been the indication that, in 1972, this turn was being taken. Here is the outline for the project of writing *différance* where the need to recall the unsayable is no longer consigned to the work of italics and quotation marks. Through a long meditation in the guise of a preface, entitled "Outwork," which concerns the essential imbalance between the form of the book and the requirements of a philosophy of *différance*, Derrida implicitly puts in place what in the later texts (*Glas*, *The Post Card*, and to a certain extent, *Spurs*) would guide the search for what must be called (in spite of the contradiction of the expression) a more adequate form of discourse. Let us look at what the first page of *Dissemination* negatively indicates are the principles that future nonbooks must attempt to follow:

> This (therefore) will not have been a book.
>
> Still less, despite appearances, will it have been a collection of *three* "essays" whose itinerary it would be time, after the fact, to recognize; whose continuity and underlying laws could now be pointed out; indeed, whose overall concept or meaning could at last, with all the insistence required on such occasions, be squarely set forth. I will not feign, according to the code, either premeditation or improvisation. These texts are assembled otherwise; it is not my intention here to *present* them.
>
> The question astir here, precisely, is that of presentation.
>
> Though the form of the "book" is now going through a period of general upheaval, and though that form now appears less natural

and its history less transparent than ever, and though one cannot tamper with it without disturbing everything else, the book form alone can no longer settle—here, for example—the case of those writing processes which, in *practically* questioning that form, must also dismantle it.[75]

Let us mention a few of the strong moments in this critique of the book:

> In principle, a book possesses a beginning, a development, and an end: this would be by definition absurd where speaking (or writing) *différance* is concerned, since such a structure presupposes that one can master the thing and explain or present it, whereas presentation cannot be presented.
>
> The book assumes that an author assembled it, which would obviously have no sense within the framework of an undertaking where the concern is not with connecting diverse elements in order to achieve coherence but with *différance* itself: For this reason Derrida has no hesitation in writing, with apparent modesty, "These texts are assembled otherwise."
>
> The book belongs to the one who signs it: logically, the nonbook should not even be signed, except through a usurping of identity (of *différance*), which Derrida will resign himself to in the future, with the reluctance one might imagine.[76]

In most of the later works, the procedures for approximating the model described are multiplied. *Glas* remains a landmark (1974) in this respect and will be worth a visit for some time to come as the surprising evidence of how *naive* such an attempt really was. Nevertheless, it contains valuable attempts to disarticulate the book:

> The text is presented as if there were no beginning or end; the preface, for example, has disappeared, since it assumes that the moment might come when, according to the metaphysical ideal of

75. *Dissemination*, p. 3.
76. Cf. the fourth cover page of *Dissèmination* (French ed.): "Qu'on appelle ceci un livre et son dos un *rempli*, que j'en soussigne la déclaration, voilà qui ne sau-

transparency and mastery, what there was to say would have been fully said.

There was an effort to suppress the mere existence of a first sentence, the text (or one of the texts that compose the nonbook) opening with a statement that has already begun: "What of Hegel anyway, today, for us, here, now?"

It goes without saying that a careful effort has also been made to avoid ending the last sentence, no subject being able to claim to "have the last word": "Today, here, now, the fragments of."

Any hope for the reader's following the *linear* development of *a* thought has been broken by juxtaposing a variety of texts in several columns, whose arrangement is supposed to defy systematic interpretation.

Thus philosophy has demonstrated the structures of its discourse, somewhat later than novelistic and cinematic works. We would like to make three short statements with regard to this dismantling.

1. This disorganization is cleverly organized, a reminder of the great naivete of this type of undertaking, which we have already mentioned. Because it is always a subject who *decides* to vanish as subject, with all the intrinsic absurdity of this approach, the author of the nonbook is just as much an author as that of the most traditional book, with the same strengths and weaknesses. In spite of Derrida's statement, "These texts were assembled otherwise," the nonbook remains the product of an intention, with all the consciousness, will, and reflection that implies.

2. One may or may not appreciate this *writing style*, though it does seem to create products that pose a problem analogous to the problem of the painting of certain avatars of cubism. However, multiplying the perspectives on an object does not eradicate the subjectivity that is still organizing the multiplication. When these efforts are new, an effect of strangeness or of a lack of understanding results, which can at least intrigue us and arouse our interest, if not

---

rait avec plus de réserve ou d'inconséquence à la lecture fermer la marche." Cf. also *Margins*, p. 330.

exactly please (in the sense of giving aesthetic pleasure). The limitation of this type of work is that this interest, which is basically an *intellectual* one, is dulled as soon as the principles governing the production of the so-called nonworks (decentering, deformation of perspective, etc.) have been grasped. Then there remains only the inherent boredom that comes from the repetition of the procedures, which at that point have only one point of interest, a *historical* one, the same interest the remnants of a period of cultural history always have.

3. Whether one appreciates this writing style or not, the works it produces have more to do with putting an idea to work than with an attempt to regenerate any kind of theoretical content. The direction *Dissemination* takes, aside from the fact that it seems to result from a choice that is incompatible with the principles of the enterprise, would still have managed to lead it onto the terrain of literature. In that case it would not have been directly included within the framework we have defined for our inquiry.

In spite of all this, there is still one philosophical point to clarify. In a context where the search for adequation had constantly been attributed to the metaphysical hegemony of presence, how could this desire for a second coming, which led to searching for a form of exposition (or of nonexposition)[77] in the nonbook that was more faithful and thus more adequate to *différance*, have been reintroduced?[78] On the one hand, this is rather comforting, we admit: Subjectivity seems strangely capable of resisting the most methodical efforts to get rid of it. But, on the other hand, inconsistency must be understood at its very roots, or critical analysis remains incomplete and suspect, having isolated only superficial, basically

77. From March 28 to July 15, 1985, the Centre Pompidou gave its visitors the opportunity to think they had returned to the flamboyant sixties through a "nonexhibition" called *Les Immatériaux*, organized by J.-F. Lyotard, and overtly presented as such.
78. This project, which was more radical in later works, motivated from the beginning the search for terms, such as *différance*, always more faithful to the idea in question.

contingent, problems that it would be easy to remedy. We have posed this very problem elsewhere,[79] with respect to Heidegger and his search for a speech closer to Being, using the language of poetry: How was it possible, even here, that the most traditional dimensions of subjectivity (like consciousness and will) would reappear, in the perspective of an *unveiling* defined as *task?* Everything indicates that, with Heidegger, the forgetting of Being is to be thought of not as the fact of a subjectivity closing itself to difference but rather as the withdrawal of being itself. In Derrida's terms, it is the appearance itself that is disappearance. In this case, if the forgetting is not a mistake, it is difficult to see how, at the same time, (1) it could be overcome and (2) this overcoming could be assigned to someone as a "task."

In Heidegger's work, the reintroduction of subjectivity seems to have been possible through an ambiguity not in the forgetting of Being but in the forgetting of this forgetting. We know that Heidegger explained that, in the process of the decline of the history of metaphysics, the forgetting of Being (the hiding of presentation) ended by no longer being perceived as such: Questioning *the being of beings* (in other words, producing an interpretation of presence), metaphysics believed it was asking the question of Being (the question of presentation), and in the course of this confusion "forgetting was established within forgetting."[80] Now, when at the level of forgetting Being Heidegger's position is not ambivalent and refers this forgetting to Being itself (as withdrawal) and not to man, his analysis of the forgetting of forgetting is somewhat blurred: It is important, he writes, to "relocate philosophy in the presence of the forgetting of Being," but "it still remains to be seen if philosophy will be capable of it." At this level, everything seems to depend on our "effort to learn to be ultimately attentive to the forgetting of Being."[81] Precisely at this point, the perspective of an error, and also that of a task to be completed, reappears, producing an ethical dimension in a philosophy that should have been entirely without

79. Cf. esp. Ferry and Renaut, *Système et critique*, pp. 92 ff.
80. *Questions I*, p. 30 ("Was ist Metaphysik? Einleitung 1949," in *Collected Works*, vol. 9, p. 371).
81. Ibid.

one. In Heidegger the principle of a (*contradictorily*) maintained reference to subjectivity resides in the inability to think of the redoubling of the forgetting of Being (in the forgetting of forgetting) from the starting point of Being itself: It pertains to the *will* to overcome the forgetting of forgetting and to have a *clear awareness* not, of course, of presentation (of Being) but of the veiling of this presentation (the withdrawal of Being).

Is there an analogous ambiguity to be discovered in Derrida? In any case, the Heideggerian theme of "the forgetting of forgetting" has an absolute equivalent in Derrida: When we read in *Margins* that "in any exposition it (appearance) would be exposed to disappearing as disappearance," the disappearing of disappearance plays an essential role in radicalizing the concealment, just as in Heidegger. So it is, then, the status of this redoubled disappearance that has to be determined. Nothing indicates that Derrida really elaborated this status.[82] At least the absence of elaboration does not exclude the possibility that at this level the process of erasing *différance* could not always be approached from *différance* itself. A more rigorous approach, more careful in questioning its progress, would have required going beyond the simple reuse of a Heideggerian structure.

Because of this *gap*, French Heideggerianism has also missed the opportunity to elaborate successfully a question that could have enriched it. Having seen the return of the possibility of a reference to subjectivity (at the level of the forgetting of forgetting) in Heidegger himself, one might have asked: If the return of a reference to subjectivity proves untenable even in the philosophies that have traced it most profoundly, would it not finally be better, rather than simply to search for a survival or a trace of metaphysics to be mercilessly tracked down, to try to confer a *legitimate status* on this

---

82. See, in the transcription of the debate that followed our presentation during the Colloque de Cerisy on *The Ends of Man*, Derrida's obvious difficulty accounting for the problem of the distinction between forgetting and the forgetting of forgetting (*Les Fins de l'homme*, Galilée, 1981, p. 51). See also the second postscript to *Eperons* (pp. 121–23): Derrida reproduces one of Heidegger's texts on the forgetting of Being but does not address the question of the forgetting of forgetting.

reference, which is inevitable in any case? Instead of attempting to extend even further the "destruction of the subject," with the intention of constructing this "hyper-Heideggerianism" that French Heideggerianism dreamed of becoming, would it not have been more useful and more illuminating to accept these traces and to question them instead of ineffectively rejecting them?

5 /
French Marxism
(Bourdieu)

To illustrate the Marxist component of '68 philosophy, we have chosen, for three reasons, the sociology of Bourdieu rather than the work of Althusser.

First, Bourdieu's work is particularly representative of a typical gesture for French philosophy of the '68 period of proclaiming the death of philosophy and announcing its replacement by another type of discourse. In this regard, the sociology of knowledge is to Bourdieu as cultural history (the history of manners) is to Foucault, as the writing of the nonbook is to Derrida, or as renewing the practice of the cure is to Lacan: In all four cases an approach, supported from time to time by one or several philosophies, is claimed to have developed beyond philosophy, independently of philosophy, against philosophy, or in the margins of philosophy. This gesture obviously takes a particular form within the Marxist domain: that of the break between *philosophy* and *science*, which we might just as well have analyzed in Althusser's work as in Bourdieu's. However, this transfer of the power, in this case from the philosopher to the sociologist, was an even more radical attempt in Bourdieu; A constant objective, the place Bourdieu gives concrete physical work, by definition, no longer seems to belong directly to philosophy, whereas Althusser always remained fundamentally an interpreter of Marx, and his disciples, for the most part, were interpreters of Spinoza. From the symbolic point of view, their work is, after all, a less open break with the traditional exercise of philosophy than Bourdieu's work on museum attendance or matrimonial strategies. From the point of view of '68 philosophy as the philosophy of the end of philosophy, Bourdieu's approach to the theory and practice of "the sociologist's work" best expresses it.

In addition (and this is no doubt related to the previous point), the French Marxism of the sixties continues to play a role in the intellectual field primarily through Bourdieu's work. Althusser, and even the work of his disciples, seems very dated, irresistibly recalling a recent but evolved past, like the Beatles' music or the early films of Godard. If we hope to understand the current phenomenon of the intellectual resurgence of the sixties, it is the development of Bourdieu's work that undeniably represents the only really lively manifestation of the Marxist "sensibility" within this resurgence.

If it is through Bourdieu that French Marxism continues and is surviving this moment of crisis within Marxism, this is probably also due to the nature of his relations to Marxism. These relations are such that the crisis of Marxism, which made Althusser a museum piece during the same period, left the symbolic capital, if we may say it that way, that Bourdieu benefited from intact. Here again, this particular quality of Bourdieu's Marxism, which is analogous to that of Derrida's Heideggerianism, or even Foucault's Nietzscheanism, is deeply representative of the intellectual style of the sixties: In all three cases what is typical of the style (and what makes up the "French" character of the enterprise) is that any reference to the founding father is euphemistic enough and is combined with enough apparent distance, or even open criticism (which is frequently an exaggeration), that the emergence of an original, new, in short, "French" position seems believable. This was not at all the case when *For Marx* or the volumes of *Reading "Capital"* were written: In that case one was exposed directly to the same experiences that the philosophy one was openly serving was exposed to. One of the great qualities of French philosophy of the sixties was its allowing its own theoretical identity be forgotten. Thus Foucault's work gained an audience that was not limited by its marked Nietzschean/Heideggerian origins; thus it was thought that Derrida was doing original work; this is how Bourdieu's Marxism was overlooked. One must not underestimate the role played by the strategy of constantly denying the model, which is among the conditions that made the survival, if not the resurgence, of these currents possible, in spite of their being very "situated": It is only natural that it be in Bourdieu's work, given that he appears the master of this type of exercise, in the Marxist register that we look for the lines of force (or weakness) of French Marxism.

Bourdieu against Althusser: Marxism Denied

Bourdieu's texts try to illustrate their irretrievable distance from Marxism at three points. It is particularly significant that they address these criticisms first to the Althusserian version of Marxism: The denial, situated in relation to what passed in the sixties for a most vigorous defense of a certain Marxist orthodoxy in France, is directed primarily at efficiency in the strategy of autonomization. So it is legitimate, in situating Bourdieu's work today, to question the real scope of this three-part criticism: (1) a criticism in the name of science of Marxism as a philosophy, (2) a criticism of structuralist Marxism on behalf of a "correct philosophy of history," (3) a criticism of simplistic materialism in the name of the understanding of the complexity of the social.

1. Against Althusserianism as Philosophy In an article of 1975 severely critical of Balibar, Bourdieu, interpolating quotations from Marx, referred to Althusser's efforts as merely a "variation on philosophical ambition," which is characterized, in imitation of the most traditional philosophy, by the "claim to have mastered empirical science and the sciences that produced it," a "theoretical" or "theoreticist" claim in Althusserianism that could cut short philosophy's necessary replacement by science. [1] The so-called science that the Althusserians had learned by reading *Capital* (the science of the possible modes of production and their transformations) in fact demonstrates a quasi-metaphysical apriorism when it attempts to deduce (like philosophy) "the essential event, the historical given of the theoretical model." Practiced in this way, the "break" produced "only 'science' with no scientific practice, . . . a science reduced to a judicial discourse on the science of others"; in short, Althusserian Marxism in fact produced only a consolidation of philosophy.

1. P. Bourdieu, "Marx lecteur de Balibar," *Actes*, Nov. 1975.

156

After reading these sharp accusations against the most fashionable Marxism of the sixties, it would seem to be somewhat mean to put *Reproduction* or *Distinction* in the same category of French Marxism as *Reading "Capital"* or *For Marx*. However, this criticism of Balibar is conducted through the use of quotations from *German Ideology*, originally aimed at Stirner and reapplied by Bourdieu to the Althusserians. On this basis, however, this first criticism is hardly conclusive from the point of view of testing Bourdieu's relationship to Marxism.

2. *Against Marxism as Structuralism* Having opened up the distance from the most authoritative representatives of the French Marxism of the sixties, Bourdieu has since been largely explained, notably in the very important book 1 of *Le Sens pratique*.[2] Directed against Althusser, this time the critique consists of accusing "structuralist readers of Marx"[3] of an odd lack of dialectical feeling and of tending to reduce historical processes to simple mechanical effects of economic structures: From this perspective, subjective practices can only be reflections or "emanations," whereas in reality, Bourdieu explains, there is obviously ("dialectical") interaction between objective structures and historical actions, between economic structures and practices.

The great banality of this proposition may seem surprising: The call for differentiating between mechanical and dialectical determinism is a ritual in the Marxist climate. Nearly a century ago, Engels was already emphasizing it in his famous, often quoted letters to Starbenkurg, Schmidt, and Bloch. In denouncing the economics of the Second International, Althusser himself had the same purpose when he emphasized that Marx did not consider the social space to be a totality organized by a single principle, that is, the development of the forces of production and their contradictions with the relations of production.[4] To have any meaning and any hope

2. P. Bourdieu, *Le Sens pratique*, Ed. de Minuit, 1980, book 1: "Critique de la raison théorique."
3. Ibid., p. 70.
4. Cf. L. Althusser, *For Marx*, trans. Ben Brewster, Verso, London, 1979, pp. 21 ff.; *Réponse à John Lewis*, p. 12.

of being effective, the repetition of this criticism would have had to demonstrate at the very least—which was certainly not impossible—that an economics survives in Althusser's work, in spite of everything, and beyond the notorious thematics of "overdetermination" of the social space, which is somewhat more subtle but no less emphatic, of course, than in the most mechanistic Marxists. In addition, this more detailed dismantling of Althusserian structuralism would have saved Bourdieu from running the risk of remaining a prisoner of what he denounced, as was always the case in the Marxist tradition, by not having rigorously isolated the generating principles of economism (and also the conditions for its avoidance).

Bourdieu takes his critique of structuralist Marxism onto the terrain of philosophy itself, in the name of what today he calls "the real logic of historical action and the true philosophy of history."[5] One might ask, having followed what he indicates such a philosophy of history is, if it preserves the autonomy of human practices in relation to the self-development of economic structures or objectives better than Althusserian structuralism. In addition to determination through objective structures (in dialectical relation with them), Bourdieu reintroduced the determination of history by historical agents, but he also specified that this dialectic between structures and actions is equivalent to that of "objective structures and incorporated structures" in that it "is at work in every practical action."[6] In other words, if, as Bourdieu says, "practical actions" make history (and if, in this way, history cannot be reduced to the mechanistic self-development of structures), it is only to the extent that any action is the place where the structures of the social world are expressed both *directly,* in the mode of a determination of action by the "objective structures" of the social world, and *indirectly* by the "incorporated structures" that *habitus* are. It should be recalled that the *habitus* in Bourdieu's vocabulary are nothing other than "systems of durable and transposable *dispositions*" that "produce . . . the conditionings associated with a particular class of existence conditions."[7] As a result, Bourdieu writes, the dialectic of struc-

5. P. Bourdieu, *Homo Academicus*, Ed. de Minuit, 1984, p. 12.
6. Bourdieu, *Le Sens pratique*, p. 70.
7. Ibid., p. 88.

tures and of their interiorization as "structured structures predisposed to functioning as structuring structures" is at play in every action. Thus the distance from Marxist structuralism seems to be, at the very least, somewhat reduced: The "real philosophy of history" that Bourdieu demands, reexploiting the schema of the "ruse of reason," consists of maintaining yet again that men (their actions) make history but without knowing the history they make, actions being nothing other than the location of a dialectics of the structures of the social world with each other (with their incorporation in the *habitus*).

Bourdieu's critique of Marxist structuralism, however problematical in content, does serve an important strategic function. It allows him to position himself today as an adversary of the elimination of the subject, just as the late Foucault did, as we have seen. We can read, for example, in *Le Sens pratique* these lines about structuralist readers of Marx who are destined to "fall into fetishizing social laws":

> To convert the constructions science must resort to, in order to explain the structured and meaningful wholes that the accumulation of innumerable historical actions produces, into transcendent entities, which are to practices in a relationship of essence to existence, is to reduce history to a "process without a subject" and merely to substitute for the "creating subject" of subjectivism an automaton subdued by the dead laws of natural history. This emanatistic vision that makes structure, capital, or the modes of production into an entelechy developing through a process of self-realization reduces historical agents to the role of "supports" (*Träger*) for the structure and reduces their actions to mere epiphenomenal manifestations of power belonging to the structure developing according to its own laws and determining or overdetermining other structures.[8]

A surprising text in view of the preceding, but one that is directed entirely against *For Marx*, that fulfills the obvious function of demarcation from a particular Marxist sociology, which is being denounced as the murderer of the subject: Bourdieu's intention is,

8. Ibid., p. 70.

therefore, presented as a critique of subjectivism, certainly, but not as a negation of subjectivity. The advantage gained by the operation is then immediately reinvested, since Bourdieu indicates that his own practice of sociological analysis, rather than destroying subjectivity, contributes to constructing the subject; a sociological analysis in fact "makes a true reappropriation of the self possible," thanks to "the objectivation of objectivity which haunts the place of so-called subjectivity"; by showing direct and indirect social determinants (*habitus*), "it offers perhaps the only means of contributing to the construction of something like a subject, if only through the consciousness of the determinants, a construction otherwise abandoned to the forces of the world."[9]

In short, contrary to certain appearances, we have to look in Bourdieu's sociology to find the true rampart of humanism and the true defense of the subject. The first chapter of *Homo Academicus* pursues the exploitation of this theme. Naturally, "the logic of scientific analysis largely transcends individual or collective intentions and desires," which is indeed why, as he indicates, it would be absurd in reading *Homo Academicus* to play the portrait game and to wonder who are these "members of the Ecole des Hautes Etudes linked to the *Nouvel Observateur*" whose role in the power relations that define the university space is discussed: One must not confuse "empirical individuals" with "epistemic individuals"[10] (the latter being the only ones involved as supports for the mechanisms of power) when one describes any "network of objective relations." In other words, one might quote Marx and the preface of the first edition of *Capital* where he states that "it is not a question of persons as they personify economic categories, supports for interests, and determined class relations." However, Bourdieu, who must have been thinking of this text, is not able to go too far. Rather than conclude from it, as Marx did, that such a method "is less able than any other to make the individual responsible for relations of which he remains the social creator, whatever he may do to disengage himself from them," he emphasizes that the depersonalization im-

9. Ibid., pp. 40–41.
10. Bourdieu, *Homo Academicus*, p. 34.

160

plied by sociological analysis in no way nullifies the notion of responsibility:

> The logic produced by scientific analysis largely transcends individual and collective intentions and desires, (the conspiracy) of the most lucid and powerful agents designated by the search for those who are "responsible." Having said that, nothing could be more wrong than to draw evidence from these analyses in order to dissolve responsibilities in the network of objective relations where every agent is held. Against those who, by stating that social laws are destiny, would like to find the excuse for fatalistically or cynically giving up, we must remember that scientific explanation, in addition to providing the means for understanding, even absolving, also allows transformation. Accumulating knowledge about the mechanisms that govern the intellectual world should not have the effect of "discharging the individual from the bothersome burden of moral responsibility," as Jacques Bouveresse fears.[11] I would rather teach him to locate his responsibilities where his freedoms are.[12]

We hope to be forgiven for quoting this instructive discussion in full. It accomplishes the feat of associating the idea of *depersonalizing* agents through sociological analysis (recognized as inevitably reifying) with the notion of maintaining *responsibility*, both through the worn-out (and intrinsically absurd) theme of the knowledge of necessity permitting it to be "transformed" and through the (unfounded) reaffirmation that a dimension of freedom exists that can substitute for the individual at the heart of sociohistorical reality: "Social necessity" does not nullify freedom when history is not regarded as a process without a subject which transforms the human agent into an "automaton subdued by the dead laws of natural history." Of course, in the "correct philosophy of history," which is supposed to establish such an assertion, no similar sphere of autonomy can appear, but no matter; since it is being *pretended* or

11. Bourdieu is citing J. Bouveresse, *Le Philosophe chez les autophages*, Ed. de Minuit, 1984.
12. Bourdieu, *Homo Academicus*, pp. 14–15.

thought that a certain distance from a rigorously determinist structuralism has been maintained, the die is cast.

Inconsistency or hoax? The truth is that the diagnosis is of secondary importance. The essential point is to emphasize that salvaging responsibility and, more generally, subjectivity is, by definition, totally excluded from the entire enterprise. Moreover, Bourdieu clearly indicates the basis of this exclusion. Describing the *habitus,* he represents them as the "generating and organizing principles of practices and representations that can be objectively adapted to their goals without claiming to have the conscious intention of goals and the express mastery of the operations necessary to attain them, objectively 'regulated' and 'regular' without resulting from obedience to the rules, and, given all this, collectively orchestrated."[13] Why is this not another representation of social functioning as a *process without subject* (as a socioeconomic "ruse of reason") at the level of the *habitus* (that is, at the level of the dialectical interaction with objective structures dedicated to naturalizing history, which is lacking in structuralist Marxism)? And in what way does taking the *habitus* into account denaturalize history and recreate a space for freedom (and responsibility)? The image of an orchestra without a conductor is meaningful here, and Bourdieu uses it quite explicitly later on, in unequivocal terms:

> As long as we are unaware of the reality of the principle of orchestration without a conductor to regularize, unify, and systematize the practices in the absence of either spontaneous or imposed organization of individual intentions, we are condemned to naive artificializing that recognizes no principle other than conscious concertation: If, in practice, members of the same group, or same class in a differentiated society, are always more in harmony than the agents know or want, it is because, "by following only their own rules," everyone "nevertheless agrees," as Leibnitz has said. The *habitus* is this immanent law, the *lex insita* inscribed within bodies by identical histories.[14]

13. Bourdieu, *Le Sens pratique,* p. 88.
14. Ibid., pp. 98–99.

No doubt this reference to Leibnitz accompanying the complete dispossession of the agent (as *knowledge* and *will*, therefore as subject) from his own practices is appreciated. As we know, Kant described the type of freedom pertaining to Leibnitz's automaton as "basically no better than the freedom that a roasting spit has which, once mounted, also performs its movements independently." In view of this amazing return to Leibnitz that fed Bourdieu's definition of a "correct philosophy of history," we will not refrain from mentioning Kant's so-called rescue of subjectivity, which he added in relation to the example of the roasting spit: "This is a poor subterfuge, which still traps some who believe they have solved, through a little play with words, this difficult problem that the centuries have worked to resolve without success."[15]

The second type of critique Bourdieu addresses to Althusser's Marxism is therefore conclusive. If indeed the model is denied, we must also admit that we are witnessing, as usual, a superb "return of the repressed." In spite of its "subtleties," Althusserianism did not really renew the Marxist approach to the social,[16] any more than Bourdieu had overturned the basic principles of what he inherited, including its inconsistencies and perverse effects. At least Althusserian Marxism had the stature to admit what it was and to dare to appear what it was.

---

15. I. Kant, *Critique de la raison pratique*, AK. V, pp. 7–8, 99–102 (*Kritik der praktischen Vernunft*, Akademie-Ausgabe V, pp. 7 ff, pp. 98 ff.).
16. In *For Marx* (pp. 207 ff.), Althusser claims his own importance in having brought to light against every "economist" reduction, the fact that if the economic contradiction is indeed determinant in the last analysis it can nevertheless exercise its determination in different ways; so, for example, during certain periods, the leading role might be played not directly by the economy but by ideology. We may judge the degree of the renewal thus produced by pointing out that Althusser specifies: "in all the social forms, it is the conditions determined by one production that assign to all the others their rank and importance." Or again, in a perfect theory of the economic "ruse of reason": "In different structures, the economy is determinant in that it determines the structure of the instances of the social structure occupying the dominant position" (*Lire le Capital*, vol. 2, p. 110). For an analysis that is further developed, cf. A. Renaut, *"Marxisme et 'déviation stalinienne,'"* in E. Pisier-Kouchner, *Les Interprétations du stalinisme*, P.U.F., 1983, pp. 199–226.

3. Against Vulgar Materialism　One last type of critique demands a less radical opposition. In an interview with Bourdieu
devoted to *Homo Academicus*, it was remarked that his work is
basically not really original since "to point out that intellectuals
have passions and interests and that they occupy a social situation
has already been done by others" before him. In his response he
agrees that, indeed, "to reduce the adversary's reasons to mere
causes, that is, to interests of a usually more or less base nature, is
the daily bread of intellectual life" (which, we note in passing,
pertains to a very specific idea of intellectual debate even today).[17]
Having made that point, he immediately stated, "there are ways and
there are ways of doing things." "What distinguishes my work from
these other behaviors . . . is that I describe the whole game that
breeds both the particular interests of intellectuals—which are
entirely irreducible to the class interests proclaimed by the heavy
Marxist artillery, which was loaded with big cannonballs but always
missed the mark—and the partial insights of others' interests."[18]

Though self-proclaimed, this new critique of Marxism is truly
clever, centered this time on the means for practicing reduction,
once the principle of reducing discourses to interests has been
accepted. A quick reading might leave the impression that Bourdieu's work is not, after all, a smoothing out of the interests that
enliven the intellectual debate around class interests and that, on
the contrary, he demonstrates autonomy of thought with respect to
the class struggle—which would indeed mark a decisive break with
Marxism. The self-image that Bourdieu occasionally tries to create—that of a Weberian sociologist constructing the logics of different behaviors without of necessity reducing this *Zweckration-*

17. An idea that is after all traditional in Marxist circles; we have already
pointed out that Althusser claimed that, "like any intellectual, a philosophy professor is a petty bourgeois" and that "when he opens his mouth, it is petty-
bourgeois ideology that he speaks." Is Bourdieu (*Actes*, Nov. 1975) doing anything different when he reduces "Heidegger's discourse" to a "variant" of "pro-
fessiorial discourse" and that, in turn, to the discourse of "the dominated portion
of the dominant class"?
18. *Le Nouvel Observateur*, interview of Nov. 2, 1984.

alität to a matter of calculating the monetary profits[19]—would be something to take seriously. The problem, however, is that a great number of texts contradict this idyllic interpretation, encouraging the impression that this sociology is less a break with the Marxist practice of reducing behaviors to the class interests that they are supposed to explain than merely a more subtle variant of the same practice.

On the one hand, the field of intellectual production is defined as a group of *relations of force*. Thus we read that "the sociology of science rests on the assumption that the truth of the product—even this very specific product that scientific truth represents—resides in a particular species of *the social conditions of production;* that is, in a particular state of the structure and functioning of the social field. The 'pure' world of the purest science is a *social field like any other*, with its relations of force and its monopolies, its struggles and its strategies."[20] In other words, scientific practice or, more generally, intellectual practice has no autonomy vis-à-vis the power relationships that define that structure of the global social field and therefore no specificity for the field of intellectual production, which is merely a "social field like any other," that is, a group of power relations. As a result, when Bourdieu, in his last writings (notably in *Sens pratique*), is delighted to take up problematics that are strictly Kantian (for example, the conditions of possibility of scientific experimentation and the limits of scholarly understanding),[21] it hardly needs to be pointed out by us that the critical enterprise being approached in this way is not so much related to the critical philosophy of Kant as it is to the critical theory of the first Frankfurt school: As it was for Horkheimer, it is a matter of illuminating the "*social* conditions of possibility" of scientific knowledge by relating it to power relations that structure the whole field of activity.

On the other hand, these power relations underlying the entire social field are described in the following terms:

19. Cf., for example, *Le Sens pratique*, p. 85, and p. 34 on the reference to Weber.
20. "Le Champ scientifique," *Actes*, June 1976.
21. Cf., for example, *Le Sens pratique*, pp. 46–47.

Each of the states of the social world is merely a provisional equilibrium, a moment in the dynamic when the adjustment between distributions and incorporated or institutionalized classifications is endlessly broken up and restored.

Before going on, let us interrupt our reading for a moment to clarify a deliberately sibylline term. We can understand the preceding assertion only if we know that Bourdieu is attempting to transpose a basic Marxist thesis, which affirms that every state of the society corresponds to an equilibrium, an adaptive relation between the degree of development of the forces of production and relations of production as the truth about class relations: By analogy, social equilibrium here is described as a state of adaptation between the actual distribution of property and symbolic capital,[22] and the way individuals are classed and class themselves according to this distribution and, most importantly, according to the representations of it they create. Bourdieu displaces to a considerable extent, at one level, the terms of the correspondence or of the adaptation where the social equilibrium is established. However, relations between social groups (relations between classes) still remain *property relations:* The social order is nothing other than "the addition of classifying and classified judgments by which agents classify and are classified,"[23] depending on how they represent the distribution of property. Bourdieu indeed emphasizes, against the "economist side of Marxist theory,"[24] that today we can no longer depend on an objectivist definition of property (that is, on an idea of property that owes nothing to the representations of it that agents create) and that therefore we have to integrate the possession of "symbolic property" into property relations. Nevertheless, for him symbolic property is basically only "material property perceived as property that distinguishes." The basis of social classification is still found in the (objective and subjective) consideration of material property. The

22. Recall here that by "symbolic capital" Bourdieu means material property *when it is perceived and appropriated as a mark of distinction* (membership in a certain golf club, etc.).
23. *Le Sens pratique*, p. 234.
24. Ibid.

description of each state of the social world as an equilibrium between distributions and classifications (of property) is then clear: Beyond the vocabulary, a banal theme of the Marxist Vulgate is being reaffirmed. We can return now to our reading of the passage:

> The struggle that is at the very origins of distribution is simultaneously a struggle for the appropriation of scarce goods and a struggle to impose a legitimation of the power relations manifested through distribution; through its effectiveness, this representation can contribute either to the perpetuation or to the subversion of these power relations.

Two remarks will again demonstrate the considerable banality of the observation: Bourdieu explicitly returns to the theme of class struggle with the additional qualification that this struggle is also a struggle for the appropriation and valorization of symbolic property; in addition, the notion of the reciprocal impact of ideological superstructures on economic infrastructures is also taken up again. The following lines attempt to confirm the latter point by using the example of the debate between sociologists on whether social classes in fact exist:

> Classifications and the very notion of social class could not be so decisively important for the (class)[25] struggle if they did not contribute to the existence of social classes by adding to the effectiveness of the objective mechanisms that determine distributions and guarantee reproduction, the reinforcement contributed by the agreement among the minds they structure.[26]

In the course of what seems to be a mere *dressing up* of Marxist discourse, the identification of class struggle as the ultimate foundation of all social practice—including intellectual and scientific practice—is entirely reaffirmed, with the information, which is nevertheless important, that the debate about the real existence and the division of social classes serves those who benefit from the class struggle, that is, a dominant class that reinforces and reproduces its

25. The parentheses are Bourdieu's, of course.
26. This text appears on p. 244 of *Le Sens pratique*.

domination in this way. It is clear that the triviality of this observation makes the sophistication of the discourse even more necessary.

Let us summarize: On the one hand, Bourdieu maintains that the field of intellectual production is a group of power relations; on the other hand, he demonstrates that these power relations have to be interpreted as class struggles for the appropriation of capital (material and symbolic). Thus, when an interview in the *Nouvel Observateur* represents the "specific interests of intellectuals" as "entirely irreducible to class interests revealed by crude Marxist artillery," one has to admire the cleverness but must carefully avoid misunderstanding: Bourdieu cannot seriously mean to say that the interests of intellectuals are not class interests; the entire analysis we have focused on here challenges this autonomization of intellectual activity.[27]

The sentence can be understood only in this way: that in the Marxist tradition class interest has too often been defined *without mediation, directly or brutally,* as the basis of intellectual production. This type of reference to class interests has been criticized by

---

27. As evidence, if indeed any is still required, we cite Bourdieu's explanation, in *Le Sens pratique,* of his own superiority as an agent in the field of intellectual production due to his specific social position. We refer to two unforgettable passages: In the first (p. 30), Bourdieu suggests that, if he is better able than others to understand the social conditions of the scholar's relations with the world (relations characterized by an "objectivizing distance"), it is because he is a "mountain peasant" and as such had "a greater awareness" of the problems posed by a distance from the object; later (p. 37), we learn that in order to elaborate a theory of objectivation one must "produce a theory of what it means to be a native," the native being one who, trapped in the object, understands it in an immediate way, but with no distance from it, therefore blindly. To understand the process of establishing a distance, which is characteristic of the scholar's relations to the object, the (practical) relations of blind proximity are taken as the starting point and an attempt is made to discover the stages one must pass through in order to overcome it. Bourdieu suggests that this theory of the native "cannot be developed through theoretical experience alone"; that is, one must have been a native oneself, one must have lived these practical relations to the world, one must not have benefited from the "distance from need" that is the prerogative of a bourgeois existence—so that one is compelled to pose the problems of objectivation in all their sharpness. The moral of the story is clear: Unless one has been a mountain peasant, preferably socially indigenous, one is in grave danger of becoming a bad sociologist.

Bourdieu in his article on Heidegger, for example. He understands
quite well that reducing Heidegger's philosophy of ontological difference to the class interests of the German petite bourgeoisie of the
period between the two wars is an attack on the Marxist-inspired
interpretations that have already developed such an analysis: He
criticizes Adorno in this way[28] for not having elucidated the "al-
chemy" that transforms a given social interest ("expressive interest") into its sublime forms. In other words, the preceding genealo-
gies of philosophical discourse were right in principle, but they
practiced a simplistic "short-circuiting" between the interest and
the sublimating discourse without explaining the modalities of the
sublimation and for that reason could not be complete, "taking account of the internal logic of the work." The entire essay devoted to
Heidegger attempts to fill this explanatory gap by showing that social interest and its sublimated version are separated by the "field of
possible philosophical positions assumed"—a philosophical field,
meaning that in any given period the philosophically acceptable or
"legitimate" problematics are not infinite and that no interest can be
expressed in discourse permitted by the "spirit of the times" unless
it flows into them. By crossing this field of the possible, expressive
interest finds its way to sublimation, the forms of sublimation being
no more undetermined than the interest itself.[29]

So it is in a very precise, *and also very restrictive*, sense that the
heavy Marxist artillery still misses its object, since its reductionism
is not disputed but only its vulgar practice of "short-circuiting." The
genealogical method, then, only needs improving, needs complicat-
ing, needs to be made less massive and, if possible, less vulgar—
but does not need to be called into question again as such. Bourdieu's position still explicitly calls for a "generalized materialism,"
which, it is true, he defines by bringing together both Marx and
Weber.[30]

Nor should Bourdieu's sociology actually appear to be a *distin-*

28. Bourdieu has *Jargon der Eigentlichkeit* in mind.
29. Bourdieu, "L'Ontologie politique de M. Heidegger," *Actes*. We have analyzed
this article (and its difficulties) at greater length in "Heidegger en question"
(1978), republished in our *Système et critique*, Ousia, 1985.
30. *Le Sens pratique*, p. 34.

guished version of vulgar Marxism.[31] It is a form of denied Marxism, and as such it constitutes one of the components of '68 philosophy, with which it shares the themes of the end of philosophy or the death of the subject through an exaggeration of genealogical practice. This is also how this approach, where the primary strategy was to confuse its own identity—not without a degree of success, in fact—can now, having been returned to its own domain, become the object of a critical examination.

A Popperian Critique of Bourdieu

This critical analysis could be focused on the assimilation of objectivity to a process of objectivizing social determinants, an important theme for Bourdieu, which he theorized most notably in book 1 of his *Sens pratique.*

To understand the basis of this critique, we must recall how Popper defines scientificity and scientific objectivity through reference to the criteria of *falsifiability.*[32] We limit ourselves here to a very short summary.

Essentially, Popper's definition of scientificity relies on a critique of the consequences that Hume believed could be derived from his analysis of reasoning by induction. As we know, Hume's skepticism rests entirely on the idea that science always proceeds by induction, that is, by reasoning consisting of the derivation of a general rule through the observation of specific facts or, more precisely, from observing the repetition of specific sequences. One may deduce Hume's fundamental skepticism from the following syllogism:

Science always proceeds by induction.

Induction never leads to certainties; strictly speaking, the generalization of the observation is always an abuse and thus is always only a form of belief.

---

31. Here we are borrowing the expression from P. Raynaud, "Le Sociologue contre le droit," *Esprit*, March 1980.
32. Cf. particularly Karl Popper, *The Logic of Scientific Discovery*, Harper, New York, 1965, chap. 4.

Thus science never attains absolute certainty, never leaves the domain of belief. In terms of a conclusion leading to *psychologism*, science is one prejudice among others, or even one feeling among others (precisely that of *belief*).

We know what Popper's position on this reasoning is: If Hume (as Kant had recognized) is right in thinking that reason by induction never leads to certain and positive truths, he is wrong, on the other hand, to conclude from this that science fails to achieve its intentions, since—and this of course is the essential aspect of Popper's epistemology—the aim of science is not to arrive at certain and positive truths. Science aims not to verify hypotheses but to try to falsify them. This redefinition of the scientific method is explained with a simple example: Although 100 thousand white swans cannot verify the proposition "All swans are white," a single black swan can prove conclusively that it is false. As a result, scientific certitudes depend only on errors, not on truths. From this derives the first and fundamental criterion for the scientificity of a discourse: its falsifiability (the possibility that it is contradicted by the facts) and not its verifiability.

In *Conjectures and Refutations*, Popper recounts a famous anecdote in this connection. In 1919, as he tells it, he was interested in Marxism and psychoanalysis, on the one hand, and in Einstein's physics on the other, but he came to see a basic difference between the two types of discourse:

Marxism and psychoanalysis are *"verificationist."* They are non-falsifiable theories in the sense that no phenomenon of the real world can ever contradict them or, even more, in that a given phenomenon as well as its exact opposite can be said to verify the theory. So it is, for example, with one of the cardinal statements of Marxism, that the socialist revolution will occur when the forces of production have achieved their maximal development. At first glance it seems falsifiable and even appears to have been in fact falsified by the Russian Revolution. But thanks to Lenin's ingenuity and to his having invented the theory of the weakest link, Marxism was immunized against reality and became nonfalsifiable.

Were the revolution to happen in Japan or in Sahel, the theory
could just as easily adjust to it.

On the other hand, Einstein *risks* his entire theory on *a single experiment* (the Eddington expedition), emphasizing explicitly that if
the experiment resulted in a contradiction of his theses he would
have to rethink them fundamentally.

On one side—where Popper places metaphysics, Marxism,
and psychoanalysis as well as astrology—there is a nonfalsifiable
discourse; on the other, there is scientific discourse, which, excluding certain possibilities of the real world, exposes itself to being
disproven.

In the light of Popper's argumentation, three criticisms of
Bourdieu's work seem possible:

1. *The discourse produced is essentially (as far as its fundamental theses are concerned), nonfalsifiable.* If we recall the theses
defended in *Reproduction*, for example, we find the idea that the
school system, which is characterized by its role in social selection,
is reproduced, *no matter what the participants' attitude*, the participants in this case being merely the unconscious, blind toys of the
system.[33] On this basis, no effort on the part of any protagonist can,
by definition, succeed in disproving the interpretation. Let us take
the example of the problem of "official channels":

> If a minister were to attempt to initiate official channels for orienta-
> tion in the secondary education system, the openness of the desire
> to make social selections would be obvious since the existence of
> official channels would mean that the destiny of the children was
> fixed forever by a process that would certainly not be neutral.

> Conversely, if this same minister were to close these channels
> down, we would see an intention to liberate free market competi-
> tion, which, as we know, always favor those who benefit from the
> greatest symbolic capital.

Unable to be disproven by any empirical reality, Bourdieu's
discourse obeys only its own logic, to which he has always already

33. We have seen, above, the theoretical basis of this thesis.

submitted the facts *a priori*. In fact, it has the structure not of a science, which it claims to be, but of an ideology, in Arendt's meaning when she defines it as "the logic of an idea."[34]

2. *This discourse rejects on principle any disagreement*, for two very clear reasons: It is not debatable, first of all, simply because it is nonfalsifiable: How can a discourse that can never be contradicted be debated? Bourdieu's discourse cannot be disputed any more than can the discourse of a dogmatic theologian: In the same way that a person who tries to demonstrate to the theologian that God does not exist finds that he cannot prove it, we do not see how it could be demonstrated that reproduction does not exist. This primary exclusion of debate itself poses a number of problems: The obverse of the *scientific* weakness of this type of discourse could well be a very great, very disturbing *political* strength, since a nondebatable proposition in its irrefutability always exercises a degree of terrorism.

Bourdieu's discourse forbids any disagreement with it for another, deeper reason: It is a discourse that considers objections to it to be only *resistances* in the analytic sense of the term and therefore supplementary confirmations of its truth. The work is supposed to lead to "terrifying" consequences for people who discover the strategies and calculations of interests through it, so any disagreement with its results guarantees *ipso facto* their confirmation, while simultaneously disqualifying itself. In fact, not only is an objection unable to disturb the theory (since the theory has been made nonfalsifiable), but any objection is exposed to being dismantled by genealogical analysis that depends on the interest that gives it its strength, and which is not an interest in the truth, we suspect. Faced with a question that expresses a reservation, he will never ask *What do you mean?* but only *Who are you to direct this critique of the theory?* The content of the objection can never be addressed, never discussed: Disagreement disappears in the face of identifying the adversary.

In Bourdieu, the elimination of disagreement becomes an

---

34. H. Arendt, *The Origins of Totalitarianism*, Harcourt Brace, New York, 1951, last section.

obsession with endlessly anticipating bad readers and denouncing beforehand any future objection, while knowing that these resistances can do nothing but be revealed, given the nature of the interests in play. For example: "You know, when I write I fear many things, that is, many bad readers. . . . I try to discourage bad readings beforehand as I have often been able to ancitipate them. But the defenses that I slip into a parenthesis, an adjective, quotation marks, etc., affect only the ones who don't need it."[35] An odd admission: having excluded from the beginning the possibility of any internal criticism of his discourse, the sociologist can depend only on the faithful, on his "believers," on those who in any case do not need the defenses—a strangely restrictive conception of scientific intersubjectivity, one must admit.

3. *This type of "scientific" approach ultimately depends, according to Popper, on an absurd, intellectually terroristic conception of objectivity.* Popper's analyses reveal two theories of objectivity to be equally erroneous:

> The so-called bourgeois theory that depends on the myth of scientific impartiality and neutrality: this is an illusion since the scholar can always be called "interested," and it is difficult to see how one could imagine any scientist whose work was not supported by "interests," unless one imagines a pure transcendental subject.

> The Marxist theory of objectivity (perfectly illustrated by Bourdieu's discourse) returns in one way, without realizing it, to defining objectivity as impartiality. Objectivity—and this is the focus of book 1 of *Sens pratique*—is defined as a process of objectivization that consists (according to a model already used by Critical Theory) of objectivizing the social determinants and historical interests pertaining to the scholar. To some extent it pertains to the practice of a social psychoanalysis where the scientific, in order to become objective, becomes aware of the interests and socioeconomic determinations that condition and enliven it, without its knowledge. While objectivity is transformed into a process, the ideal of this objectivity fundamentally assuming self-*mastery* by controlling its

35. Interview in *Libération*, Nov. 4, 1979.

social interests and the *consciousness* of its determinants is preserved.

Following Popper, who often ridiculed this falsely clever attitude (in reality so naive), we offer two criticisms of this definition of objectivity: First, it is an *absurd definition*. Given that the interests in question can in principle always be unconscious and therefore escape us, this conception of objectivity necessarily engenders skepticism (or it should if we are intellectually rigorous). It is clear that one can never be sure of having mastered his individual or social unconscious, by definition. But, more importantly, this work, which is no doubt useful on the personal level (no one would dream of denying it), is totally useless *on the truly scientific level:* What is important here is not who speaks and why but only whether the discourse produced is falsifiable (thus debatable) or not. In other words, the objectivity of science does not depend on how it is produced or its conditions of production; it depends on the conditions for its being effectively debated by a subject who is an interlocutor and who can be recognized as such. This possibility is in principle excluded from the materialist epistemology that is Bourdieu's, and the true scientific figure of objectivity can only remain entirely foreign to the discourse practiced. We can measure the specificity of this conception of "science" by confronting Bourdieu's text, quoted above, with Popper's direct appeal for dialogue:

> If you were to ask me: How do you know? What is the source or basis of your information? . . . I would answer: I do not know; my statement was merely a conjecture. No matter the source or sources it may have come from—there are many possibilities and I may not be aware of them all: questions of origin or of genealogy in any case have little to do with questions of truth. But if the problem I have tried to resolve through my hypothesis interests you, you can help me by criticizing it as severely as you can, and if you can design an experiment which you think could refute it, I would gladly help you.[36]

36. K. R. Popper, *Conjectures and Refutations*, London, 1969, p. 27.

Second, *the definition of objectivity as a process of objectivation again manifests the intellectually terrorist character of this method.* If in listening to and judging the objectivity of the discourse of others, the actual identity of the person upholding the discourse has to be accounted for (in Bourdieu, in Foucault, and elsewhere), how far do we have to go to discover (to make him reveal) this identity? Is it enough to discover the existence of symbolic capital in him or to reveal his class position? Do we also have to unmask his political opinions or his religious convictions? And why not also question his ethnic origins? In short, where exactly is the boundary that genealogy will not cross in its desire to disqualify *a priori* the discourse of others? In what way, for example, is it more legitimate to judge the discourse of others as a function of class position rather than ethnic origin? We can see here precisely how the very idea of this attitude is *intrinsically terrorist*, if we understand, parodying A. Besançon, that "pseudoclass" has no more scientific value than the "pseudorace" and that in this situation the "pseudo" counts more than the "race" or the "class."[37]

Obviously, the meaning of this last criticism, which in a Popperian framework can be applied to Bourdieu's work, should not be misunderstood. We do not mean to imply that Bourdieu's discourse is a "racist" discourse. Nevertheless, it is true that certain forms of *zdanovism*—for example, the talk against "philosophers," regarded as undifferentiated and interchangeable representatives of a homogeneous category (we know the terms used)—in particular historical circumstances are not entirely exempt from danger either: A general category is always disqualified in the name of a pseudoscience that first attacks the man and only then the ideas.

Toward a Criticist Critique of Sociologism

The critique inspired by Popper can be usefully complemented and reinforced through an analysis more directly inscribed within

---

37. Cf. "Des difficultés de définir le régime soviétique," in *Passé russe et présent soviétique*, Livre de poche, "Pluriel."

the framework of criticism. Such an analysis could demonstrate easily the total absence in Bourdieu's sociological discourse of the kind of *self-reflection* which, when criticized, is the most effective antidote to dogmatism, and rightly so.[38] More simply stated: the characteristic of all dogmatic discourse is that it is of no value even to the person who holds it, its content inapplicable to its author.

Here, at least at one level, is the objection Habermas addressed in *Knowledge and Interest* to the first Critical Theory, that is, to historical materialism in all its forms, including the most refined. However simple it may be, this objection is a powerful one and has consequences of considerable importance. It merits a precise formulation.

According to the theses of materialist epistemology, all discourses are historical and express historically determined interests. The distinction between traditional theory, which attempts to be autonomous from history, and critical theory, which is considered to be totally immersed in history, is founded on this simple statement. Of course, Bourdieu adopts the affirmation of the historicity of all discourse, as the following text, among others, reveals: "The sociology of science rests on the claim that the truth of the product—even the very specific product of scientific truth—is contained in a particular species of social conditions of production or, more precisely, in a determined state of the structure and functioning of the scientific field. The 'pure' universe of the 'purest' science is a social field like any other."[39]

Here it is clearly stated (1) that discourses, including scientific discourses, are products and (2) that therefore they are immersed in sociohistorical reality.

This conviction leads to a real contradiction:

> Either the sociology of science, like all other discourses and in conformity with its own presuppositions, is itself entirely historical, in which case the problem of defining the "break" between ideology and science (between traditional theory and critical the-

38. The model for this critique is provided by Fichte's refutation of Spinoza in *Principles of the Doctrine of Science* (1794).
39. *Actes*, June 1976, p. 89.

ory) does indeed appear to remain insoluble; from this perspective, no discourse is ever privileged in any way, and there exists only a battlefield where the different discourses gather and where the only criterion of validity is success or failure. In other words, if the sociology of knowledge as Bourdieu practices it is self-reflective and applies its theories to itself, it can only regard itself as one force among others in the middle of a battlefield where all considerations of the truth are excluded. Science, then, is not superior to ideology in any way, and the distinction between science and ideology becomes particularly problematical.

Or else, in order to avoid this difficult situation, the sociology of knowledge *decrees* an "epistemological break," declaring itself to be superior to ideology, and indeed superior to any other discourse, in a constitutive gesture of sociologism. It could then escape from the demand for self-reflection, since with this decree it would no longer have to apply its own criteria to itself: It then becomes dogmatic by giving itself an excessive and illegitimate privilege by its own standards.

In view of this contradiction, two solutions were considered: A perfectly defensible solution can be found in returning to the notion of "the pure interests of reason" as it was used by Kant in *Critique of Pure Reason*. Elaborating it, however, poses a number of problems. This perspective has the obvious advantage of preserving the notion of "the interests of science" without being vulnerable to the consequences of these interests being interpreted exclusively in terms of class. This is the direction Habermas took in *Knowledge and Interest*, by way of Kant and Fichte, which assumes, then, not the celebration of the death of philosophy but a renewal of philosophical activity in order that the status and function of "pure interests" be rigorously determined.

Bourdieu adopted another solution consisting not of resolving the problem but of declaring it insoluble by decreeing that it is an insurmountable contradiction which would be presented from then on as a rich tension, when it is in fact merely a gross contradiction within which, nevertheless, it is possible to play on all the registers, once the pill has been swallowed. This is an example of the type of assertion we used in our first chapter to illustrate the philosophists exaggerated taste for paradox: Bourdieu writes that, if the conditions of production of scientific truths have to be analyzed, it is "in the name of the conviction, which itself is a product of a history, that the reason for the paradoxical progress of a reason that is historical through and through and yet irreducible to history has to be looked for in history."[40] It is not difficult to see that this time the hoax consists of presenting as a solution what is in fact an enormous problem, given that the notion of an entirely historical reason that is irreducible to history, at first glance and at second, makes absolutely no sense.

It goes without saying that Bourdieu, like everyone else, in fact finds himself forced to distinguish between the ahistorical interest in the truth and the historical interests that feed strategies for acquiring power (including, it goes without saying, intellectual power). He simply goes endlessly on attributing pure interests to himself, both naively and foolishly, and reserving historicostrategic interests for others. Let us return to the interview in the *Nouvel Observateur* on the occasion of the publication of *Homo Academicus:* If Bourdieu is always angry with philosophers, he says, it is because they regard themselves as "the cleverest defenders of intellectual narcissism," because "these people who talk endlessly about radical doubt, about critical activity, about deconstruction, . . . always omit doubting the belief that leads them to accepting this position of doubt, . . . this prejudice about the absence of prejudice that confirms its distinction with respect to common sense." In other words, it is philosophy that is characterized by an absence of self-reflection. Let us admit it (even if we cannot see how this definition can be applied to the whole of philosophy, from Parmenides to Nietzsche), but then we could legitimately wait for Bourdieu himself to begin practicing the self-reflection of which philosophers are congenitally incapable. However, let us read the rest of the interview. There Bourdieu explains that professors might greatly profit from the assiduous reading of his works, if they would consent, of course, to doing their self-analysis (here their socioanalysis) and to

40. Ibid., p. 88.

becoming aware of the unacknowledged interests supporting them. The interviewer asks if they really have an "interest" in it, and the sociologist answers with stunning dogmatism: "From my point of view, which is *that of genuine scientific gain*, I am sure that they would. I would even say that they could derive a great ethical advantage from such a socioanalysis."

A simple question: What exceptional status does Bourdieu give his own thought since it and *it alone*, pure and disinterested, corresponds to the "point of view . . . of genuine scientific gain" and not to a point of view determined by an unacknowledged socially and historically situated interest, like everyone else's thought?

Throughout Bourdieu's texts, one can readily find an indefinite number of indications of such an absence of self-reflection that are difficult to ignore (*let us be very clear; we do not deny that Bourdieu questions himself on the conditions of possibility of his own discourse, but since he looks for them only in the "objective" world of social determinants, it is less like self-reflection than, if we can put it this way, self-reification*). Thus, for example, in the case of the use of quotation marks in scientific discourse, an insignificant detail no doubt, but a detail that Bourdieu himself seems particularly attracted to:

> From Heidegger speaking of the "masses" and the "students" in the highly euphemistic language of the "authentic" and the "inauthentic" to American *politologues* reproducing the official vision of the social world in the semiabstractions of a descriptive-normative discourse, the same strategy of *a false break* always defines *scholarly jargon* as opposed to scientific language. Whereas scientific language uses quotation marks, as Bachelard observes, to indicate that words from ordinary language or from a prior scientific language are being completely redefined . . . , scholarly language uses quotation marks and neologisms only for symbolically demonstrating a distance and a fictional break from common sense."[41]

Thus there is also a good and a bad use of quotation marks, one marking a true epistemological break from common sense and the

41. "Le Champ scientifique," ibid., pp. 100–1.

other a false break. The fact by itself seems plausible. But in this situation can one authorize only oneself to establish the criterion for such a "distinction"? In an interview given in November 1979 to *Libération*, Bourdieu denounces the discourse of the ecology movement for being "full of scornful references" to "subway–work–sleep" and to the vacations that the "ordinary petit bourgeois" take like "sheep," while he serenely explains in parentheses: "Quotation marks have to be used everywhere. It is very important—not to indicate the prudent distance of official journalism but to signify the gap between analytical language and ordinary language, where all these words are instruments of struggle, arms, stakes in the battle for distinction." Yes, but will he ever tell us the exact nature of the "distinction" separating the "distance" from the "gap"? The answer that science manages to advance without paying any attention to these subtleties would mean—which might have been preferable under the circumstances—that the sociology of knowledge might have done better to stay away from any epistemological considerations, since it is ultimately proving to be quite simply incapable of resolving the most minimal question in all epistemology, the question of the difference between science and the ideology of common consciousness.

The Confrontation with Kant

It is understandable in view of the foregoing why a confrontation with Kant must have seemed to Bourdieu like an unavoidable move. Was not his primary concern addressing the analysis of the conditions of possibility of discourse from the sociological perspective, as the modest subtitle of *Distinction* indicates: *A Social Critique of the Judgment of Taste?*

The few pages devoted to the *Critique of Judgment* deserve analysis on this decisive point in their own right, so well do they demonstrate the purely sophistic nature of the intellectual pottering on which they are based. Here is what he says in what passes for an introduction to a deconstruction that is described as severe and rigorous:

It is no accident that, when one sets about reconstructing its logic, the popular "aesthetic" appears as the negative opposite of the Kantian aesthetic and that the popular *ethos* implicitly answers each proposition of the "Analytic of the Beautiful" with a thesis contradicting it.[42]

At first glance, however, it is difficult to grasp exactly how obvious it is that popular taste is the opposite of Kant's valorization of, for example, the "beautiful natural countryside," or even his critique of intellectualizing in artistic matters. No doubt the statistics indicate to Bourdieu that the working masses hurry to concerts of serial music and that avant-garde intellectuals visit Niagara Falls. But, be that as it may, let us look at his demonstration aimed at refuting two central themes of the *Critique,* according to which (1) the beautiful is not the agreeable and (2) the beautiful is the beautiful representation of a thing and not the representation of a beautiful thing.

The *Critique of Judgment* is entirely concerned with the idea (and it is still difficult to see what it has to with "the antipopular") that the beautiful is neither agreeable nor true and that between the two terms there exists a specific feature of the aesthetic dimension. Moreover, reason can very briefly sketch it out since it coincides with common sense, unlike what Bourdieu asserts. In Kant's view, the indisputable sign that the Beautiful cannot be confused with, for example, culinary art is that, contrary to the well-known adage, one never stops *arguing about* the Beautiful. The Beautiful is an object of communication, even of interpretation (in the musical sense of the term), which is the case to a lesser extent with the agreeable, we must add: We do not often try to convince someone who prefers tea to coffee that he is missing some essential dimension and that his choice reveals an unfortunate lack of taste! Nor is the Beautiful the true, however: If we argue about it, we do so with the feeling that our disagreement cannot be resolved by demonstration, as a scientific dispute might be, at least in principle.

42. On this entire discussion, cf. *Distinction,* trans. Richard Nice, Harvard University Press, Cambridge, Mass., 1984, pp. 41 ff.

It is not important here, however, that Kant seems to be saying something essential when he places the aesthetic at an equal distance from the true and the agreeable. What we have to understand is: How can it be claimed that this analysis is the polar opposite of popular aesthetics, prototypical of the aesthetics of the dominant class?

This is Bourdieu's argument: Contrary to the Kantian distinction between the beautiful and the agreeable, "working-class people, who expect every image to fulfill a *function*, if only that of a sign, refer, often explicitly, to norms of morality or agreeableness in all their judgments."[43] The strength of the reasoning is simple: What Bourdieu wants to demonstrate is that "for the people" there is no pure aesthetics and that what finally counts is the content of the representation and not the representation itself—in short, that they do not differentiate the beautiful from either the agreeable or from the representation of the thing.

This statement seems to us gratuitous, false, and incredibly contemptuous. But the most incredible thing is the example Bourdieu evokes to support his "demonstration." For—and a reader of the third *Critique* could never have dreamed of it—the example is that of photography![44] As far as we know, the problem of photography is not a central one in Kant's work. Even if we were to assume a thing that is already hypothetical and, to tell the truth, quite pretentious, that we could speak, as Bourdieu does, of Kant's position on a subject he never addressed, and for good reason, the example of photography would be particularly badly chosen for two obvious reasons: first, because Kant's aesthetic is above all an aesthetic of natural beauty (Hegel reproached him for it often enough); and also because Kant never allows, in his opposition to classical French aesthetics, anything into the aesthetic domain that could be assimilated as a form of *imitation* in any way (which is why he claims to prefer baroque art and English gardens to the geometric art of French-style gardens). But that is not all. Not satisfied with choos-

43. Ibid., p. 41.
44. Bourdieu also uses the example of cubism, of which Kant was a great theoretician, as we know!

ing photography as his example for refuting Kant, Bourdieu's argument becomes frankly comic when he decides to discuss only two types of photographs: nudes and war photographs of violent death. In other words, *Playboy* and *Paris Match* are models of art for the third *Critique*. Under these conditions the reader has no choice but to follow Bourdieu: In fact, the thesis that the representation of the thing counts more than the thing itself fails here: "Photographs of nudes are almost always received with comments that reduce them to the stereotype of their social function: 'All right for Pigalle,' 'it's the sort of photos they keep under the counter.' "[45] Similarly, "the photograph of a dead soldier provokes judgments that, whether positive or negative, are always responses to the reality of the thing represented."

We have only two comments: We do not see how a reaction that shows an interest in the content of these photographs can be called the exclusive prerogative of "popular aesthetics." In the reactions to such images on the part of high school students, executives, or nuns of any social class, one can bet that the contents of the representation would be more important than the form. As a sociologist of publishing, Bourdieu really should know that the large number of magazines devoted specifically to photography are in fact competitors of *Lui* or *Playboy* that are simply easier to buy and read in public and that the sometimes considerable price that is paid for war photographs published in the sensationalist press has very little to do with their aesthetic value, if there is one.

On the other hand, and keeping in mind the reservations we made above, it is quite probable that precisely for these reasons Kant would not have considered these photographs to be works of art since it is so difficult to separate the representation of the thing from the thing represented. Kant's thesis is clear enough not to be deformed here, however: It states simply that a painting may be beautiful even if it represents garbage, which is why we cannot see how it challenges the taste of the popular classes, classes Bourdieu obstinately decides to treat like dumb animals.

In order to refute the *Critique of Judgment* sociologically,

45. *Distinction*, p. 42.

which in principle is not a scandalous or impossible goal, it would have been necessary—this is a minimal requirement—to test its theses rather than set up examples of "arts" in opposition to it that (1) it quite simply has no knowledge of and that (2) it would probably have rejected as art. It has simply not been demonstrated that privileging natural beauty over artistic beauty, distinguishing between the beautiful and the agreeable, the beautiful and the true, and so on, is "antipopular." Moreover, these are all things that Bourdieu is no doubt perfectly well aware of.

One question remains. After reading these aberrant criticisms of the Kantian aesthetic as prototype of the bourgeois aesthetic, we are interested, after all, in knowing something about the aesthetic judgments that Bourdieu himself, like anyone else, cannot avoid making. This is a difficult problem since the underlying principle of *Distinction* is that any aesthetic judgment or, more generally, any judgment of taste in the larger sense has to be regarded as a strategy of differentiation. To clarify, we may say that, if a bourgeois serves chitterlings, it is because he is acting "like the people" out of snobbery, a typically bourgeois attitude; and if he prefers to offer smoked salmon, the diagnosis is no longer in doubt (My God, but it's a sure thing!).[46] Under these conditions, how is it that Bourdieu has not died of hunger? A journalist from *Libération* once asked him—and this is a more serious example: "If all cultural practices, all classical tastes, have a defined place in the social space, then a counterculture has to be viewed as a differentiating activity like any other. . . . What, then, would a real counterculture be like?" Here is his unfortunately quite predictable answer: "I do not know if I can answer that question."[47]

46. We borrow this humorous note from the wonderful P. Raynaud.
47. *Libération*, Nov. 1979.

6 /
French Freudianism
(Lacan)

Lacanian psychoanalysis is at least modest enough that it has never claimed to have any merit other than being the most legitimate interpretation of Freud. It could be given various representations, numerous interpretations, but for two reasons we have chosen to focus our examination of Lacanianism exclusively on the theory of subjectivity. The first is the necessity of situating Lacanian philosophy with respect to the question of humanism, a question Lacan brings into the very center of his own theory of the subject. The other is more immediately related to the thing itself: Lacan expressly stated that the theory of the subject, particularly the opposition of "subject" and "ego," was the central axis around which Freud's thought had to be reconstructed: "Everything Freud wrote aimed at reestablishing a precise perspective on the subject's eccentricity in relation to the ego. I claim that this is the essential thing and that everything must be organized around it."[1]

Before addressing this theory of subjectivity and specifying the meaning of the "subject's eccentricity in relation to the ego" (an element, as we will see, in disqualifying humanism as the ideology of autonomy), we would like to situate our own perception of Lacan's reading of Freud by stating again[2] that it seems to us that interpretations of Freud, with respect to this question of the status of subjectivity, can be organized in terms of three different logics.

---

1. *Le Séminaire*, vol. 2, Ed. du Seuil, 1978, p. 60.
2. Cf. our interview with the journal *Esprit*, "Qu'est-ce qu'une critique de la raison?," *Esprit*, April 1982.

186

The Three Interpretations of Freud and the Question of the Subject

1. The Rationalist Interpretation (the Absolute Subject) This interpretation, which almost seems to be systematically hidden by the current, commonplace claim that Freud's philosophy is the philosophy of the irrational in man *par excellence*, is nevertheless the only one that permits the *whole body* of Freud's texts to be taken into account without fear of one day being contradicted (we will see why in a moment).

This interpretation is also the most obvious one, which only reinforces the paradox. In order to understand it, we only have to pay some attention to how Freud presents his theory of parapraxis as the intellectual matrix of his theory of dreams and neuroses, for example, in *The Introduction to Psychoanalysis* in the *Psychopathology of Everyday Life*. In keeping with a wholly Hegelian model that we have analyzed elsewhere,[3] Freud demonstrates that what is devoid of meaning, even inexplicable *in appearance*, can be shown to be completely meaningful *in reality* and *based on reason*, provided that the reality of unconscious psychic life is taken into account: "Certain insufficiencies in our psychic functioning . . . and certain acts that seem unintentional, are revealed to be entirely motivated and determined by reasons which are outside consciousness when we examine them psychoanalytically."[4] In other words, it seems that on this point Freud considered the principle of rationality (determinism) to be absolutely valid—and this is why we call this reading "Hegelian" or "rationalist"—since it reaches even into what seems to be rationality's *other* (lapses, dreams, madness, etc.) in such a way that the control of rationality can be applied (from the point of view of a hypothetical absolute subject) to *everything that exists*. In this sense, for Freud as much as for Hegel, "the real is rational," as the following text, among a thousand others we might have chosen, illustrates:

3. Cf. our *Système et critique*, Ousia, 1985.
4. *Psychopathologie de la vie quotidienne*, trans., Payot, p. 257 (*The Psychopathology of Everyday Life*, in *Basic Writings*, trans. A. A. Brill, Modern Library, New York, 1938). (Quotations are from the French edition.)

When one part of our psychic functions is left out, because it is
not amenable to explanation by representing the intended goal it
would reach, we fail to understand the scope of the determinism
that our psychic life is subject to.

In truth, it is a *total* scope, Freud continues, since the arbitrary does
not exist:

> For a long time I have known that it is impossible to think of a
> number or a name entirely arbitrarily. If we examine a number of
> several digits composed in an *apparently* arbitrary manner, for fun
> or out of vanity, it can be seen that *invariably* it is *rigorously deter-
> mined*, that it *can be explained by reasons* that would never have
> been considered possible in *reality*.[5]

In short: *nihil est sine ratione*. Such an interpretation, as we
have said, can never be contradicted on the basis of the texts of
Freud. This statement is shocking only if it is not understood. Let us
briefly explain why. Some may be tempted to regard these texts as
tangential to Freud's work (even though the examples can be multiplied almost indefinitely). They may then object, somewhat naively,
that other, non-"rationalist" texts (in the sense given here) do
indeed contradict the first with the result that Freud's philosophy
becomes "more complex" than the rationalist reading would indicate, penetrated as it then appears to be by contradictions and other
"rich" tensions. The proof is, of course, either that with his hypothesis of a dynamic unconscious Freud makes the Hegelian idea of an
absolute subject a permanent illusion, or else that accounting for
man's libidinal dimension causes the framework of the traditional
metaphysics of the *cogito* to break apart, and so on. These argu-
ments are in fact nonsense and can carry conviction only by means
of a simple blocking of thought: To maintain the Hegelian reading in
the face of these objections, all that is required is to recall that the
claim that reality is rational does not in any way mean that we, finite
beings, ever achieve absolute knowledge, a full understanding of
this rationality. There is no doubt that the hypothesis of the unconscious distances us even further from it. However, this does not

5. Ibid., p. 258.

change the fact that Freud did indeed postulate, at least in our opinion, the complete rationality of reality (the absolute validity of the principle of reason), the belief in chance or indeterminism for him being basically only a form of ignorance (in the best case) or, more often, a form of superstition (itself entirely explainable, moreover).

2. *The Nietzschean/Heideggerian Interpretation (the Split Subject)* In order not to be impossible, this second interpretation delivers a sharp blow to strict "philology." To state its basic principle simply, we will say that it consists of demonstrating that Freud's thought is a psychoanalytic version of the famous Nietzschean adage (we have seen that it supplied May '68 with one of its slogans): "There are no facts, only interpretations." If we return to the text of *Gay Knowledge* entitled "Our New Infinite," we can read (para. 374): "I hope, however, that today we are far from the ridiculous pretension that our own little corner is the only place where one has the right to a point of view. On the contrary, the world has become infinite for us once more in the sense that we cannot refuse to give it the possibility of infinite interpretations." Why? "Because in the course of analysis, man's mind always sees according to its own perspective and can see itself only in terms of itself. We can see only with our own eyes." Let there be no mistake: There is no question of Nietzsche's defending a flatly empiricist relativism. On the contrary, perspectivism depends on an implicit critique of Hegel's notion of absolute knowledge (subject), on the idea that all human value judgments are symptoms and that there is no metalanguage, no absolute truth on which interpretation founded in reason could be definitively based: "Judgments, value judgments about life, can never in the last instance be true; their only value is as symptoms, they should only be considered as symptoms, for in themselves such judgments are mere foolishness."[6] It is quite clear that Freudian psychoanalysis could be lost in this philosophical model; for that to happen, we only have to consider that the hypothesis of a dynamic unconscious makes the aim of a discourse closed upon itself, the aim of a subject

6. F. Nietzsche, *Twilight of the Idols*, trans. R. J. Hollingdale, Harmondsworth, Penguin Books, 1969, "The Problem of Socrates," para. 2.

perfectly transparent to itself, impossible forever, at least for man. In other words, the analyst does not possess absolute knowledge; his interpretations are themselves interpretations through another analyst, whose interpretations can in turn be interpreted, and so on infinitely. There are then no facts, only interpretations. Lacan, whose reading of Freud clearly has to be situated within this link to Nietzsche, wrote: "Now extended to the analyst's knowledge, the question derives its power from not allowing the answer that the analyst knows what he is doing, since there is the patent fact that he does not know, in theory and in technique."[7] The analyst must not give in to that illusion which consists of looking for "true explanations"; at most he must "locate" a "relevant interpretation."[8] If we call this reading of Freud both Nietzschean *and Heideggerian*, it is simply because Lacan explicitly depends on the Heideggerian concept of the truth as an "unveiling," as the idea that absolute knowledge is impossible and that, as Heidegger wrote, "the unveiling of being itself is simultaneously and in itself the hiding of being in its totality."[9] Any manifestation is carried out on a foundation of absence or invisibility.

3. The "Criticist" Interpretation (the Subject as Tension between the Finite and the Infinite)   This interpretation offers a critical solution to the paradox constructed by the first two *taken absolutely*. In our view, it corresponds to Freud's intention, if not literally to the texts, which would clearly agree with the first interpretation, as we have already said. From this perspective, the subject seems irremediably finite (thus destined endlessly to confront this obscurity we might well call the unconscious) but nevertheless *extended* toward that demand for autonomy that the illusion of an absolute, perfectly transparent, self-mastering subject both translates and betrays. Contrary to certain of Lacan's theses that we are going to examine, the intention of psychoanalysis according to Freud is indeed to return self-mastery to the *ego* as much as possible (that is,

7. J. Lacan, "Variantes de la cure-type," in *Ecrits*, Ed. du Seuil, 1966, p. 350.
8. Ibid., p. 353.
9. M. Heidegger, *Questions I*, Gallimard, p. 188 (*Vom Wesen der Wahrheit*, in *Collected Works*, vol. 9, p. 198).

never completely) and not the "subject," as this excerpt from the *Outline* shows: "The best we could do for him (the patient) is . . . to transform what had become unconscious, what had been repressed, into preconsciousness in order to return it to the Ego."[10]

It is important to understand which of these theses on subjectivity Lacan is employing to initiate his radical challenge to this conception—a conception which is, after all, "human" in that it is supported by the humanist ideal of autonomy—of the psychoanalytic cure.

The Status of Subjectivity: "The True Subject" versus "the Ego"

The Lacanian doctrine of subjectivity may not be as original and complex as has often been thought. In fact—apart from the question of Lacan's style, to which we will return—his comparative unintelligibility is due more to importing into another field philosophical models that are not made explicit[11] and are unknown to the majority of his disciples than to some indefinable intrinsic profundity. Using a genetic approach, we would like to recall the most important moments in this doctrine in order to demonstrate that many of the major theses responsible for the insertion of Lacan's philosophy into the very heart of the French antihumanism of the 1960s can be deduced from them.

A few quotations will serve as a guideline:

> Human knowledge, and at the same time the sphere of conscious relations, is made up of a certain relationship to this structure that we call the *ego*, around which the imaginary relation is centered. The latter has taught us that the *ego* is never merely the subject, which is essentially a relationship to the other. . . . All objects are seen from the point of view of this *ego*.

10. S. Freud, *Abrégé de psychanalyse*, trans., P.U.F., pp. 50–52 (*Outline of Psychoanalysis*, trans. James Strachey, Norton, New York, 1969). (Quotations are from the French edition.)

11. Moreover, this importing is clearly acknowledged, as for example in *Ecrits*, p. 240, referring to the "latest problems in philosophy, where psychoanalysis often only has to go claim its belongings."

But it is indeed the subject, an originally out-of-tune subject fundamentally cut up by this *ego*, that desires all objects. . . . And it is from the tension between the subject—which could not desire without being fundamentally separated from the object— and the *ego*, which is where the glance originates to go toward the object, that the dialectic of consciousness takes its departure.[12]

No doubt the true *I* is not the ego. But that is not enough. . . . The important thing is reciprocity, which must always be present to our minds—the ego is not the *I*, is not a mistake in the sense that classical doctrine makes it a partial truth. It is something else— . . . an object that fulfills a certain function that here we call the imaginary.[13]

The subject is posited as operative, as human, as *I* from the moment the symbolic system appears.[14]

The primary motifs of Lacan's conception of subjectivity are already apparent in these three quotations—excerpts from a seminar of 1954, at the time his style was still clear—what has to be called his university style. We will indicate from the start exactly what has to be understood from them:

The ego is associated with the dimension of the *imaginary*, whereas the subject proper is associated with the *symbolic*.

The subject is essentially *desire*; the ego is the *look*.

The ego is *reified*, literally even an object; the authentic subject is *schism* or *tension*.

Before examining the articulation of these motifs in Lacan's analysis of the transition from the mirror stage to the Oedipal stage, let us represent their meaning by translating it into the philosophical language of existentialism, to which they are clearly related. This thesis is well known as it was broadly developed by Sartre: The authentic subject is "nothingness" since it escapes any attempt to capture it in a definition. This is the freedom by which he distin-

12. *Séminaire*, vol. 2, pp. 209–210.
13. Ibid., p. 60.
14. Ibid., p. 68.

192

guishes himself from manufactured objects, which in order to exist had to be conceived, thus defined, from the start by the mind of an artisan. [15] If, therefore, objects are "something" (definite), the true, properly human subject is *nothing* determined, is *not* identifiable; in other words, he breaks with himself since he is always beyond everything that might define him, even in his own eyes. However— and here the possibility appears of the alienated and reified face of the ego as subject—man can give himself up to "bad faith," that is, accept being identified with a character, a role, in his relations with others. When he does this he stops being nothing (being neither here nor there); he becomes something (reification) and loses the freedom that is the basis of his humanity or, if you wish, of his authentic subjectivity. He becomes, by and for others, an image that he decides to *cling* to. In this way he suppresses the distance (the nothingness, the schism) he still maintained from that "round full-ness of being" that characterizes the man of bad faith, for whom the most unauthentic figure is the "bastard."

There is no doubt that Lacan invests in this opposition between Being and Nothingness in order to "get his money back." He fills it with the psychoanalytic dimension that had in fact been missing from existentialism. Philosophically armed, Lacanian psychoanaly-sis could posit itself as an antimetaphysical war machine and as anti-Hegelian, whatever Lacan's fascination with Hegel may be elsewhere:

> The ego we are discussing is absolutely impossible to distinguish
> from the imaginary inveiglings that constitute it from head to foot,
> in its genesis and in its status, in its function and in its actuality,
> by and for an other. In other words, the dialectic underlying our
> experience is to be found at the most enveloping level of the sub-
> ject's efficiency, obliging us to understand the ego from one end to
> the other in a progressive movement of alienation, where self-
> consciousness is located in Hegel's phenomenology."[16]

15. See, for example, the famous analysis of the paper cutter in *L'Existentialisme est un humanisme.*
16. *Ecrits*, p. 374.

Lacan is interested in describing the genesis of this quasi-Hegelian alienation of the ego through imaginary relations with the other from the mirror stage to the Oedipal stage. This is a decisive moment in Lacanian philosophy since it was to determine irrevocably the meaning of the cure (its signification and orientation): If the ego is alienation from true subjectivity, how could the goal of analysis be anything but the work of progressively undoing the ego's certainties in order for it to become a subject again? And, under these conditions, why refuse to define psychoanalysis as a humanism, as Lacan insists?[17]

The so-called mirror stage, which has been described so many times in similar terms,[18] denotes, as we know, that moment when the child acquires the feeling of his own body's unity through a process of identification associated with the functioning of the imaginary. In the early phase,[19] the child does not appear able to differentiate himself from others very well. Still centered as he is around imaginary relations, he takes himself for someone else, says he "has been hit" when he is hitting someone else, "cries" when he "sees someone fall," and so on. But in a second phase he gains a certain distance from the imaginary phase and soon succeeds in understanding that the image and the reality are different, and also that the image of himself that he sees in the mirror is indeed *his own*. This mirror stage is ultimately "formative for the functioning of the *I*," since it serves a structuring function with respect to the body, which was experienced before that as cut up and, more importantly, truly immature. More importantly, the experience undergone in the course of this phase prefigures the opposition between the subject and the ego that interests us here. In fact, Lacan writes, the mirror stage "seems to us to demonstrate in an exemplary situation the symbolic matrix where the *I* is precipitated in primitive form, before it is objectified in the dialectics of identification with the other, and

17. Cf., for example, *Séminaire*, vol. 2, pp. 87 ff.; "La Chose freudienne ou sens du retour à Freud en psychanalyse," in *Ecrits*, p. 401; etc.
18. Cf. particularly in *Ecrits*, pp. 93 ff.; "L'Agressivité en psychanalyse," ibid., pp. 401 ff.; "Propos sur la causalité psychique," ibid., pp. 180 ff.; etc.
19. "L'Agressivité en psychanalyse," ibid., p. 113.

before language restores its function as subject to it, in the universal."[20] So the idea is suggested that at its emergence subjectivity is immediately destined for alienation in the imaginary relationship with the other but that this relationship is suspended again, or at least somewhat disturbed, by the symbolic function of language, which "restores" some part of nonalienated subjectivity. An analysis of the Oedipal phase will allow us to clarify this structure further.

In a seminar of 1956–57 on the "formations of the Unconscious,"[21] Lacan proposed to distinguish three moments of the Oedipal phase. The first phase, which extends and completes the subject's alienation in the ego, can be described, as it is by Lacan, in the terms of the *Phenomenology of Mind:* As the dialectic of master to slave illustrates, desire can exist only when it is redoubled, when it becomes the desire of desire. Based on this model, Lacan describes the child in this first phase as "desire for the mother's desire." Desiring to *be* everything for her, he tries to identify himself with the *object* of the mother's desire or, in other words, the phallus. From this we can see that in this imaginary relationship (since it concerns identification with the supposed, or imagined, object of the other's desire) the child's subjectivity tends to be entirely *reified*, to be caught up in the problematics of being (and not of nothingness). Indeed, the answer to the question "to be or not to be the object of the mother's desire" stipulates that in order to please the mother "it is necessary and sufficient to *be* the phallus." At this stage the child "has no symbolic substitute for the ego, and as a result he is deprived of individuality, of subjectivity, and of a place in society: This is the phase of imaginary capture (identification with the mother through identification with the object of her desire) and the reign of primary narcissism."[22]

In the second phase of the Oedipal stage, the symbolic dimension and true subjectivity (nothingness, schism) are simultaneously introduced. In this respect the father is decisive: He intervenes both

20. Ibid., p. 94.
21. Unpublished seminar; a report can be found in the *Bulletin de Psychologie,* 1956–57.
22. A. Lemaire, *Jacques Lacan,* Brussels, 1977, p. 141.

to *frustrate* the child's desire for the mother and to *deprive* the mother of the phallic object represented by the child. He thus appears as the one who affixes his *law* to the mother's desire and the one whom, as a result, the child must suppose possesses the phallus. So "the close link between the mother's reference to a law that is not hers and the fact that the object of her desire is 'supremely' possessed in reality by this same 'other' whose law she refers to," provides "the key to the Oedipal relation."[23] In fact, the child, referred to this third term in the relations represented by the father, finally has to decide to emerge from the imaginary and reifying problematics of *being* (being the phallus in order to correspond to the mother's desire) in favor of the problematics of *having:* "Shaken in his certainty that he himself is the phallic object desired by the mother, the child is then forced by the paternal function into accepting not only that he is not the phallus but also that he does not even have one, in imitation of the mother whom he perceives as desiring it where it is supposed to be and where it then becomes possible to have it,"[24] that is, with the father.

This second Oedipal phase is obviously marked by the permanent appearance of the symbolic and of authentic subjectivity. The father in this triangular relationship is not in fact merely the "real" father but also the *symbolic father:* He only intervenes in the relationship invested with *meaning,* which arises from his seeming to possess the phallus; that is, he intervenes as the lawmaker to the mother's desire. In other words, "the father is not a real object . . . the father is a metaphor," that is, "a signifier that replaces another signifier."[25] Through this discovery of the symbolic and this transition from the problematics of being to those of having, the child becomes a subject too: Giving up (originary rejection) being the phallus, the *object* (and not the subject) that fulfills the mother, he can become the subject of his own desire, which is oriented toward an indefinite chain of substitutive objects (what Lacan calls "demand") from then on: "The operation necessitates the child's posit-

23. J. Lacan, *Les Formations de l'inconscient.*
24. J. Dor, *Introduction à la lecture de Lacan,* Denoël, 1985, p. 111.
25. Lacan, *Les Formations de l'inconscient.*

ing himself as a 'subject' and not merely as an 'object' of the desire of the other."[26]

The third Oedipal phase is, then, its resolution through this primal repression. The difference between Lacan and Freud is particularly notable here since this rejection proves to be beneficial by introducing both the symbolic and subjectivity. Irrevocably entered into the problematics of having (the phallus), the boy can identify with the father (it is clear why) and the girl with the mother, by imitating her since "she knows where it is, she knows where she has to go to get it, that is, to the father, to the one who has it."[27] We also know that one of the unfortunate results of the Oedipal phase can be the psychotic foreclosure of the symbolic dimension of the father so that in some way the child continues to identify with the phallus (to *be* the phallus), thus remaining a slave (in the imaginary relationship) to the mother's desire.[28]

In order to complete this theory of subjectivity, it still remains to be stated that the subject's emergence by way of the symbolic dimension is quite paradoxical since the subject is immediately exposed to a tripartite—and *inevitable*—alienation:

First, if it is the case that, by bringing about the primal repression that causes the child to move from the problematics of being to those of having, the name of the father is a metaphor for the desire of the mother, the child is destined never to be able to name his desire adequately: As we have suggested, he enters into an inextricable relationship with an indefinite series of substitutive objects, which are merely metonymic signifiers (a part designating the whole) for the original object, forever lost.

On the other hand, one can say that in a sense the subject, properly speaking, seems to be only an "effect of language" since, as we have seen, it really only appears with the rupture introduced through the symbolic dimension (the paternal metaphor) in the reifying and imaginary relationship to the mother's desire. This is the source of the well-known thesis stating that the subject is not the

26. Dor, *Introduction*, p. 116.
27. Lacan, *Les Formations de l'inconscient*.
28. Cf. on this point *Ecrits*, pp. 531 ff.

cause of language but its effect. [29] However, if it is true, as another of Lacan's preferred formulations asserts, that "the word is the murderer of the thing" and that "the thing must disappear in order to be represented," then, in this very way, in language the subject splits. The subject is only represented in discourse through a signifier, which is to say that the subject is immediately absent from it so that language simultaneously and indissolubly indicates both the birth and the death of the subject. If we can say that the Other denotes the symbolic, this paradox of subjectivity is clearly explained in these terms by Lacan: "The signifier being produced in the place of the (not yet located) Other gives rise to the subject of being which does not yet speak, but at the cost of being frozen. What was ready to speak there . . . disappears for being only a signifier."[30] This "fading" of the subject, as Lacan also calls it, can also be found (it is basically the same problem) in the notorious distinction between the subject of the *énoncé* and the *énonciation:* The subject of the *énoncé* (for example, the *I*) is the subject as it is represented in discourse; the subject of the *énonciation* is the subject of desire/subject of the unconscious that is alienated and lost the moment it is articulated in language. This splitting or cleaving (*Spaltung*) of the subject irrevocably proves to be both its possibility condition and its impossibility condition. Where we rediscover, as we were suggesting, the idea that the subject is nothingness, a tension between two imperceptible moments of the self.

At this point we can locate the third, equally inevitable, alienation to which the paradoxical emergence of subjectivity is exposed. Endlessly deformed in the subject of the *énoncé* and betrayed by it (but is there "something" deformable and betrayable that preexists it?), the true subject can ultimately only perish in the ego, which can now be defined as a recollection, in the course of the imaginary relationships of identification with the other, of the different events of the subject of the *énoncé*. "Thus the ego is always only half the subject,"[31] whereby we come once again to the Sar-

---

29. See esp. "Position de l'inconscient," in *Ecrits*, pp. 835 ff.
30. Ibid., p. 840.
31. Ibid., p. 346.

trean idea of a bad faith which is constitutive of the ego, with this difference, that here in Lacan this "bad faith" really ceases to be bad faith in order to appear instead as an inescapable destiny of subjectivity.[32]

Effects of the Splitting of the Subject: Lacan's Antihumanism

If the subject is radically split, if it always escapes itself into its various alienations, one thing at least is sure: The philosophy of the *cogito* as it fundamentally expresses the essence of humanism is the illusion *par excellence*, the *Ur-Ideologie*, since it does not recognize "the radical heteronomy that Freud's discovery revealed is gaping in man," which is "the radical eccentricity of the self to itself with which man is confronted."[33] So it is indeed, we suggest, the analytic experience of the "function of the I" that motivates Lacan to write, whatever the relationship to Descartes's meditations may be,[34] that it is the opposite of "all philosophy emerging directly from the *cogito*."[35] Because based on the evidence, what Lacan is once again questioning in humanism is any claim on man's part that he is the author not necessarily of his own acts but of the meaning and value he gives them: "The subject does not know what he is saying, and for the best reasons—because he does not know what he is."[36]

From this point on locating himself in the philosophical tradition of deconstruction, Lacan determines to attack what he considers the pinnacle of humanism, which is Hegelian Absolute Knowledge where "discourse is closed upon itself, wholly in agreement with itself, where everything that can be expressed in discourse is wholly coherent and justified."[37] If one can say that "Hegel is at the limits of anthropology, Freud has gone beyond it. His discovery is

---

32. The expression "bad faith" (*mauvaise foi*) is not, however, challenged by Lacan; cf. ibid., p. 352.
33. Ibid., p. 524.
34. Cf. A. Juranville, *Lacan et la philosophie*, P.U.F., 1984, pp. 140 ff.
35. *Ecrits*, p. 93.
36. *Séminaire*, vol. 2, p. 286.
37. Ibid., p. 89.

that man is not entirely within man; Freud is not a humanist."[38] So
in answer to the question of whether "psychoanalysis is a humanism," Lacan unhesitatingly gives a negative answer.[39]

We will not analyze at greater length here this thematics of
antihumanism, so familiar has it become by now. We will add only
that it governs a certain number of consequences through which
Lacanian psychoanalysis deserves most admirably to be included in
what we call in this essay the ideal type of the sixties philosopher.
We will merely supply certain indications of it.

1. The Critique of Truth as Identity/Adequation It is clear
that, if the truth is to be located in the splitting of the subject, the
traditional discourse on truth, defined as adequation or identity, is
ideological in that it "forgets" (in the Heidegerrian sense of forgetting) the real (the difference): "The word seems even more a word
when its truth is based less on what we call adequation to the thing;
the true word is thus paradoxically opposed to true discourse." This
paradox, we claim, is not a very great one for anyone with the
slightest knowledge of Heideggerian phenomenology: The theme
that states that the truth as adequation (identity) is an illusion and
that it plays a role in hiding the dimension of invisibility, the
dimension of the absence in the heart of all presence, is well known
within the tradition. We have found the echo of it in Derrida;
Hegelian Absolute Knowledge, which is the culmination of the
philosophy of identity, is the apex of the illusion. If it is still
accepted (which is somewhat naive) that Freud "discovered" the
split in the subject (radical heteronomy), one could then say that,
"in order to purge the truth as it deserves, one must enter analytic
discourse."[40] *From this perspective,* however, Lacanian thought is
well within "the movement of contemporary philosophy (first of all
Heidegger's)," to use the fortuitous phrasing of A. Juranville, since
it "extends and even 'surpasses' [contemporary philosophy's] critique of metaphysics" through a movement of radicalizing antihumanism, which is typical of '68 philosophy, as we have already seen.

38. Ibid., p. 92.
39. Ibid., p. 87.
40. *Séminaire*, vol. 20, p. 98.

200

Any rational discourse, whether philosophical or scientific, appears
to be the very prototype of ideological discourse, since any dimension of otherness disappears in it, the split, heteronomous subject
being radically foreclosed in favor of the Ego's illusions. "From this
point of view," J. Dor has no hesitation in stating, "certain strategies
of discourse are shown to be very radical in evicting the subject from
the unconscious. This is particularly obvious in all the strategies of
rational discourse, and *a fortiori*, in scientific discourses, mathematics, and logic, where the subject of speech creates for itself the
beautiful illusion that it is the subject itself."[41] Under these conditions, it is also clear that psychoanalysis cannot fail to take sophist
dialectics as its model in order to avoid this supreme alienation
(scientific discourse being shown to be even worse than psychotic
discourse in this regard): "Analysis, in terms of progress in non-
science, is related to the state of the history of science before
Aristotle's definition, which is to say, dialectics."[42] According to
Lacan (who translated Heidegger, as we know), Freud's references
to the pre-Socratics would suggest this.[43]

Without referring to the oddly naive aspects of the belief, also
typical of contemporary antihumanism, that considers a return to
the "pre-Aristotelian" to be a definite form of progress, let us say
that it allows us to illuminate one aspect of Lacan's work that is
singularly lacking in illumination, namely, his style.

2. The "Neoclassical" Style   We have no intention of taking up
that worn-out exercise of literary criticism of Lacan's style. We will
say only that its complexity—whether real or apparent is of little
significance—makes real sense in relation to the idea of the subject
and of truth that we have just described, perhaps because his style,
though still lucid during the formative years of his doctrine, continued to "split" while his doctrine, on the other hand, was becoming systematized. Because: "the true word, interrogating true discourse about its meaning, discovers that meaning always refers to
other meanings, that nothing is revealed except through signs, for

41. Dor, *Introduction*, p. 164.
42. *Ecrits*, p. 361.
43. Ibid.

which reason it is destined to error."[44] The reasoning, though not very convincing (as we will explain later), is quite simple in itself: If the true word is the word that knows it does not know what it is saying,[45] if true discourse, on the other hand, is wrong to believe that it knows what it is saying, is it ultimately coherent to be incoherent? In this regard, what Freud proposes that we achieve, according to Lacan, does not comform "to the useless adage, 'know thyself,' " as an inattentive reading might lead us to believe: "What he proposes that we achieve is not anything that might be the object of knowledge but, as he says, what creates my being and which he teaches us that I evince just as much and more through my caprices, my aberrations, my phobias, and my fetishes as in my more civilized person."[46] From this come the critique of rational discourse and its derivatives such as "academic discourse when it makes its case for this fiction known as the author."[47] So we are to invert the traditional criteria for judging discourses and affirm "the consistency of discourses where the truth limps, and precisely when it openly limps, and the inanity, on the other hand, of scientific discourse when, affirming its closure, it makes the others lie."[48] In other words, since the real is the impossible, since the truth is not adequation but split difference, only broken discourse can be *adequate* to it. Here, as with Derrida, we nevertheless discover at the root of a certain practice of writing or of the practice of a certain style the traditional definition of truth as adequation (which, in spite of everything, is annoying in terms of the whole proposition) and, correspondingly, the *classical* ideal of the true word as adequate or faithful to its "object," with the difference that in this case it is a matter of being adequate or faithful to difference instead of to identity.

We are then free to judge Lacan's *neoclassical* style as attractive or repellent according to our taste. On the other hand, what the analysis reveals is that his statement is not original. Basically, it is the analogue in the field of psychoanalysis of Nietzsche's aphoristic

44. Ibid., p. 61.
45. Dor, *Introduction*, pp. 131–32.
46. *Ecrits*, p. 526.
47. Preface to Lemaire, *Jacques Lacan*, p. 6.
48. Ibid.

style, or of Heidegger's poetic style.[49] In all three cases, paradoxically, it is a matter of creating a discourse adequate to its "object," and since the "object" is split, it is a matter of splitting discourse as well. Those who do not understand this procedure because they are unable to grasp it, even intuitively, are destined to be its victims forever.

3. Communication as a "Dialogue of the Deaf"[50]   If we accept that subjectivity—in the generic sense of the word—is made up of these two opposite moments represented by the subject and the ego, the only relationships that can be called "authentic intersubjective relationships"[51] are those established directly between one subject and another without the knowledge of the "ego." Unfortunately, such relations are unimaginable, at least at the conscious level, since the subject can only be perceived as alienated in the Ego, the alienation obviously not being perceived as such. Given that it is *structural* alienation, it cannot be eliminated, "even at the end of analysis."[52] The subject is unavoidably doomed to believing that "this is the ego that he is, that everyone is in the same situation, and that there is no way out."

This is Lacan's perspective in his summary of the structure of all human communication in the "*L* schema":

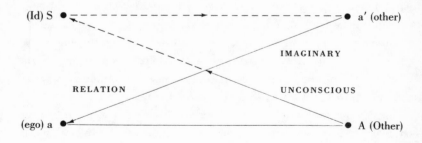

(Id) S   a' (other)

IMAGINARY

RELATION   UNCONSCIOUS

(ego) a   A (Other)

49. To be accurate, we would have to state that of the three the only real writer was doubtless Nietzsche, an aesthetic judgment that makes no claim to universality, of course.
50. Dor, *Introduction*, pp. 160–61.
51. *Séminaire*, vol. 2, p. 285.
52. Ibid.

S designates the true subject (the subject of desire or the subject of the unconscious = *Es*, the Id); *a* is the ego of this same subject; *a'* denotes the ego of the other, and *A* its subject. Conscious relationship is always an "interego" relationship, so, for example, the relationship between *a* and *a'* is an imaginary and alienated relationship between two individuals who do not know what they are saying,[53] without even knowing that they do not know. Thus a doubling of forgetfulness is achieved, a "forgetting of forgetting," so to speak, so that, parodying Ionesco, one could say that all conscious communication is carried out "between two others": "I always search for true subjects and I must be satisfied with shadows. The subject is separated from the Others, the true ones, by the wall of language."[54] This is because it is always the subject of the *énoncé* (the ego) that is present in language and never the subject of the énonciation.[55] A certain conception of intersubjectivity follows from this, which we hope we may be permitted to consider a not very heartening one: "If the word is based in the existence of the Other, the true, language is made to refer us to the other objectivity, to the other whom we can do what we want with, including thinking of him as an object, that is, that he does not know what he is saying."[56]

We will not return here to the criticisms we have already directed to the genealogical and historicist attitudes (discourse is always a historically situated "product," and under these conditions a metalanguage is impossible). Instead, we would like to conclude by describing the difficulties, even the dangers, inherent in the emergence of this approach within the field of psychoanalysis. Unlike the situation in Heideggerianism or Nietzscheanism (the situation for Marxism is more problematical), French Freudianism is a theory with a direct opening onto the practice of a cure. This authorizes us to inquire what the practice of that cure might be in terms of the conditions dictated by the theory.

53. Ibid.
54. Ibid., p. 286.
55. In other words, representation always concerns beings, never Being.
56. *Séminaire*, vol. 2, p. 286.

From the Theory of Subjectivity to the
Destruction of the Ego

The function and end of the Lacanian cure can be logically deduced from its theory of subjectivity: "If we train analysts, it is so that there will be subjects whose ego is absent. This is the ideal of analysis, which remains a potential, of course. There is never a subject without ego, a fully realized subject, but that is indeed what one must aim to obtain from the subject in analysis. The analysis must aim for the transition to a true word that joins the subject to another subject on the other side of the wall of language."[57]

Analysis according to Lacan must be devoted to avoiding the three errors of traditional analysis:

1. The error of "causal analyses" is that the analyst naively attempts, from the starting point of his interpretations, to intervene actively in the life of the patient; there is no question of "transforming the subject in the present through wise explanations of his past."[58]

2. In a more general way, there is no motive for the psychoanalyst's attempting to "come to the aid" of the subject through his falsely illuminating interventions: "That the expedient he has recourse to may at times be of some use to the subject has no importance other than as a stimulating joke and will detain us no longer."[59]

3. Finally and most importantly, he must avoid reinforcing to any degree the subject's ego since, as we have said, this ego is the place of his alienation *par excellence.* The supreme error of "traditional" psychoanalysis is "wanting the subject to combine all the more or less shattered and shattering pieces of that in which it misrecognizes itself. . . . If in the end the subject believes in the ego, it is a form of madness. Thank God the analyst rarely succeeds, but there are a thousand indications that he is being pushed in this direction."[60]

57. Ibid., p. 287.
58. *Ecrits*, p. 251.
59. Ibid.
60. *Séminaire*, vol. 2, pp. 287 ff.

"Bad analytic practice" is then directly related to a theoretical error: that of believing in "this mirage that it is the individual, the human subject—and why him among all possible subjects?—who is truly autonomous and that somewhere in him . . . there is the little man who is in man who makes the machine work."[61] Now, according to Lacan, "the whole of analytic thought, with few exceptions, is currently moving back" toward this error when it "talks about the autonomous ego, the healthy part of the ego, the ego that must be reinforced."[62] The truth is the ego must be simply "liquidated": "The analyst's art is to suspend the subject's certainties until its last mirages are consumed"[63]—a nice little project whose application suggests certain pages of Kafka. Using a "sustained silence" that confines him to the role that, "in bridge, is the role of the dummy,"[64] the analyst must deprive the patient of any response so that, confused, even "driven mad," he undoes his certainties and effects this "analytic regression," which should take him from the ego to the subject. As one woman disciple writes with touching naivete, in this matter "the analyst lends only a distracted ear to the historical narrations. . . . The patient, more sensitized than usual to the effects of an open dialogue [?], *paralyzed* by an attentive listening and a sustained silence, *aroused* by the immanence of the unveiling, in his *panic* will open himself up to the *slippages* of his language."[65]

Apart from the revulsion that might legitimately be inspired by this practice—especially when we consider that it is intended for somewhat fragile individuals—it obviously confronts a number of difficulties. We note first that this practice is quasi-mechanically deduced from the theory that supports it and that it thus presupposes genuine scorn for experience or for "prudence," if you like, in the Aristotelian sense: "The imbecilic recourse to the word 'lived' to define the knowledge that he (the analyst) gains from his own analysis, . . . is not enough to distinguish his thought from that

61. Ibid., p. 87.
62. Ibid., p. 88.
63. *Ecrits*, p. 251.
64. Ibid., p. 589 (in French, the "role of death"—Trans.).
65. Lemaire, *Jacques Lacan*, pp. 331 ff.

which attributes to him the fact of being a man "who is not like other men."[66] Is it really so "imbecilic" to believe that psychoanalysis, like education or politics, neither can nor should be more than an "art"?

Next, we would point out that in this Lacanian practice the subject who is "driven crazy" by "sustained silence" is being treated, in conformity with the theory, as nothing other than an object. For all intents and purposes, "we can do whatever we want" to the "other," given that he is merely a reified ego, "including believing that he is only an object, that is, that he does not know what he is saying."[67] On the contrary, would it be better to believe that even in his extreme aberrations the "madman" or the "sick person" remains in some way, to use Swain's fine formula, the "subject of his madness"?[68] Lacanian theory and practice are indeed at opposite poles from this kind of humanism since in that theory and practice the "madman" appears only as an "intermediary thing" between the human and the inhuman: It is not enough "that we be this imaginary ego in order to be men. We can still be this intermediary thing called a madman. A madman is precisely the one who simply hangs on to this imaginary"[69] and who, as such, is no longer even the subject of his own madness. So any communication with him is excluded *a priori*.

However real these difficulties may be, we recognize that they are still not the essence of the problem. One might respond that if it is true that subjectivity is entirely consumed in the division between the authentic subject and the alienated ego, humanist sentimentalism is not called for: The ego has to be destroyed at whatever cost.

The problem is, finally, to see whether this theoretical opposition—the practice is only its scrupulous working out—is well founded. Let us reformulate the question in terms of psychoanalysis itself: Does Freud's "discovery"—the radical heteronomy of the split subject—make any reference to the Idea that the ego's auton-

66. *Ecrits*, p. 350.
67. *Séminaire*, vol. 2, p. 286.
68. G. Swain, *Le Sujet de la folie*, Privat, 1977.
69. *Séminaire*, vol. 2, p. 284.

omy is definitively mistaken, which, let us remember, Freud himself did not think, as the passage from the *Outline* we quoted early in the chapter indicates. Ultimately, does not Lacan make the same mistake, common to the "all or nothing" logic of contemporary anti-humanism, which states that since *real* autonomy is manifestly illusory, the very *Idea* of autonomy is meaningless in terms of orienting the practice?

If this were the case, and we will attempt to show that it is in the following chapter, we would have to apply to him the formula Lacan reserved for "orthodox" Freudians: "Thank God experience is never pushed to the limit, one is not doing what one says one is doing, one remains very far to this side of one's goals. Thank God we are not successful at the cures, and for that reason the subject escapes them."[70]

70. Ibid., p. 283.

7 /
Return to the
Subject

As has been clearly apparent in the course of the preceding chapters, it would be absurd to deny that, if antihumanism was in fact a virtual rallying cry for French philosophy of the sixties, it developed through very different strategies and from very different perspectives. In other words, if the trial that '68 philosophy brought against man always resulted in the same verdict, at least the subject has been given its own choice of death, to a certain extent. Two deaths of man and two corresponding antihumanisms can be clearly distinguished depending on the way this heteronomy is conceived that they wanted to construct from a human condition finally free from the illusions where metaphysics had kept it.

The Deaths of the Subject

We have seen that in the Marxist register the claim of the metaphysical subject to mastery over its thoughts and actions, its claim to *autonomy,* has consistently been denounced as simple mystification. Bourdieu's sociology has no other intention, beyond certain appearances, but to reveal what in the "last instance" can only be called the *causal* determination of consciousness and will through the socioeconomic relations that thoroughly condition, directly or indirectly, the existence of the "subject". Penetrated by relations of force, what used to be called the *subject* no longer, in fact, appears, in the process of this intrinsically *reifying* approach, to be anything but an *object* or a *machine* whose gears, it is claimed, are being dismantled and whose mechanisms are being uncovered.

The constitutive autonomy of subjectivity also appears to be an illusion from the Heideggerian perspective, where the other currents of '68 philosophy have established themselves, both as the product of a forgetting and as an obstacle to overcome: a product of the subject's forgetting (and of the forgetting of this forgetting) of the dimension of otherness (Being, *différance*, the unconscious), which marks its own identity; an obstacle to overcome in that, dispossessed of its would-be self-mastery and mastery of the world, *Dasein* returns to its authentic ipseity—to be not a subject but a "site," the "there" where Being takes its stand.

In both cases, reduced to a "site" (a "site" where relations of force are expressed, a "site" where Being is manifested at the same time it is withdrawing), man as that dimension of autonomy that humanism had wanted to be the essential mark of what is not a thing also disappears. It should be pointed out that, in view of these two deaths of man (and two condemnations of humanism that underlie them), two conditions appear to be necessary if humanism is to retain any meaning:

> In order for *humanity* to be opposed to *thingness*, one of course has to attribute to man the capacity not to be closed upon himself like a thing or, in other words, not to be what he is. It is this *openness*, as opposed to the *closedness* of the thing, that properly constitutes man as *ek-sistence*, the reaffirmation of which is still the undeniable achievement of the various deconstructions of metaphysics to which contemporary philosophy has devoted itself.[1]

> But in order that humanism not be destroyed at the same time metaphysics is deconstructed, the *meaning* of this openness that is constitutive of *ek-sistence* still has to be accounted for. If one attempts to specify what the opposition between openness and closedness (humanity/thingness) *means*, one is forced to admit that openness is the very thing that governs a *free* being's capacity, in relation to what is and what he is, to posit the goals defining what must be and what he must be. *Ek-sistence* as openness seems to have meaning only if it is thought of as *autonomy:* The idea of humanity as such arises only if openness can be thought of beginning

---

1. This is simply a restatement since the "existentialist" thesis that "every animal is what it is, man alone being originally absolutely nothing," had already been fully explored from Rousseau to Kant and Fichte (J. G. Fichte, *The Foundation of Natural Law* [1796–97]).

with this area of autonomy that confers meaning and repre-
sentability on it.

So it seems that the problem posed by contemporary antihumanism has to be formulated in the following terms.

Counter to the reifying discourses of metaphysics, or at least to
certain figures of metaphysics (the prototype being the Hegelian
system, which conceives of the subject as entirely enclosed within
itself), it was indeed necessary and useful to bring to light this
dimension of openness that defines *ek-sistence* (or, if you wish,
finitude): This reminder that the human condition escapes the status
of the thing, instead of generating any type of antihumanism, is the
indispensable precondition of all humanism of whatever type. We
will remark only that in the various currents that make up '68
philosophy this precondition is not really fulfilled except when the
Heideggerian reference plays its antimetaphysical role and, on the
other hand, that the reifying discourse of Marxism, measured by
this philosophy of *ek-sistence*, is rather the apex of the metaphysical
destructions of authenticity.[2]

Apart from that, there is every indication that contemporary
philosophy has often and paradoxically conflated the idea of *closure*
and that of *autonomy* into a single critique. The latter has also often
been denounced as constitutive of the metaphysical illusions that
must be deconstructed and destroyed in order for this dimension of
openness that is the sign of non-thingness to be restored. This
confusion is understandable in a way. At least it has a logic: If in fact
autonomy could be considered effective and integral, it is clear that
the (absolute) subject thus postulated (where the Idea of God can
ultimately be perceived) would be entirely enclosed in itself, with no
determining outside, and devoid of any openness to an otherness of
any kind. The temptation to believe that the destruction of the ideal
of closure also assumes renouncing the idea of autonomy that had

2. From this, Heidegger's constant and harsh criticisms of Marxism; cf. *Lettre
sur l'humanisme,* trans. R. Munier, Ed. Aubier, 1964, p. 45 (*Brief über den Humanismus,* in *Collected Works,* vol. 9, pp. 319 ff); *Questions IV,* p. 115 ("Das
Ende der Philosophie und die Aufgabe des Denkens," in *Zur Sache des Denkens,* Tübingen, 1968.

defined the humanist man derives from this. This is also the source of the condemnation of *all* humanism as metaphysics and, ultimately, contemporary antihumanism.

However, we will dispute this logic by demonstrating its erroneous character. It does not follow that, having established that man is not really (*hic et nunc*) autonomous (that he is open to his other), one has to go to the extreme of withdrawing all meaning and function from the idea of the ideal, in short, from the very Idea of autonomy. In this case, and if we assume that humanism is defined by thinking of man from the perspective of this Idea, neither is it obvious that antihumanism has to be the inevitable focal point of any critique of the reifying figures of metaphysics.

It also seemed necessary to identify our positions further with respect to the Heideggerian side of contemporary antihumanism, in order to give these hypotheses body and to limit our study. Although we have no doubts about our previous position with respect to Marxian antihumanism, we do share to a certain extent the first moment of Heideggerian antihumanism, the moment of denouncing all forms of philosophy, beginning with Marxism, that might lead the "subject" back to close in upon itself and in this way to be destroyed as a subject. If it were possible, in view of reifying discourses, to grasp clearly what distinguishes a Heideggerian critique (or a critique inspired by Heidegger) from a no less radical critique of the closure of the subject that still does not go so far as to eliminate all the meaning of the idea of autonomy, the ultimate definition of what a *nonmetaphysical humanism* might be would no longer be merely a future project.

We propose to question the Heideggerian critique of subjectivity from three directions: (1) What exactly do the expressions "metaphysics of subjectivity" or "metaphysical subject" mean? (2) What is the nonhumanist philosophy of man that can replace the defunct metaphysical subject after its deconstruction? And (3) what is left of the subject after its deconstruction?

In order to avoid certain misunderstandings in what follows, we would like to explain that for us it is less a matter of providing philological commentary on Heideggerian philosophy (a duty we have often undertaken elsewhere) than one of leading an open

212

discussion with it, as far as possible. For this reason, at times we maintain a certain very deliberate distance from the orthodox terminology.

On the Metaphysical Subject

To state the essential, the metaphysical subject as understood can be said to be defined as *representation*, as *will*, and finally as the *will to will* (technical).

1. In the dimension of representation, the metaphysical subject is defined as consciousness (*Bewusstsein*): The Cartesian *cogito* is the prototypical illustration for modern humanism of this first definition of subjectivity. If metaphysics is fundamentally characterized as the forgetting of Being, as the forgetting of the aspect of invisibility or mystery inscribed in the very heart of all presence, the philosophy of consciousness there *is* only what is *present* to a consciousness at the heart of a *representation*. Thus the philosophy of consciousness, along with Hegelian idealism, ultimately culminates in the idea of absolute Knowledge, in the idea of an omniscient subject for which the totality of what is would be fully intelligible and transparent (or, if you will, a subject without an unconscious, however the word is understood).

2. Although this view of subjectivity as the center of a world that is *represented* as fully rational in the self-transparency of an omniscient consciousness is very important, it does not exhaust the classifications of the metaphysical subject: It still has to be thought as *will*, as we have said: "Here man's way of being begins which consists of occupying the sphere of human powers as a space where the mastery and possession of being in its totality can be measured and fulfilled."[3] The reference to Descartes is extended through a reference to Kant and Fichte's pragmatic philosophy. Why is will "metaphysical" in the sense of the forgetting of Being? One might venture one simple response among other possibilities: For the philosophy of will, the actions of men, historical events, for exam-

3. M. Heidegger, *Chemins qui ne mènent nulle part*, trans. W. Brokmeier, Gallimard, p. 83 (*Holzwege*, in *Collected Works*, vol. 5, p. 92).

ple, are ultimately *founded* in the intention of subjects, which plays the role of ultimate cause in this respect. From this perspective, the dimension of mystery that characterizes all events disappears in favor of exhaustively founding the event on subjectivity. Here again there is the "forgetting of Being," then, in such a way that the illusion of *practical mastery* can be considered as parallel to that of *theoretical presense.*

Again we note that, if Hegelianism occupies a very specific place in the history of the metaphysics of subjectivity, which it in some respects completes, it is because it is constructed from a synthesis of these two moments of metaphysical subjectivity, the absolute Subject, according to a well-known formula, being the "reconciliation of will and intelligence" (through which Hegelian philosophy takes the form of a *system*).

3. Finally, in post-Hegelian philosophy, and particularly in Nietzsche, according to Heidegger, metaphysical subjectivity is classified as the will to will or as *technique.* What distinguishes the will to will from "simple" will is this: In the metaphysics of simple will, the goals of mastery forged by the subject are still subjugated to an objective end; at issue is, for example, the mastery of nature *in order* to assure the material happiness of humanity, or the mastery of social and political organization *in order* to assure men's freedom. On the other hand, for the will to will all ends disappear in favor of the goal of "mastery for the sake of mastery." Will no longer wants anything other than itself, which is its own increase. Here we have the emergence of *technique* understood as "instrumental reason" (*Zweckrationalität*), which never reflects on ends, but only on means: "The will to will denies any end in itself and tolerates no end unless as means,"[4] so that in the world of technique the man of metaphysics has stopped believing even that the mastery of beings could in some way ameliorate his fate, for the simple reason that the question of such an amelioration itself has disappeared, so to speak.

To summarize these three classifications we could say that the metaphysical subject is a *self-transparent* subject that lays claim to

4. Heidegger, *Essais et conférences*, trans. A. Préau, Gallimard, p. 103 (*Vorträge und Aufsätze*, Pfullingen 1954, p. 89).

the mastery of *everything* that exists, both for itself and the world. It is, then, a subject without an "unconscious," a *closed* subject in that any *transcendence* (ek-sistence) in it, any *openness* to Being as withdrawal (to the invisible, to mystery), has disappeared. In other words, this subject is deluded to the extent that it thinks of itself no longer as a finite and temporal being but as an absolute and atemporal subject.

Before addressing our second question, we will note that in Heidegger's view these different classifications of metaphysical subjectivity succeed each other, are even added to each other, throughout this long "decline of philosophy," which the history of modern philosophy is, ultimately to take the form of *the* metaphysical subject, first in Hegel and then in Nietzsche.

From the Metaphysical Subject to *Dasein*

In *Kant and the Problem of Metaphysics*, and particularly in the course of the Davos debate against Cassirer in March 1929, Heidegger clearly located his own intention with respect to the question "What is man?"—the question Kant had made the center of his philosophy. There is no doubt that these texts are the appropriate point of departure for determining what Heidegger designates as *Dasein*.[5]

Here is what the Davos debate has to say on this point:

> Kant was led by his radicalism to a position he could not help but turn away from.
>
> This position means: the destruction of what until then had been the foundations of Western metaphysics (the Mind, the Logos, Reason).
>
> This position required radically regenerating and uncovering the foundation of the possibility of metaphysics as the natural propensity of man, that is, a metaphysics of *Dasein* directed at the possibility of metaphysics as such. Such a metaphysics must ask the

5. We will return to the questions raised by the *Kehre*, the "turn" that eventually took place in Heidegger's thought.

question of the essence of man in a way that is *anterior* to all philosophical anthropology as it is to all philosophy of culture.[6]

"Metaphysics of *Dasein*" and "metaphysics as such" are understood
here as an echo of *Critique of Pure Reason:* Heidegger, at least for
the moment, likens the intentions of fundamental ontology to metaphysics understood as the natural propensity of man. In terms of the
direction of the Copernican revolution, it is fundamentally a matter
of looking for what makes up the unity of the meaning of being in
Man/*Dasein* (instead of naively, in a flatly "realist" way, looking for
this unity and meaning in the object). So "metaphysics as such,"
which is related to *Dasein* in an analysis of finite reason (a "critique
of pure reason"), designates "general metaphysics," which Heidegger, in a *coup de force*, likens to the transcendental question of
objectivity as it is established in the doctrine of categories: These
define the structure of objectivity (of beingness) in general. And,
indeed, it is in the transcendental subject that they are unified in
terms of the thrust of the Copernican revolution, for Heidegger the
whole question being to specify the difference separating *Dasein*
from this transcendental subject which, in his view, is in some way
still metaphysical. Counter to Cassirer's neo-Kantism, then, it has
to be demonstrated that "The analysis is not only an ontology of
nature as the object of the science of nature but a general ontology, a
critically based *metaphysica generalis*," that is rooted in the structures of *Dasein*, thus in a metaphysics as the natural propensity of
man, as man's ability to transcend being in order to question himself
about his being.

Reading these texts, the motifs of the *Kehre*, this "turn" that is
claimed to divide Heidegger's philosophy into a "Heidegger I" and a
"Heidegger II," retrospectively appear clear enough (as we will see,
in reality the idea of the turn has to be particularly nuanced, as
Heidegger himself repeatedly insists). If *general metaphysics* (the
question of the meaning of being) is "critically based" on metaphysics as the natural propensity (the question "What is man?"), is
the philosophy of the first Heidegger still a prisoner of humanism? Is

6. *Débat de Davos*, Ed. Beauchesne, 1972, p. 24.

the interpretation of the meaning of being still based on subjectivity, in the last instance?

In fact, the question is more complex than it seems, precisely because Heidegger, from the *Kantbuch* on, is careful to distinguish *Dasein* from the metaphysical subject; it is even one of the main issues in the Davos debate.

We will briefly recall the intellectual context of the polemic. One of the major objections of the neo-Kantians to *Being and Time*—an objection that had even more weight in Heidegger's view since it was also Husserl's, it is useful to point out—bore on the problem of the suspected "psychologism" of the 1927 work: In basing the interpretation of the meaning of being on *Dasein*, does not Heidegger—and this is Cassirer's question—take the risk of reducing the truth to a simple evaluation in relation to the subject? More importantly, if *Dasein* is different from the transcendental Kantian subject precisely because—and Heidegger always emphasizes it—it is thoroughly immersed in historicity (because it is not an abstract subject, if you will, which is atemporal and eternal), does not the truth also take the risk of being thoroughly historicized and relativized? Thus, "Heidegger poses the problem of truth and says: there can be no truths in themselves, no eternal truths, but truths to the extent that they are that, are relative to *Dasein*. Thus a finite being absolutely cannot possess eternal truths." For Kant the problem was just this: How can there be, in spite of this finitude that he himself had demonstrated, necessary and universal truths?[7]

Cassirer's question is perfectly legitimate, we admit. This is the very question, as it was conveyed by Husserl, that led Heidegger to state his philosophy precisely in the *Kehre* (the meaning of being "founded" on Being and no longer on *Dasein*).

It is not clear, however, that from 1929 on Heidegger did not possess a convincing response to this question with his definition of *Dasein*, a response that the *Kehre* made more precise without in any way nullifying it. But this response, as we will see, was so "Kantian" that if it had been formulated directly it might have jeopardized the originality of *Being and Time* itself.

7. Ibid., p. 32.

Heidegger is careful to indicate the limits of the neo-Kantian interpretation of Kant in this debate: Cassirer wrongly retains only the epistemological or methodological aspect of *Critique of Pure Reason* and considers the doctrine of categories to be only a theory of natural science and not a general ontology. And in fact Cassirer's aim, as it appears in *The Philosophy of Symbolic Forms*, is essentially to produce the analogue for the field of culture of what *Critique of Pure Reason* was for the natural sciences: One must begin from the facts (there exist cultural objects that transcend the specificity of empirical subjects in the same way objects in mathematics and physics do) in order to question, in terms of the motion of transcendental thought, their conditions of possibility in order to discover something like "cultural categories."[8] In Heidegger's view, Cassirer abandons the question of ontology to turn to anthropology. According to Heidegger, Kant's authentic project is, on the contrary, that of an articulation of ontology to the analysis of *Dasein*. Now, it is precisely the specificity of *Dasein* that Cassirer lacks: As an orthodox Kantian he defines man either as a transcendental, atemporal subject or as an empirical subject (as consciousness). This raises two difficulties:

> If we retain the classical definition of the transcendental subject, we "do not leave metaphysics" since, as an ahistorical subject, *constituting* beings, it continues to suggest the ideal of a *primary foundation.*[9]

> If we consider, on the other hand, only the empirical subject, we seem to confront the problem of psychologism, which is itself only a degraded form of metaphysics.

8. "I remain with Kant's position on the question of the transcendental, as it was formulated by Cohen. Cohen believed that the essence of the transcendental is that it begins with a fact so as to question the possibility of this fact; but he restricted this general definition by considering only the mathematical science of nature as properly worth interrogating. Kant, however, did not stay within this limitation. For my part, I question the possibility of the fact of "language." How is it possible, how is it thinkable that we can understand each other from *Dasein* to *Dasein* through the medium of language?" (ibid., p. 49).

9. Obviously, this argumentation can be disputed since the transcendental subject is in no way being; therefore, how can it be a foundation?

Dasein then has to be defined—man as he is thought nonmetaphysically—in some other way than as the transcendental or empirical subject. This is why Heidegger suggests that the word *Dasein* may have no equivalent in orthodox Kantian language: "I believe that what I designate as *Dasein* has no translation in Cassirer's concepts. If one said consciousness, that would be precisely the word I myself rejected."[10]

What is this *Dasein* then, and is there really no possible translation of the word within the framework of Kantianism, as Heidegger suggests? We need to point out three of its characteristics here:

Dasein is temporal: "The task will be to place in evidence the temporality of *Dasein* within the perspective of the possibility of the understanding of being."[11]

If it does not constitute but rather *interprets* the meaning of being, this can only be (and it is on this point that Heidegger begins to respond to Cassirer's objection) in the way of a subjective interpretation: "When I say: truth is relative to *Dasein*, this is not an ontic utterance, as if I were saying: the only truth is what man the individual thinks. But my statement is metaphysical;[12] truth itself cannot be, and the truth in general has no meaning unless there is *Dasein*."[13]

It is necessary, then, though at first glance it seems paradoxical, to consider *Dasein* as *historical* and yet at the same time as not relativizing the interpretation of the meaning of being. Contrary to Heidegger's polemical assertion during the Davos debate, but in agreement with the basic theses of his *Kantbuch*, this paradox can be easily unraveled within the framework of Kantianism, and from there *Dasein* can be translated into the language of the *Critique: Dasein* is quite simply *the man of schematization* in that the latter

10. *Débat de Davos*, p. 44.
11. Ibid., p. 38.
12. *Metaphysical* is evidently to be understood here in a nonpejorative sense, as what transcends the ontic sphere. The articulation between metaphysics as a natural disposition (fundamental ontology) and general metaphysics (ontology) is thus still at issue here.
13. *Débat de Davos*, p. 36.

specifically mediates between the transcendental subject and the empirical subject. We should pause on this point: It not only in fact allows us to understand what Heidegger designates as *Dasein* but in addition leads us to locating with great precision what separates an antihumanist critique (Heidegger) from a humanist critique (Kant) of metaphysics.

On this point let us briefly recall what one has to know about schematization in order to follow the argument. Formally, a schema is a synthesis between concept and time effected in the imagination. To make sense of the formula *schema = category + time*, we should add that, at least for Kant, it can resolve the difficult problem raised by the *antinomy* of Cartesianism and empiricism. Against the Cartesians who accept the existence of general, innate ideas, that is, of eternal, atemporal truths, the empiricists objected that such general ideas have no meaning from the psychological point of view: Anytime I create for myself a representation of a triangle and its various mathematical properties, for example, I inevitably create a representation, *in the time* of my consciousness, of a *particular* triangle with a *particular* form and dimension. From this come the skeptical consequences proper to all empiricism, since the notion of a general idea itself is disqualified by simply considering the psychological conditions of its incarnation in a consciousness.

Kant's position on this antinomy is well known: The empiricists are evidently right on the psychological plane, since it is effectively impossible to represent a so-called general idea without *particularizing* it and *temporalizing* it; but on the epistemological plane one must nevertheless maintain the Cartesian demand for a critique of skepticism if one is to avoid psychologism, the relativization of the truth, and its decline to the rank of merely one belief (Hume) among others.

It is the theory of schematization, then, that constitutes the formulation of the Kantian solution of this antinomy. This solution must show how *a priori* concepts, notably categories, can be *particularized* and *temporalized* in a consciousness (in the internal sense) without losing any of their *universality* and *demonstrability*. All that is required for this is to define concepts as schemas, that is, not as images or general representations (which would be effectively devoid of meaning, the empiricists being right on this point) but as general *methods* for constructing objectivity. To take once again the example of the triangle, one could thus say that the schema of the triangle is nothing other than the series of operations one must effect *concretely in time* in order to succeed in tracing an image of a triangle with ruler and compass.

There are two advantages to this solution with respect to the antinomy it resolves. On the one hand, it permits psychologism (skeptical empiricism) to be avoided since concepts do not lose their universality and their apodicticity by being represented (the method of construction of the triangle remains the same in all places and times and for all triangles—this is a matter not of belief but of science). On the other hand, conceptual thought becomes *thoroughly* temporal, so that here *temporalizing categories does not have the effect of historicizing them.*

It is understandable that the theory of schematization must have seemed crucial to Heidegger for his conception of *Dasein*. If one accepts—which is not difficult—that the doctrine of categories answers the question of the meaning of being (that it is, in other words, an ontology), one could say that the place where it is rooted is not in consciousness (the empirical subject) or in the transcendental subject but in *Dasein*, understood as the "subject" of schematization. If general metaphysics refers to metaphysics as the natural propensity of man, it is in the sense that this man is the man of schematization—which is how Heidegger effectively avoided Cassirer's and Husserl's accusations of psychologism.

Subjectivity after Its Deconstruction

Before measuring what is left of the metaphysical subject after this temporalization of subjectivity, it is important once again to indicate some of the philosophical stakes in this theory of schematization.

We note first—since Heidegger emphasized it—that schematizing activity indeed is related to the imagination. The imagination, as common sense suggests, is the faculty we use to create representations of objects for ourselves "in the absence of the objects." It is, so to speak, a perception without the object. If we think about it we can see that in this sense categories, once schematized, are indeed an "ontological precomprehension," that is, a general definition of beingness: As schemas they represent all that we can know of being in general *even before* it is present to our eyes (transcendental imagination).

It is with Kant that there appears, then—Heidegger, as we have seen, only follows him in this respect—a conception of subjectivity which is radically regenerated by comparison with what was current in Cartesianism or empiricism. One can even say that the concept as schema is essentially no longer a *representation* but rather an *activity*, and that is essentially why there will always be a certain primacy of practical reason over theoretical reason in critical philosophy.

Finally, the theory of schematization implies a theory of meaning that is the basis of Kant's critique of metaphysics: Only what can be schematized, that is, particularized in the internal sense, has meaning. Therefore, the discourse of the absolute (metaphysics as special metaphysics) is devoid of meaning, properly speaking, since it can never be "practiced" by a finite subject.

Consequently, *Dasein*, as the subject of schematization, presents three aspects:

Insofar as *Dasein* is first of all the schematization of the transcendental subject (of the unity of categories), it is the place of *transcendence:* It alone has the faculty of rising above the ontic sphere to question the meaning of being (ontologic preunderstanding).

Insofar as it is thoroughly temporal, *Dasein* cannot be considered the constitutive foundation of beings: In fact, this temporality means that it is not a subject closed on itself but an open subject, as its rootedness in imagination indicates. It is in this way that the *Kehre*, rather than fundamentally modifying the philosophy of the "first Heidegger," particularizes it: If *Dasein* is a subject that is not closed upon itself in a *self-foundation*, its interpretation of the meaning of being can be thought beginning from the nonclosure itself, thus beginning from Being as Difference.

Finally, *Dasein* contains within itself the possibility of its own negation in inauthenticity: It can always yield to the metaphysical illusion that consists either of thinking itself as absolute subject (paralogisms) or of producing for thinking itself the idea of an absolute subject whose creature it would be (theological Idea).

Dasein as the subject of schematism stands in a threefold relation to Being, to beings, and to inauthenticity, as we attempt to represent in the following diagram. In each case we indicate the Heideggerian terminology above the line, and the corresponding Kantian terminology below:

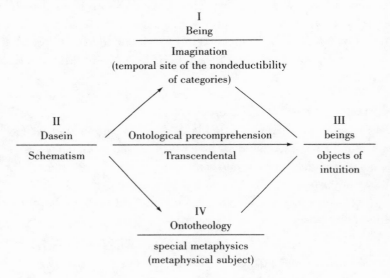

I
Being

Imagination
(temporal site of the nondeductibility
of categories)

II
Dasein

Schematism

Ontological precomprehension

Transcendental

III
beings

objects of
intuition

IV
Ontotheology

special metaphysics
(metaphysical subject)

The *Kehre*, if we were to indicate it in relation to this configuration of thought, which corresponds to the "first Heidegger," could be described as a simple displacement of stress from II to I, a displacement intending to suggest with greater clarity, as opposed to Husserl and Cassirer, that *Dasein* is neither the metaphysical subject nor the empirical subject.

What remains of "humanism" in this conception of the subject still has to be measured. The question could seem strange, so strong is our feeling that there is nothing separating Heidegger from Kant here (at least from the Kant of the "first edition" of *Critique of Pure Reason*, if we hold to this rather dubious restriction). The proximity is so great that the reader might even experience some difficulty in locating the origins of Heideggerian antihumanism in the preceding analyses.

Here it is, nevertheless. As distinct from what happens in the "criticist" tradition, everything that happens in Heidegger (and *a fortiori* whenever one behaves like an epigone to radicalize the method), as if bringing human finitude (the temporality of *Dasein*) to light, has to lead to withdrawing all meaning from the concept of autonomy. There are two reasons for this.

1. As a result of the *Kehre*, Heidegger seems to abandon the problematic of schematization in the state the *Kantbuch* left it. He develops no thought on the conditions under which man, as subject of schematization, appropriates his finitude: Ontological difference will be thought of from then on as the difference between Being and being, without the point of view of *Dasein* being taken into account. The philosophy of Being, then, receives the form of a new *dogmatism*, if one can call dogmatic any position that makes an abstraction of the conditions of *finite consciousness*. On the other hand, the *Critique of Judgment*, through the problematics of reflecting judgment, questioned the modalities of the finite subject's grasp of the radical contingency of reality with respect to the requirements of rationality—requirements inevitably conveyed by the structure of ontological understanding.[14] And it is precisely in this way that it already offers the model for a *critical* philosophy of ontological difference.

2. Consequently, we have the essential deficiency (in the sense of a lack) of Heideggerian phenomenology: The dimension of mastery of self and world implicitly included in the subject of metaphysics is everywhere referred to the domain of illusions to be overcome based on the "discovery" of ontological difference. From the heart of Heideggerian philosophy, no legitimate status, however minimal, could be conferred on this ideal of autonomy. Here again, on the other hand, the *Critique of Judgment* (and it is no accident that it shines by its absence in Heideggerian commentaries on Kant)

14. Cf. on this point our article, "D'un retour à Kant," in *Ornicar*, 1980, reprinted in Ferry and Renaut, *Système et critique*, Ousia, 1985.

offers a model: Carefully elaborating the theory of schematization to its ultimate limits, Kant in fact questions, in the wake of *Transcendental Dialectics*, the conditions of possibility of a legitimate role for metaphyscial Ideas after their deconstruction. That is, it is a matter for him of grappling, apparently paradoxically, with the question of the *schematization of metaphysical discourse*. From this perspective, the whole contribution of *Critique of Judgment* consists of demonstrating that, if the metaphysics of absolute mastery is stripped of all meaning when one attributes the status of a truth to it, on the other hand, by virtue of being a regulating principle of thought it can constitute a *horizon* of meaning for human practice, in the scientific order as much as in the ethicopolitical order.

Heidegger was denied the possibility (and the opportunity) of preserving some meaning for the *legitimate* requirements—in this case, of autonomy—that had been explained in *deluded form*, in that he conceived of metaphysics only as an obstacle to overcome and pursued the critique only in the mode of an *overcoming*. Certainly, this overcoming of metaphysics, at first rather awkwardly presented as a "destruction,"[15] later took on the apparently less imperious attractions of the *Verwindung*, the "rising above" (in the sense that one rises above some distress or mistake). Must this lexical displacement, however, provoke us into thinking that in the "last Heidegger" the relations with metaphysics must have been reconsidered in the direction where exclusion had given place to a maintained proximity (perceived as indispensable)? Nothing could be less obvious when one pays attention to how Heidegger himself justifies abandoning the slogan that called for "overcoming metaphysics": For philosophy today, he explained, it is a matter of "thinking about being without looking back at metaphysics"; now, "looking back at metaphysics still controls the intention to overcome it. That is why it is useful to give up the overcoming and to

---

15. M. Heidegger, *Sein und Zeit*, para. 6 (*Being and Time*, trans. John Macquarrie and Edward Robinson, Harper and Row, New York, 1962, pp. 41 ff.).

leave metaphysics to itself."[16] Abandoning the vocabulary of "over-coming" is no evidence of an attempt to consider the relation to metaphysics as other than an *abandonment* of it by a philosophy that is seeking to occupy an *other* place from then on: The intention explained in the idea of "overcoming" simply culminated in the pursuit of a methodological indifference to a former trajectory which had been "overcome" and which there is no longer any reason to look at. From then on, it would no longer be a matter of worrying, in whatever mode it might be, about reinvesting what had been the content of metaphysics, now transformed, into the future work of philosophy. Under these conditions, the idea of autonomy that had been closely associated with subjectivity in metaphysics could only be "left to itself" and stored on the shelves of the prop room along with all the other elements of what, *in the same spirit*, Engels had called "the old metaphysical bric-a-brac," where the principle of reason, and even the idea of system, might also be found.

Why was this gesture particularly serious when it came to the idea of autonomy (and correlatively of humanism, which was defined as the will to make such an idea the "property of man")? To be convinced of its seriousness, we have only to put three kinds of texts together:

1. The texts where Heidegger describes what must become of man as *Dasein*, he whose ipseity will be thought of no longer in (metaphysical) terms of autonomy but in terms of *Gelassenheit*—this "serenity" which consists of "letting things be":

> I have tried, freed from all representation, to rely absolutely only on the free Extension and to persist in this behavior. . . . The relation to the free extension is waiting. And to be waiting means: to let oneself be engaged in opening onto the free Extension. . . .
> The essence of philosophy resides in this: that the free Extension takes serenity into itself and assimilates it. . . . To arrive at serenity is to detach oneself from representative thought with a transcendental structure and to renounce will brought back from the horizon. This renunciation no longer proceeds from a will, unless,

16. *Questions IV*, p. 48.

however, the impulse to move toward adherence to the free Extension itself needs a last vestige of will; a vestige that moreover is effaced in the course of our progress and completely disappears in Serenity.[17]

2) The typical texts of '68 philosophy, in which Deleuze and Guattari describe the "desiring machines" that take over from humanist man: on the "surface," where these "machine effects" are inscribed, which used to be called "actions," "something on the order of a *subject* can be discerned on the recording surface. It is a strange subject, however, with no fixed identity, wandering about over the body without organs, but always remaining peripheral to the desiring machines, being defined by the share of the product it takes for itself, garnering here, there, and everywhere a reward in the form of a becoming or an avatar, being born of the states that it consumes and being reborn with each new state. . . . A part adjacent to the machines. And if this subject has no specific or personal identity, it is because it is not only a part that is peripheral to the machine, but also a part that is itself divided into parts that correspond to the detachments from the chain (*détachements de chaîne*) and the removals from the flow (*prélèvements de flux*) brought about by the machine. Thus this subject consumes and consumates each of the states through which it passes, and is born of each of them anew, continuously emerging from them as a part made up of parts, each one of which completely fills up the body without organs in the space of an instant."[18]

3. The texts where G. Lipovetsky describes, with great finesse, the "contemporary individual": "floating space, with no attachment, no reference, pure availability, adapted to the acceleration of combinations, to the fluidity of our systems," this new Self of the "end of will" corresponds to "the more and more aleatory individuals, . . . combinations of activity and of passivity improbable until now," whose "personal identity becomes problematical"; in the

17. "Pour servir de commentaire à Sérénité," in *Questions III* ("Sur Erörterung der Gelassenheit," in *Gelassenheit*, Pfullingen, 1959).

18. G. Deleuze and F. Guattari, *L'Anti-Oedipe*, Ed. de Minuit, 1972, pp. 16 ff. (*Anti-Oedipus*, trans. Robert Hurley, Mark Seem, and Helen Lane, University of Minnesota Press, Minneapolis, 1983, chap. 1, pp. 16–40).

period of "disunification" and of "the breaking up of personality," "to the extent that objects and messages, psy and sport prostheses invade existence, the individual is breaking up into a heteroclitic patchwork, into a polymorphic combination, the very image of postmodernism"; at the horizon of this process of "dispossession," "the disparate fragmentation of the self, the emergence of an individual obeying multiple logics in the manner of the compartmentalized juxtapositions of pop artists or the flat and chancy combinations of Adami."[19]

There is no question of conflating these texts, all three of which obey their own logic. Yet it is the case that there is an obvious point in common between *Dasein*, whose last vestige of will consists in letting itself be assimilated by the emergence of things, the desiring machine where the Self without identity only garners the reward of a future or an avatar, and contemporary individuality, well understood by Lipovetsky as heteroclitic submission to multiple logics: the inscription of what was called the "subject" into the multiform register of *heteronomy*. What Heidegger established, then, and what the sixties radicalized in various modes are cultivated throughout the period in the form of this "indifferent Self, with a failing will, a new zombie traversed by messages" that define "a new type of personality." From the *Dasein* to desiring machines and the contemporary figure of the zombie: this is a single process of destruction of the ideal of autonomy that is being achieved. Perhaps this process is not necessarily catastrophic and not inevitably preparing the way for a "submissive and alienated humanity."[20] At the very least, however, it must seem paradoxical and problematical that what passes for postmodernism, withdrawing any meaning from an ideal of man that had in fact made up the main contribution of modernity itself, acquires the strange appearance of a regression, once again substituting for the ideal of a "nature which is subject to a will" the premodern ideal of "a nature to which the will is subject."[21]

19. G. Lipovetsky, *L'Ere du vide: Essais sur l'individualisme contemporain*, Gallimard, 1983, pp. 65, 80, 125.
20. Ibid., p. 64.
21. I. Kant, *Kritik der praktischen Vernunft*, Akademie-Ausgabe, pt. 1, book 1, chap. 1.

Conclusion

To conclude this essay we will return to our starting point. Is there some paradox, some contradiction, emphasizing the essential character of the individualist component of May '68, as we have done, and in using the expression " '68 philosophy" to designate these philosophers, when, as diverse as they are, they had in common not only their critique of humanism but their lack of sympathy (which is the least one can say) for the "consumer society" where individuality of the most exaggerated kind has flourished and dominated?

This whole book provides an answer to this objection, but since we wish to be clear we will repeat that the critique of truth as Absolute Knowledge, though perfectly legitimate in itself *when not accompanied by a consideration of the regulating value that the demands of reason can ideally nevertheless preserve*, can be wonderfully reconciled with the individualist sentimentality that the formula "To each his own truth" expresses so well. If the truth must be shattered, if there are no facts but only interpretations, if all references to universal norms are inevitably catastrophic, then is not the essential thing to "participate," as they say? And, from this point of view, do not deconstructions of modernity accompany democracy, in the Tocquevillean sense of the word, to its farthest point, making authenticity the supreme value, *whatever its content may be?* The most spontaneous and naive ideology, for example, the ideology of those *lycéens* who saw their philosophy professor as combating popular opinion, meets the most elaborate philosophy when it valorizes the "plural," the "open," the "complex," "fertile tensions," even "contradictions" in and of themselves. In short, as the song says, "everyone does his own thing," everyone has the absolute right to heterogeneity (to difference) since, as we have noted, everyone agrees with J.-F. Lyotard: "Consensus obtained through discussion, in Habermas' sense? That violates the heterogeneity of language games."[1]

Quite simply, there are two questions: If freely consented to and discussed, what is so terrible about such a consensus? And if consensus is not sought through free discussion, where will it emerge, if not from violence? Even though he was writing with his right hand, it is true, Marx taught us at least one thing: Merely left to themselves, heterogeneous interests are nothing other than the law of the fittest.

No doubt our essay in its rustic *will* to *clarify* the debates, to *identify* positions, to perform critiques as *delimitation*, to *reveal* contradictions, will be called simplistic, an amalgam, and negative reaction will frequently limit itself to pointing out that things are not so simple, that the questions are more complicated than they appear, and so on.

The truth is, however, that it is the critique of humanism, of the subject, of metaphysics, of autonomy, of anthropology, and of the truth that reveals a surprising and persistent simplicity. In this respect, a *history of the subject*, or rather of the modern representations of subjectivity, still has to be written. Such notions as humanism, individualism, and the metaphysics of subjectivity are not homogeneous in any way. What is more, the *plural* facets of the subject, which is *nontotalizable* in a single concept, are not several stages in a linear history that was crowned by the Hegelian Absolute Subject. So this book will have to have a sequel: From the appearance of the Cartesian *cogito* to the empiricist deconstruction of the ideal of substance, from the Kantian critique of rational psychology to its dialectical rehabilitation with Schelling and Hegel, there are gaps and breaks to be illuminated. In the same way, it is important to restore in all its diversity, that far-off history of the German antihumanism that '68 philosophy all too often merely slavishly prolonged.

1. J.-F. Lyotard, *La Condition post-moderne*, Paris, 1979, p. 8.

Name Index

Tocqueville, Alexis de, 42, 47, 48, 50
Touchard, J., 34, 37
Touraine, Alain, 36

Velázquez, Diego, 101

Veyne, Paul, 11

Wahl, J., 83
Weber, Max, 49, 168
Wittgenstein, Ludwig, 96